Making Inclusive Higher Education a Reality

Revealing higher education inclusive practice in action, this key title showcases a range of international case studies from a number of universities in order to highlight approaches to developing a culture of access and inclusion. It provides detailed information on how to transform institutional commitment to access and diversity into systemic change and the creation of a university for all.

By deconstructing assumptions and practices and offering a range of inclusive techniques and case studies to challenge and enhance instruction, this book moves the conversation about inclusivity from a concept to a reality. It evokes and prompts solutions to everyday challenges experienced by those working in higher education and offers the reader a ringside seat to its application, implementation and unearthing of inclusive practice gems which showcase inclusive practice at its best.

Providing a whole-institution perspective of student access and inclusion, citing case studies and sharing real world experience, this book will appeal to academic leaders, faculty, and professionals in higher education, as well as policy makers. In particular, those charged with addressing issues of access, diversity, and inclusion in higher education will find this a vital read.

Anna M. Kelly is Director of Access and Lifelong Learning, University College Dublin. Anna offers leadership to the University community to realise its strategic objective to be a university for all. She has significant expertise in Inclusive Design, organisational change in the fields of access, widening participation, mainstreaming and inclusion.

Lisa Padden is Programme Manager for University College Dublin's University for All initiative. Lisa has particular expertise in change management, capacity building, and professional development in the areas of Universal Design and Universal Design for Learning.

Bairbre Fleming is Deputy Director of Access and Lifelong Learning in University College Dublin. She has extensive experience teaching and supporting under-represented students with particular emphasis on mature students and part-time programmes.

"This inspiring and timely book demonstrates that it is possible to have a university for all. Inclusion is constantly talked about in higher education but rarely reaches the lives of students. *Making Inclusion in Higher Education a Reality: Creating a University for All* reveals how to make inclusion a reality that permeates every aspect of life in higher education institutions. Drawing on a richly theorised case study of University College Dublin, it shows that once access and inclusion become everyone's business, all students, regardless of background, can feel they belong."

Diane Reay, *Emeritus Professor of Education, University of Cambridge*

"This is an important book addressing one of the abiding challenges for those involved in higher education – ensuring that the life benefits provided by university education are available to all who have the ambition and ability to undertake third level studies, irrespective of their background. From an institutional perspective, the mainstreaming diversity and inclusion is addressed, while practical guidance is provided for embedding inclusive practice at all levels in the institution, down to curriculum design and IT services. I strongly recommend this book to everyone interested in making their university more inclusive."

Professor Andrew J. Deeks, *Vice Chancellor and President, Murdoch University, Australia*

"In this volatile and uncertain world, one thing is clear: we need all the talent we can get, to strengthen our societies and our economies, and to ensure a just and sustainable future. To do that, we have to create opportunities for everyone, particularly in higher education.

Making higher education a Reality is, therefore, most welcome, as it brings us one step closer to creating that university for all."

Dr. Imran Uddin, *Director of the KU Leuven Association*

"As the pressure to improve inclusion, access, and equity grows in many systems of higher education, scholarly work that is both insightful and practical, is a true find.

The authors of this volume have the knowledge and experience to offer both. Some chapters focus on specific obstacles that stand in the way of inclusive access to HE. Others offer solutions for an institution-wide approach to combatting exclusion.

The book is certainly a worthwhile read!"

Eva Egron-Polak, *Former General Secretary, International Association of Universities (IUA), France*

"The editors of this volume have led a revolution in University College Dublin, developing the concept of University for All as a rallying cry for mainstreaming broad and deep approaches to more inclusive approaches to higher education. In this volume they bring together a wide range of expert contributors to offer a reflective and practical guide which shares and makes accessible the experience of effectively advancing University for All for a wide readership interested in further widening participation and effective support for all students."

Professor Colin Scott, *Vice President for Equality, Diversity and Inclusion, University College Dublin*

"This work has a very ambitious title but, unlike some which have gone before it, a wide-ranging and very relevant content to match. There are chapters focused, not only on non-European countries (as we should expect these days), but also those which connect broad themes in policy and practice with case study and other types of research. The work deals with 'enabling change', alongside 'data as a driver of change' and 'IT infrastructure and digital accessibility'. It covers perhaps more anticipated topics like 'programme and curriculum design, teaching and learning'. And there is much more. In my view, a work not to miss."

Stuart Billingham, *Emeritus Professor of Lifelong Learning, York St. John University*

"University for All is a tour de force of evidence-based research which will make a significant positive impact on the reality of Inclusive Design for Education in our global universities and higher education institutes, with life-changing results for students of all backgrounds, ages and abilities. The reality is that there is no 'typical student', no one curriculum or approach that works across disciplines or cultures. And now we must move together to the next frontier of Inclusive Design for Education. This excellent book provides the evidence, examples, and toolkit to support educators and students to move forward with scaffolding to that new frontier!"

Professor Lizbeth Goodman, *Chair of Creative Technology Innovation, and Inclusive Design for Education, University College Dublin*

"*Making Inclusive Higher Education a Reality* is a must-read for each of us working towards more equitable colleges, more equitable higher education systems, or more equitable national higher education policy. The authors take a practical approach that recognises the constraints under which higher education operates and offer realistic steps any institution can take to become more inclusive, more diverse, more prepared to assure that 21st-century students are welcomed and can excel."

Maureen Hoyler, *President, Council for Opportunity in Education, USA*

Making Inclusive Higher Education a Reality

Creating a University for All

Edited by
Anna M. Kelly, Lisa Padden and Bairbre Fleming

Routledge
Taylor & Francis Group
LONDON AND NEW YORK

Designed cover image: Getty

First published 2023
by Routledge
4 Park Square, Milton Park, Abingdon, Oxon OX14 4RN

and by Routledge
605 Third Avenue, New York, NY 10158

Routledge is an imprint of the Taylor & Francis Group, an informa business

British Library Cataloguing-in-Publication Data
A catalogue record for this book is available from the British Library

ISBN: 978-1-032-15477-0 (hbk)
ISBN: 978-1-032-18259-9 (pbk)
ISBN: 978-1-003-25363-1 (ebk)

DOI: 10.4324/9781003253631

Typeset in Times New Roman
by Taylor & Francis Books

Contents

List of figures xi
List of tables xiii
List of contributors xiv
Foreword xxi
Acknowledgments xxiii

1 Introduction: How do you create a University for All? Moving from theory to action with a framework for inclusive change in higher education 1
ANNA M. KELLY, LISA PADDEN AND BAIRBRE FLEMING

CHAPTER 2
Foundations and Scaffolding: Strategic Approach and Organisation 19

2.1 Adopting an institutional approach – moving from silos to mainstreaming inclusion 21
ANNA M. KELLY

2.2 Creating universities for all: 30 top public research universities in the US respond to anti-Black violence 33
LESLIE A. WILLIAMS, PATRICK KENT RUSSELL AND FRANK TUITT

2.3 Inclusive post-secondary education: Is there such a thing? 40
VIANNE TIMMONS

2.4 Applying the values and principles that underpin Universal Design at a national level 43
GERALD CRADDOCK

CHAPTER 3
Data as a driver of change 49

3.1 Driving change – using data to tell the story of inclusion 51
BAIRBRE FLEMING

3.2 Student engagement and retention through a data driven approach in higher education: A case study of developing inclusive practice addressing the attainment gap 65
MARILYN HOLNESS AND HAMEED MOZAFFARI

CHAPTER 4
From vision to practice: A Toolkit for Inclusive Higher Education Institutions 71

4.1 Tell me how! Development, methodology, and use of the Toolkit for Inclusive Higher Education Institutions 73
LISA PADDEN

4.2 Who 'does' inclusion? Using the Toolkit to create change from the margins 87
MARY FARRELLY

4.3 "It has to come from the top!": Using the Toolkit for bottom-up planning for inclusion 90
GRAHAM FINLAY

4.4 Embedding inclusion in the Engineering discipline: Using the Toolkit for Inclusive Higher Education Institutions both online and in person 93
MARK FLANAGAN

CHAPTER 5
Programme & Curriculum Design, Teaching & Learning 97

5.1 From national collaboration to grassroots implementation: Achieving widespread inclusion through Universal Design for Learning 99
LISA PADDEN

5.2 Drawing from the global to act local: How Universal Design for Learning lends itself to facilitating inclusion in Moroccan higher education 110
MUSTAPHA AABI AND SEÁN BRACKEN

5.3 Achieving culturally inclusive teaching utilising the Universal Design for Learning framework 118
LINDA HUI YANG

CHAPTER 6
Student Supports & Services 125

6.1 The structures and status of student support 127
BAIRBRE FLEMING

6.2 Putting student support centre-stage to improve diversity, belonging, and success – the #Ibelong project 145
LIZ THOMAS

CHAPTER 7
Physical Campus & Built Environment 153

7.1 The campus as a canvas: How the built environment embodies a university's journey towards inclusion for all 155
KIM LOMBARD

7.2 Universal Design Patterns for enabling physical environments 164
HUBERT FROYEN

7.3 Mainstreaming inclusion and accessibility of the University built environment through collaboration with and empowerment of Campus Services 174
FIONA SWEENEY AND TINA LOWE

7.4 Beyond compliance: Embedding accessibility and creating community through inclusive design of the university built environment 178
TADGH CORCORAN AND THOMAS HAMILL

CHAPTER 8
IT Services & Infrastructure 185

8.1 Facilitating inclusion in an evolving digital world 187
DANIEL ELLIOTT

8.2 Embedding inclusion and accessibility in higher education IT 192
SINÉAD O'ROURKE, RYAN TEEVAN AND JANET COLLINS

8.3 Digital accessibility in the UK context 201
ALISTAIR MCNAUGHT

9 Conclusion – carpe diem – seize the day! 206
ANNA M. KELLY

Appendix 221
Index 227

Figures

1.1 University for All Implementation Framework 3
1.2 Student responses to the statement: 'In my experience, UCD's policies, procedures and university strategy support the development of a University for All, providing an inclusive educational experience' 9
1.3 Student responses to the statement: 'In my experience UCD's Teaching, Learning and Assessment meet my needs and are inclusive for all students' 10
1.4 Student responses to the statement: 'In my experience UCD's Student Supports and Services meet my needs and are inclusive for all students' 11
1.5 Student responses to the statement: 'In my experience UCD's physical campus meets my needs and is inclusive for all students' 12
1.6 Student responses to the statement: In my experience UCD's technological environment meets my needs and is inclusive for all students 13
2.1 The seven element Universal Design system within a human ecological framework 46
3.1 Sample of the university as a village of 100, used to convey the relative proportions of under-represented cohorts in the university c. 2015 53
3.2 Elements of storytelling using data 54
3.3 Key moments in identifying the 'data problem' 56
3.4 Timeline and rollout of Quantitative Data Measures 56
3.5 Mixed data options to inform a University for All – the elements required to tell the story 58
3.6 Knowing your audience – segmentation allows different data approaches 59
3.7 Illustration of use of data to identify and prompt action to drive change 61
3.8 Using data and finding compromises 61
3.9 RAFA2 data entry qualifications 67
3.10 The RAFA Way 68

4.1 Toolkit for Inclusive Higher Education Institutions (Kelly and Padden, 2018a) 74
4.2 University for All components 76
4.3 University for All implementation process including workshop 80
4.4 The scoring mechanism of the digital toolkit 83
4.5 Capturing good practice in the digital toolkit 84
4.6 Capturing participant ideas for possible actions in the digital toolkit 84
5.1 System implementation of UDL 101
5.2 Lessons learned on why this digital badge model works for UDL training, based on feedback from participants, facilitators, and coordinators 103
5.3 Building an inclusive organisational culture; attributes for consideration 112
6.1 UCD Student Experience Map, 2019 128
6.2 A statement from the summary of students' perspective of their UCD experience documented as part of the UCD Student Experience mapping project 129
6.3 Coding of Student Goals from incoming students who described their key goal for the semester ahead 133
6.4 Student Support as a detailed map offered to students at Orientation 135
6.5 Revisiting a Student Experience Map to consider Universally Designed student supports 137
6.6 The identification of a Third Space 139
7.1 Person–Environment–Occupation Model of Occupational Performance 156
7.2 Approaches to creating an inclusive physical campus and built environment 161
7.3 (a) Artist's rendering of the UD Living Lab (Hasselt, B) in 2011. (b) The renovation project was completed in 2013 166
7.4 Smaller room (166 cm × 203 cm). Existing situation (left) and UD concept for more "Care & Well-being" (right) 170
7.5 Larger room (178 cm × 297 cm). Existing situation (left) and UD for more "Care & Well-being" (right); Graphics: dr. arch. Elke Ielegems, dr. arch. Anne Bosserez, interior arch. Kaat Berben. 171
7.6 UCD Belfield campus 179
7.7 Andrzsj Wejchert's sketch of his proposed campus layout 180
7.8 UCD Tierney Building 1972 181
7.9 Architect's impression of the UCD Centre for Creativity 182
8.1 IT Supports and Services for students 193
8.2 IT implementation process 194
9.1 University for All Implementation Framework 209
9.2 Key Take Aways for creating a University for All 217

Tables

1.1 Qualitative student responses on inclusion in Foundation and Scaffolding: Strategic Approach and Organisation 9
1.2 Qualitative student responses on inclusion in Programme & Curriculum Design, Teaching & Learning 10
1.3 Qualitative student responses on inclusion in Student Supports & Services 11
1.4 Qualitative student responses on inclusion in Physical Campus & the Built Environment 13
1.5 Qualitative student responses on inclusion in Information Technology Systems & Infrastructure 14
2.1 The key components of the University for All Implementation Framework as indicated in Figure 1.1 (previous chapter) 27
5.1 Individualist /collective societies and teaching and learning 120
5.2 Power distance and teaching and learning 120
5.3 UDL for CIT 121
7.1 Sample responses to Physical Campus & Built Environment question on the 2020 University for All Student and Staff surveys 160

Contributors

Dr Anna M. Kelly is Director of Access and Lifelong Learning in University College Dublin. Together with a team of access professionals, she offers leadership and support to the University community to realise its strategic objective to be a University for All, where access and inclusion is embedded and everyone's business.

Her PhD is in Inclusive Design in Higher Education, where she investigated the implementation of national policy to mainstream access and inclusion in higher education, gathering the views of the leaders of Ireland's seven universities. Her research interests are in the areas of organisational change in the fields of access, widening participation, mainstreaming, and inclusion.

She chairs a consortium of six higher education institutions, working to address access and participation to higher education, including Trinity College, National College of Art & Design, the Institute of Art, Design & Technology, Marino Institute of Education, RCSI (University of Medicine and Health Sciences), and UCD. She represents UCD on the Irish Universities Association (IUA) Access Steering Group, also chairing the IUA sub-committees on Supplementary Entry Routes, and Flexible Education, respectively. She is a member of the European Access Network.

Prior to joining UCD, Anna held a range of senior positions in further education, access, and diversity fields, including Director, Curriculum & Quality Assurance in FÁS, the State Training & Employment Authority. She was Regional Director with the National Rehabilitation Board (NRB), Ireland's statutory body for services for people with disabilities.

Dr Lisa Padden has worked in University College Dublin (UCD) since 2012, having joined the university from a role in the National University of Ireland, Galway. Lisa's current role is Programme Manager for UCD's University for All initiative, based in UCD Access and Lifelong Learning. Lisa works with academic and professional colleagues across the University to implement University for All – UCD's whole-institution approach to student inclusion, encompassing strategy and policy, teaching, learning and assessment, student supports and services, the built environment, as well as technological infrastructure. Lisa has particular expertise in capacity building in the areas of Universal Design and Universal Design for Learning, working with colleagues across the higher education and further education and training sector in Ireland through joint coordination of the Digital Badge for Universal Design in Teaching & Learning, now with almost 3,000 awardees in Ireland. Lisa has been lead editor on four collections of Universal Design for Learning Case Studies and co-wrote the Toolkit for Inclusive Higher Education Institutions. Lisa's research interests include Universal Design for Learning, widening participation, equitable access to higher education, and student inclusion.

Dr Bairbre Fleming is Deputy Director of UCD Access and Lifelong Learning. She has extensive experience working with under-represented students through the UCD Access programmes, with particular emphasis on mature students and part-time programmes. Her PhD drew on a sociological analysis of the experiences of mature students in higher education.

She leads on post-entry student supports, working with her team to design and provide coherent and integrated supports for all students, including academic skills workshops, needs assessments, and student referrals. This focus facilitates students as they transition to independent learning. Bairbre is leading a national project to develop a digital badge in Student/Learner Support for further and higher education staff, as well as leading on a number of projects to develop innovations around post-entry student support.

Finally, Bairbre leads on the Data project for UCD, developing strategies for visualising, democratising, and using data in order to lever change.

Bairbre has experience of working with adult learners and under-represented students. She has created an innovative way of offering part-time learning in the university through leveraging spare capacity in existing classes. Her focus is on mainstreaming projects, including the transition of university access programmes to university governance, developing progression pathways for part-time learners and the democratisation of data.

Mustapha Aabi is an Associate Professor at the University of Ibn Zohr University, Agadir – Morocco, currently serving as Horizon NCP for Culture, Creativity and Inclusive Society/Civil Security for Society. He is a member of the steering group of the International Collaboratory for Leadership in Universally Designed Education (INCLUDE), co-leading the team for 'learner voice'. His research interests lie in the areas of trans-linguistics and education. He has collaborated actively with researchers in several other disciplines of education, particularly inclusive education, leadership, and early education on issues at the linguistic, cultural, and pedagogical intersections.

Seán Bracken is a Principal Lecturer at the University of Worcester in the UK, as well as a Principal Fellow of the HEA. He has worked in a diversity of countries as a primary and secondary teacher, a teacher educator, a lecturer, and an educational project manager. Seán's research and pedagogy have a strong and consistent focus on learner voice, engagement, and empowerment, especially as these pertain to course design in higher education. He is co-founder of the International Collaboratory for Leadership in Universally Designed Education (INCLUDE) and is a member of the Steering Committee for the International Conference on Education Quality (ICEQ), an initiative based at Ibn Zohr University in Agadir, Morocco.

Janet Collins (BSc Computer Systems, MSc Project Management) is a project manager with UCD EAG, IT Services. Janet has over 20 years' experience in software development and project/programme management, working in a range of organisations, from start-ups to large multinationals, with expertise in the financial, educational, and non-profit sectors.

Tadgh Corcoran is Director of Estate Services at University College Dublin. Tadgh joined UCD as Technical Services manager in 2005 and was appointed as the Director of Estate Services in 2018, which includes responsibility for the sustainable development of a rapidly growing university. UCD recently approved an updated Strategic Campus Development Plan 2016–2021–2026 which focused on three key objectives: planning accommodation needs for a growing university, enhancing the campus experiences (including adaptation of existing buildings), and preparing the university to transition to low carbon estate to meeting the obligation of the Climate Action Plan. In conjunction with UCD Access and Lifelong Learning, UCD Estates promotes inclusive design in the planning of UCD building projects.

Gerald Craddock is the inaugural Chief Officer of the Centre for Excellence in Universal Design, a statutory body established by the Irish Government in 2007. It is part of the National Disability Authority, which is the lead state agency on disability in Ireland. The Centre's key domain areas are the built environment, products and services, and information and communication technologies (ICT). The centre's focus is on infusing Universal Design into educational curricula at all levels, developing standards in professional and industrial services, and creating awareness of the benefits of Universal Design within Ireland, as well as at European and international level.

Daniel Elliott is Project Officer supporting the University for All strategic initiative in UCD, as well as the UCD Widening Participation Committee and the Faculty Partnership Programme. He is currently supporting the development of new Universal Design professional development micro-credentials for the higher and further education sector. He is project lead for the rejuvenated John Kelly Awards for Universal Design in Further & Higher Education. He has previously worked in higher education in the UK.

Mary Farrelly is an Assistant Professor in Spanish Studies in the School of Languages, Literatures and Cultures, University College Dublin. She has worked as a Widening Participation Fellow at the University of Manchester and College of Arts and Humanities Widening Participation Representative and a University for All Faculty Partner at University College Dublin. She is especially interested in UDL and the relationship between multilingualism and accessibility in the classroom.

Graham Finlay is Vice Principal for Widening Participation in the College of Social Sciences and Law, University College Dublin. He is also an Assistant Professor in the School of Politics and International Relations, where he teaches and researches human rights, equality, and justice, including justice in education and migrants' rights. He has been principal investigator at UCD for a number of grants and research networks in these and other policy areas.

Mark Flanagan is an Associate Professor in the School of Electrical and Electronic Engineering and represents Engineering on the UCD Widening Participation Committee. He leads the UCD Communications and Signal Processing research group, authoring more than 150 peer-reviewed papers in international journals and conferences. In 2014, he was a Visiting Senior Scientist with the Institute of Communications and Navigation, German Aerospace Centre, under a DLR-DAAD Fellowship. He is currently serving as TPC Co-Chair for the IEEE Global Conference on Communications (GLOBECOM) 2022, as well as serving as an Editor for the journal, *IEEE Transactions on Communications*.

Hubert Froyen is an emeritus professor in the Faculty of Architecture in UHasselt (B). Hubert studied architecture in UHasselt (B) and in Leuven (B), and anthropology at KUUniversity Leuven (B) and at UC Berkeley (USA). He holds an additional M.Arch. degree from the University of California, Berkeley (USA), which he achieved in 1979. From 1973–2012, he taught architecture in Belgium, Hasselt University (UHasselt), Faculty of Architecture and Arts, and was appointed professor in January 1996. His ongoing research focuses mainly on *Universal Design: A Methodological Approach* (Froyen 2012). On 1 April 2012, he was awarded emeritus status. He is the holder of the Universal Design 'Ron Mace / Designing for the 21st Century Award', Rio de Janeiro 2004.

Thomas Hamill is the Operations Manager for University College Dublin's Estate Services. Tom has worked in the University Facilities Management sector for over 20 years and, in that time, has developed an excellent understanding of the importance of providing an outstanding campus environment and support service. He has invaluable experience on how the University operates from a facilities and operational viewpoint. Having joined UCD Estate Services in March 2020, his current role involves a diverse portfolio of responsibilities, but Tom is particularly proud of his role in promoting inclusivity and accessibility. Prior to joining Estate Services, Tom worked as the Facilities Manager for UCD Research and Innovation.

Marilyn Holness is Professor of Education Engagement and Practice and Dean of Students at the University of Roehampton. She was awarded an OBE for services to Teacher Education. Working with the executive team, she plays a key role in shaping and implementing the University's strategic vision and leading on the academic aspects of the student experience, as well as supporting students to succeed in and progress from higher education with successful outcomes, including work to close the degree-awarding gap (https://rafa2.org/). She is passionate about the transformative power of education and the positive difference it can make to lives – her own included. She works to help students realise their potential by taking control of their experiences and developing agency over their lives.

Patrick Kent Russell is a PhD candidate in the Department of English, University of Connecticut. His research focuses on the cultural logics of neoliberalism. In particular, he focuses on the cultural project that spreads neoliberal logics into the spatial sites of everyday American life, including institutions and entertainment. He has published and presented on crime fiction as a coherent representation of neoliberalism's uneven spread during the twentieth century. He currently serves as the Communications Coordinator for the University's Office for Diversity and Inclusion, where he facilitates inward and outward facing communications about the institution's diversity programming and initiatives.

Kim Lombard is an Occupational Therapist practising in Access and Lifelong Learning, University College Dublin (UCD). Kim qualified with a BSc in Occupational Therapy from Trinity College Dublin and joined the Occupational Therapy Service in UCD in October 2017, working 1:1 with students with disabilities, as well as facilitating various training and workshop sessions for students and staff, and developing online resources for ALL. Kim acts as a Supervisor for the Disability Access Route to Education (DARE) scheme in Ireland. Kim is currently undertaking PhD research which aims to improve the evidence base of Occupational Therapy Services for students with disabilities in higher education using a statistical methodology known as Rasch analysis.

Tina Lowe is a University College Dublin graduate who has been working in UCD since 2008. Tina works as the Campus Accessibility Officer in Access and Lifelong Learning. Tina's role is to assist in creating a universally accessible campus, in collaboration with UCD's Estate Services. Tina is a guide dog owner who has worked on many building projects throughout the campus and continues to strive to make it universally accessible.

Hameed Mozaffari is an early career researcher whose cross disciplinary work lies at the nexus of Cultural Studies and Education, with a focus on exploring the educational inequalities that have emerged as a result of mass academisation over the last decade. Dr Mozaffari's research interests are in representation, media and popular culture, identity and race, islamophobia, and educational common sense. Hameed is especially passionate about studying the intersections where power and popular media meet and shape cultural identities and normality in the UK educational landscape.

Alistair McNaught spent 20 years as a mainstream teacher committed to developing student skills and independent learning. This led to early adoption of e-learning, which, in turn, paved the way for an abiding interest in making teaching and learning content more accessible to more students. Alistair spent ten years as a senior advisor for TechDis – a national advisory service for technology and disability – followed by four years as an accessibility specialist for Jisc, before setting up Alistair McNaught Consultancy. He is a regular conference speaker and trainer, specialising in making accessibility accessible to non-specialists.

Sinéad O'Rourke is a Communications Officer with UCD IT Services. Sinéad has worked extensively in the areas of Customer Service and Communications and has over 25 years' experience in the higher education sector.

Fiona Sweeney is Head of Outreach, Engagement and Transition in University College Dublin Access and Lifelong Learning (UCD ALL). Her portfolio of responsibilities includes UCD's Outreach programme for students from under-represented groups; UCD's access scholarship programme – Cothrom Na Féinne; student transition, including the ALL Student Welcome and student finances. Fiona has over 20 years' experiences of leading strategic projects in the community and education sector, as well as representing ALL at a cluster and national level. In collaboration with UCD Estates and the Campus Accessibility Officer, she brings her practical approach to ensuring that UCD's built environment is accessible for all users.

Ryan Teevan is a Senior Project Manager with IT Services. Ryan has over ten years' experience in the higher educational environment in Ireland, working in both administrative and IT roles, delivering on university-wide projects.

Vianne Timmons was raised in Newfoundland and Labrador and became the first female president and vice-chancellor of the Memorial University of Newfoundland in April of 2020, having served as president of the University of Regina since 2008. Dr Timmons OC, has extensive teaching experience across Canada, with wide-ranging research interests, with particular emphasis on family literacy and inclusive education. She has received numerous awards, including Officer of the Order of Canada in 2017, and the 2019 YWCA Women of Distinction Lifetime Achievement Award. She was also named one of Canada's Top 100 Most Powerful Women, on four occasions.

Liz Thomas is a UK higher education researcher and consultant. She has been researching widening access, diversity, and success for about 25 years, undertaking academic and applied research and evaluation for national bodies, charitable foundations, and higher education institutions. Her work has affected national policy and institutional practice in the UK and beyond, including ensuring that equity is embedded within the Teaching Excellence and Student Outcomes framework (TEF) and providing evidence underpinning aspects of Access and Participation Plans (APP). TEF and APP have been engaged with around 300 higher education providers, affecting approximately 1.5 million undergraduate students.

Frank Tuitt, EdD, is the University of Connecticut's Vice President and Chief Diversity Officer and Professor of Higher Education and Student Affairs in the NEAG School of Education. In 2019, he received the National Association of Chief Diversity Officers in Higher Education Individual Leadership Award, in recognition of "outstanding contributions to research, administration, practice, advocacy, and/or policy, and whose work informs and advances understanding of diversity and inclusive excellence in higher education". He is a co-editor and contributing author of five books, including *Plantation Politics and Campus Rebellions: Power, Diversity, and the Emancipatory Struggle in Higher Education* (SUNY Press, 2021).

Leslie A. Williams, EdD, is a Lecturer in the Higher and Postsecondary Education program at Teachers College, Columbia University. He recently served as the Racial Equity and Inclusion Research Fellow in the Office for Diversity and Inclusion at the University of Connecticut, where he led a study investigating the responses of public flagship universities to state sanctioned anti-Black violence. Leslie's career in education has spanned more than 25 years as a practitioner and scholar, and his work has always focused on improving the educational experiences and outcomes of all students, particularly those from historically excluded communities.

Linda Hui Yang is the Associate Partner at Hofstede Insights, a global intercultural consultancy. Before moving to Australia, she was the Programme Leader for the Intercultural Development Programme (ICD) from 2018 to 2022 at UCD Michael Smurfit Graduate Business School, University College Dublin, Ireland. She has a PhD degree in Intercultural Studies from Durham University in the UK. Linda has over 24 years' experience working in China, UK, Ireland, and Australia. She has extensive experience in delivering intercultural consultancy and training to diverse participants from more than 86 nationalities, from business sectors, NGOs, and the higher education sector. Her current research interests include intercultural education, intercultural communication, intercultural competence, and cultural differences in teaching and learning.

Foreword

In 1852, UCD's founder, St John Henry Newman, the nineteenth-century educational visionary, set us a challenge, to "turn our eyes to a hundred years from now". Let us reflect on that; what ideas do we have for a 2123 university? One that is radically different, where access and inclusion are no longer mentioned, where the term 'mainstream' is unknown, there is no 'access' office, no targeted entry routes, no reserved quotas, or affirmative actions? One which will embrace all students equitably, with the learning experience universally designed and configured to meet the needs and aspirations of all students? A University for All.

Any transformation of this nature is not without its challenges. This publication will help to untangle those challenges and provide a practical guide to implementation. It offers all higher education leaders a ringside seat on the implementation of University for All and an opportunity to learn from experts who have led the University for All initiative. I am delighted to welcome this long overdue publication; it will be an invaluable resource to anyone tasked with leading change in this area.

Uniquely, the publication offers an institutional lens on the implementation of the systemic change needed to embed access and inclusion into everyday university life. However, although having a diverse student profile is a laudable objective, this belief does not easily translate into institution-wide good practice and culture change. Regrettably, access remains a marginal activity in higher education. As such, this publication is a unique addition to the discourse on access and inclusion in higher education and moves the conversation from concept to reality. Grounded in research and practice, it reveals the key ingredients to developing inclusive higher education, creating an inclusive culture, as well as promoting systemic change that will enable all students to belong.

Creating a University for All is underpinned by the philosophy of 'a student is a student'. This simple concept is predicated on the need to design university systems, processes, and approaches so that all students, wherever they come from and whatever their background, receive a tailored educational experience that meets their needs, without the need for labels.

This publication, in my view as a university leader, is an essential resource that will propel the development of inclusive higher education institutions, enabling them to move beyond opening doors, beyond the development of a pipeline of diverse students, beyond affirmative actions, labels, and rhetoric. It translates the vision for diversity and inclusion into tangible change across all aspects of campus life: from institutional 'add-on' to making access and inclusion everyone's business. Inspired by Newman, this publication sets a path to envisage and, critically, to realise the future of our universities.

Professor Mark Rogers, Acting President UCD

Acknowledgments

> I look towards a land both old and young; old in its Christianity, young in the promise of its future... I contemplate a people which has had a long night and will have an inevitable day. I am turning my eyes towards a hundred years to come, and I dimly see the island I am gazing on become the road of passage and union between two hemispheres, and the centre of the world...
>
> John Henry Newman (1891, p. 32).

We wish to acknowledge the leaders of University College Dublin, who, evoking the spirit of Newman, invested their trust, support and confidence in us, as we aspired to envision a university for all.

Likewise, the Higher Education Authority (HEA) and the Department of Further and Higher Education, Research, Innovation and Science (DFHERIS), whose support enabled and accelerated this work.

The role played by our university colleagues is pivotal. We salute their engagement and commitment; their contribution enabled the development of a blueprint for a whole-institution approach to inclusion in higher education. We appreciate the insights shared and their willingness to accept the challenge presented.

A very special acknowledgment to the team of access professionals in UCD Access & Lifelong Learning. Their expertise, enthusiasm, and commitment to inclusive higher education is unrivalled. We are fortunate to work with such wonderful people.

We also recognise the contribution of students who, enthusiastically and generously, shared their lived experience and used their voice to prompt, propel, and promote the idea of an inclusive university.

Our contributors to this book have shared their wisdom, expertise, and practice, offering a global perspective and adding to our understanding of inclusion across continents. We thank them one and all.

We are indebted to our partners, families, and friends for their unconditional support and encouragement throughout.

Finally, the authors will donate the proceeds of this book to the UCD Cothrom na Féinne scholarship fund for access students.

Reference

Newman, J. (1891). *Historical Sketches.* Volume 3 of *Rise and Progress of Universities; Northmen and Normans in England and Ireland; Medieval Oxford Convocation of Canterbury.* London: Longmans, Green, and Co, New York.

1 Introduction

How do you create a University for All? Moving from theory to action with a framework for inclusive change in higher education

Anna M. Kelly, Lisa Padden and Bairbre Fleming

Why this book?

This book answers the 'how' question – 'how to make access and inclusion everybody's business – how to create a university for all'. Time and time again, we are asked this question. Despite terms such as 'inclusion' and 'diversity' featuring in higher education discourse, embedding inclusion has remained elusive (Callaghan, 2000; May and Bridger, 2010; Thomas, 2011; Thomas et al., 2009; Tuitt, 2016). Inclusion policy requires higher education institutions "to integrate the principle of equity of access more fully into the everyday life of the HEIs so that it permeates all faculties and departments and is not marginalised as the responsibility of the designated access office" (HEA, 2015, p. 25). However, the implementation of this policy objective, remains a challenge, with "ambiguity surrounding the concept and practice of mainstreaming ... and how it should function" (HEA, 2018a, p. 14).

The student population is increasingly diverse and reflective of the society's population mix (HEA, 2018a, 2018b) and higher education institutions are no longer universally seen as the sole preserve of an elite group (Walsh, 2014). Higher education institutions are now different places. Their doors are open, the range of entry routes has been extended, quotas are increasingly common, and more financial support is available. In short, the sector has made much progress. How do we build on this success?

This book, *Making Inclusive Higher Education a Reality: Creating a University for All*, answers this question. It describes how to embed and mainstream access and inclusion; how to move from 'opening doors' – from access and inclusion being an 'add on' to it being integral, a core belief, and a value practised and demonstrated by all. This is a complex challenge, best undertaken 'one bite at a time'. The partially eaten apple, depicted on the cover, is a metaphor for incremental change, evoking evolution rather than revolution, gradual and progressive, and is an invitation to begin taking small steps.

Forging research and practice in the fields of Universal Design, access, inclusion, change, and institutional transformation, this book offers real-world

DOI: 10.4324/9781003253631-1

insights to enable higher education to create an inclusive university for all. Using an institutional lens, we have developed first-hand knowledge and practice of what works to embed and mainstream inclusion. There is no magic answer, no single action that can be taken, with no silver bullet for this complex task. Rather, we offer a tried and tested set of ingredients, tools, and contextual solutions to create an inclusive university.

Terminology and definitions

Terms such as access, equality, diversity, inclusion, and widening participation feature in higher education discourse, often used interchangeably. Throughout this book, we use the word 'access', which we define as meaning the participation and inclusion of groups who are under-represented in higher education. While this varies from country to country, these groups typically experience low participation on the grounds of age, disability, socio-economic status, race and ethnicity, family status, gender, or sexual orientation.

We recognise that terms such as mainstreaming may be contested and understood differently. We use this term to mean a whole-institution systemic response that weaves access and inclusion into the fabric of the organisation at every level, recognising that it is everyone's business. Hence, mainstreaming extends access beyond entry to include an inclusive learning environment, designed for all students, and encompassing teaching and learning, student support, and the built and technology environment.

Finally, we define a university for all as an institution where all students feel they belong.

University College Dublin (UCD) – a case study in making inclusive higher education a reality

This book is anchored by our experience of leading UCD's University for All initiative – a whole-institution, evidence-based systemic response to embed and mainstream access and inclusion. Launched in 2017, and characterised as an institutional transformation process, University for All is designed to weave access and inclusion into the fabric of the University so that "it permeates all faculties and departments, and is not marginalised as the responsibility of the designated access office" (HEA, 2015, p. 25). In short, the UCD University for All case study shows how to make access and inclusion everyone's business (UCD, 2021, 2020, 2018). The implementation of this change process has shaped our thinking, informed our learning, and provided us first-hand implementation experience. This book, therefore, is based on the evidence underpinning this case study, from which we have developed our implementation methodology. The location of this case study is UCD, which is ranked within the top 1 per cent of higher education institutions (HEIs) worldwide. It is Ireland's largest University, with more than 33,000 students from 144 countries. Research and teaching are at the core of UCD's mission, with a strong focus on innovation and research output. The undergraduate population includes 29 per cent international students, with almost 35 per cent of students from groups identified as under-represented in higher education in Ireland. The development of this UCD initiative was informed by a wide range of contextual factors, including, the university culture; its status as a research-intensive institution; its size, scale, and complexity; the organisational structures; and the wide range of stakeholders.

The University for All initiative was prompted by Anna Kelly (2017), whose study of implementation of access policy in Ireland's seven universities identified an 'inclusion implementation gap', despite the policy imperative that explicitly promotes the integration of access and inclusion into everyday life of the university (HEA, 2015). In response to this gap, University for All was developed as a whole-institution, evidence-based and systemic response to ensure that all students feel that they belong (Kelly, 2018; Kelly and Padden, 2018). Using an institutional lens, University for All frames the creation of a culture of inclusion necessary to embed and mainstream access in higher education. It engages a triumvirate of implementation actors – leaders, university community, and students – thereby ensuring that all voices are heard, contextual issues are considered, and ownership is fostered. It uses a top-down and bottom-up strategy to percolate change through the entire University community (Greenbank, 2007). It moves beyond 'opening the door' to higher education, and instead, promotes universally designed inclusive systems, processes, and approaches that meet the needs of all students, without labels. One size does not fit all, but a universally designed higher education institution will.

We have distilled the implementation to seven key components, shown below in Figure 1.1. Chapter 2 discusses these in more detail.

Figure 1.1 University for All Implementation Framework

Structure of this book

We have structured this book to reflect the answers to the 'how' question: how do we make access and inclusion everyone's business? In other words, how do we successfully implement a whole-institution approach to inclusion, engaging the entire university community?

This book is informed by our experience of leading the University for All initiative in UCD. We have also drawn from international research and practice, inviting authors from the USA, Canada, the UK, Morocco, Belgium, and Ireland.

The overarching message of this book is that institutional transformation change, while complex, is achievable with an informed understanding of the essential ingredients and tools to enable this change. Hence, over the course of nine chapters, this book takes the reader through this process, offering practical insights, while providing the theoretical and research basis for our implementation approach.

Chapter 2 addresses an institution-wide approach to inclusion. Kelly sets out the key ingredients to move diversity and inclusion, from 'add on', to 'intrinsic', describing policy context, the translation of the vision to reality, and setting out an Implementation Framework. Chapter 2 also showcases three case studies. Two are North American: 'Creating universities for all: 30 top public research universities in the US respond to anti-Black violence' by Williams, Russell and Tuitt; and by Timmons, who asks, 'Inclusive post-secondary education: Is there such a thing?' In the third case study, Craddock explores the role of the National Centre for Universal Design in Ireland.

Chapter 3 presents the case for data and evidence as a driver of change. Fleming discusses the deliberate use of a 'burning platform' to convey urgency, acting as catalyst for change, to build momentum, and enhance understanding. This chapter explores storytelling and its role in gathering, sharing, and reporting on data metrics, and its visual representation to illustrate impact. Chapter 3 also showcases Holness and Mozaffari, who share a UK perspective on a relevant topic: 'Student engagement and retention through a data driven approach in higher education: A case study of developing inclusive practice addressing the attainment gap'.

Chapter 4 discusses the Toolkit for Inclusive Higher Education Institutions (Kelly and Padden, 2018). Padden discusses its genesis and highlights the key aspects of this practical resource, which reinforces a 'one bite at a time' approach. Offering an institution-wide lens to assess inclusion progress, it identifies opportunities for improvement and creates bespoke action plans. The Toolkit comprises the four typical institutional pillars: 1) Programme & Curriculum Design, Teaching & Learning, 2) Student Supports & Services, 3) Physical Campus & the Built Environment, and 4) Information Technology Systems & Infrastructure, as well as foundation and scaffolding components. This chapter also spotlights three academic staff who have used the Toolkit: Farrelly uses the Toolkit in the Arts & Humanities discipline, and questions

'Who 'does' inclusion?'; Finlay, from a Social Sciences perspective, argues that 'It comes from the top'; and, lastly, Flanagan discusses the use of the Toolkit in the Engineering discipline.

The next four chapters discuss the four institutional pillars, highlighting key inclusion considerations and challenges. Chapter 5 discusses Pillar 1 – Programme & Curriculum Design, Teaching & Learning – examining how Universal Design for Learning (UDL) can be embedded in practice, highlighting UCD's Faculty Partner Programme, designed to accelerate the implementation of UDL, by developing a Community of Practice of UDL advocates and role models across all disciplines. This chapter also presents two case studies, which explore the use of UDL in international contexts. Here, Aabi and Bracken discuss 'How Universal Design for Learning lends itself to facilitating inclusion in Moroccan higher education', while Yang explores the following: 'Achieving culturally inclusive teaching utilising the Universal Design for Learning framework'.

Chapter 6 addresses Pillar 2 – Student Supports & Services. Fleming discusses two discrete but relevant strands of student support in a university for all, examining the universality of design and delivery to maximise the impact of support for all students, and the status afforded to those staff who provide such support. Using Bourdieu's capital lens, Fleming considers the changing nature of student support, its sequencing, and its delivery. Citing student aspirations, their emphasis on making friends, Fleming argues that assumptions made, and priorities attached, may be misplaced. In this complex and often-contested area, Fleming presents the challenges and potential solutions to an inclusive approach to student support. This chapter features Thomas, who describes the UK-based #Ibelong project, designed to place student support centre-stage to improve diversity, belonging, and success.

Chapter 7 addresses Pillar 3 and focuses on the Physical Campus & the Built Environment. Lombard advocates the adoption of a Universal Design approach, which "goes beyond mere compliance" and which seeks to design environments for all. Highlighting how Universal Design can be used within the physical environment to include people with disabilities, she also stresses the need to expand the scope to include the needs of people from other diverse backgrounds. Lombard also makes the case for the inclusion of all voices to best understand the user experience of the physical campus, built environment, and institutional contexts. The chapter features two case studies, one based in Ireland, where Sweeney and Lowe, and Corcoran and Hamill discuss UCD's strategy to move beyond compliance and to illuminate the practical actions to build an inclusive campus. The second, a Belgian case study, features Froyen, who charts the evolution of Universal Design education for the built environment. He cites UHasselt (Hasselt University, Belgium) and "Rooms for Care & Well-being", as examples of good education practice.

Chapter 8 addresses the final Pillar – Information Technology Systems & Infrastructure. Elliott discusses some of the most pressing issues around digital accessibility and how HEIs can, and are, building their IT infrastructures and services to tackle these. He elaborates how higher education responds to the myriad barriers that make up the 'digital divide' and illuminates some of the challenges and solutions. This chapter offers two case studies. The first is from Ireland, where O'Rourke, Teevan, and Collins describe UCD's journey towards the development of inclusive information systems and infrastructure, citing the use of a selection of practical tools to assist. Acknowledging the scale and complexity of systems, O'Rourke, Teevan, and Collins stress that student-centric systems are needed. In the second case study, from the UK, McNaught discusses digital accessibility, observing that digital accessibility involves complex, multi-layered issues, concerning stakeholders at government and community levels. He stresses the need for good stakeholder communications in order to identify the issues, barriers, and solutions.

Finally, Chapter 9 offers a conclusion and outlines the Key Take Aways from this book: seize the day and begin; have courage and accept imperfection; engage with the entire university community; adapt for your own context and start where you can; use data and storytelling tailored to your audience to create a sense of urgency; use the Implementation Framework as a guide; use and adapt the Toolkit for Inclusive Higher Education Institutions to facilitate your journey; apply Universal Design across the institution; recognise the central role of student supports and scaffolding; design and provide tailored Universal Design professional development opportunities for all stakeholders; and, finally, inclusion means moving beyond compliance.

Student as catalysts for change in a University for All

Students are powerful catalysts for change and their role as 'ally' is integral to the implementation process (Chapters 1 and 6). Increasingly the pivotal role of students is being recognised (R. Brooks et al., 2015; Czerniawski and Kidd, 2011). Not only are we asking students to be the catalysts, but we are aiming to challenge their thinking around their entitlement and participation in higher education. Durkheim, and many more since, remind us that talent is equally distributed, but opportunity is not. This perspective, which is one we have started to share with incoming access students, generates occasional disbelief and debate. Students, their advocates, and the system in which we work, are too persuaded by meritocracy. Reay challenges the ease with which we have accepted the satirical concept of meritocracy and notes: "privilege is represented as advantage that the privileged have earned through hard work and ability rather than social, cultural and economic benefits they amass simply by being born into already privileged families" (Reay, 2020, p. 405).

This sense of privilege is not new. In Hardy's exploration of conditions of the working-class poor, *Jude the Obscure*, a stonemason, is repelled in his attempt to go to university:

> Biblioll College. Sir, – I have read your letter with interest Judging from your description of yourself as a working-man, I venture to think that

> you will have a much better chance of success in life by remaining in your own sphere and sticking to your trade than by adopting any other course
> (Hardy and Ingham, 1895, p. 136).

Jude the Obscure's dismissal is a striking reminder of the ease with which an agent of a university can so readily refute or negate the aspirations and expectations of applicants. On that basis, we must recognise that students' awareness of issues of social justice and equity is essential to their educational experience, which, in turn, informs their role as implementation actors. The students' lived experience is a most effective antidote to the received wisdom and associated assumptions, and thus serves as a powerful persuader (CFE Research, 2020).

Empowering students to tell their own stories is important, and it lends authenticity, context, and credibility. We have deployed a range of strategies to weave the voice of students into the implementation of the University for All initiative. Access Leaders are UCD student champions who guide, mentor, and encourage students from their communities to engage with the university. They foster an inclusive and welcoming environment and help us create a university for all, assisting us in our work.

Access Leaders are involved in a variety of activities, both on and off the campus. These range from assisting at annual events, such as the Student Welcome and various symposia, peer mentoring, at outreach events, and acting as Digital Ambassadors, who offer digital and technological support to students. Through such activities, Access Leaders have moved from a passive position, of supporting the programme, to a proactive role, whereby they plan, facilitate, and coordinate the programme. Importantly, Access Leaders also represent the student perspective at university committees and at national conferences. Access Leaders are also ambassadors for the University for All initiative, being part of the development team for an introductory module for all incoming students and at the core of our 'University for All Roadshow', where they 'meet and greet' their fellow students and talk about the student role in an inclusive university.

The student voice is central to the implementation of a university for all, and we argue that this voice is an essential part of the triumvirate of actors. Our students are encouraged to challenge us and not necessarily to have to change themselves. A university for all approach is, by definition, a cultural and institutional change programme that requires our sector to consider moving out of our sphere and amending our structures. In the spirit of Jude the Stone Mason, and captured later when we consider Seamus Heaney's words on Scaffolding, our students are helping us to reframe and build again.

Gathering baseline evidence and demonstrating impact: University for All research

The change process, which is the creation of a university for all, requires a robust evidence-based approach to show impact, shape conversations and thinking, and offer a basis for action. Gathering such evidence and data is the hallmark of implementation, as outlined in Chapter 3.

At every step of our journey, we have foregrounded the student voice and, in 2020, we undertook research with both the student and employee population. This baseline study of views, knowledge, and understanding, offers a window to the university community's thinking, which has moved the conversation, from storytelling of individuals, to gathering evidence systematically to allow for analysis and comparison. This study gathered information in key aspects of university life, which has informed the understanding of the challenges, identified the priority areas for action, and shaped the opportunities for change. The findings offer an insight to student and staff perceptions of inclusion, and also reflect the commitment to impact measurement and to demonstrate the results of the University for All initiative.

Results

Focusing on the student voice, we received 2,839 responses to the anonymous survey issued to the full university population. Responses from students were received as follows: 64 per cent undergraduate, 36 per cent postgraduate; 87 per cent fulltime, 13 per cent part-time. Just under one fifth of respondents disclosed they were linked with the university's access service (i.e., students with a disability, low-income students, mature students, part time learners, further education award holders, refugees/asylum seekers/protection applicants). Some results from the survey will be found in the later chapters of this book, so here we offer only a flavour of how students perceive inclusion in our institution. For each of the five main areas, as delineated in the Toolkit for Inclusive Higher Education Institutions (Kelly and Padden, 2018), we offer you both quantitative data (responses on a Likert scale) and qualitative data (the results of thematic analysis of open text comments – only primary codes are provided here).[1]

Foundation and Scaffolding: Strategic Approach and Organisation

This quantitative response saw the highest number of 'neutral' responses ($n = 719$) and it was clear both in this result and in the qualitative results, students don't necessarily feel an awareness of this area of the university structure. Quite often, students don't see themselves in university strategies and policies, although, of course, the student should always be central in these aspects of university development and processes. In the qualitative responses, students spoke positively about institutional supports, with many commenting specifically on the provision of disability supports. Students also noted the inclusive approach of staff and faculty and their fellow student population. Negative comments most frequently mentioned affordability – an issue at the forefront of Irish higher education currently, specifically in relation to accommodation, as Ireland has been in a rental crisis now for some time

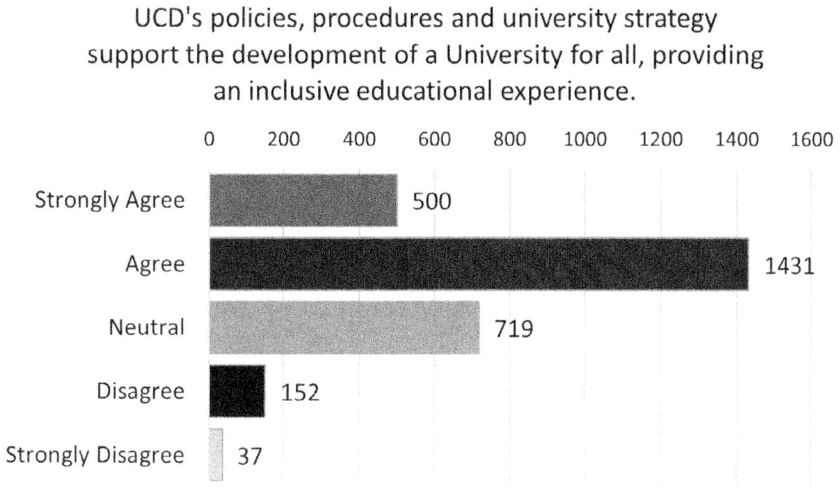

Figure 1.2 Student responses to the statement: 'In my experience, UCD's policies, procedures and university strategy support the development of a University for All, providing an inclusive educational experience'

Table 1.1 Qualitative student responses on inclusion in Foundation and Scaffolding: Strategic Approach and Organisation

Positive (n = 437)	*Negative (n = 235)*
Good institutional support provision	The university is not affordable
Good disability support policies and procedures	Staff/Faculty are not inclusive in their approach
Staff/Faculty are inclusive in their approach	
Student population is diverse and inclusive	
The university is equitable as a whole	

(Reynolds, 2021). The issue of affordability can often be the one most difficult to address, but it must remain a priority for all HEIs, especially with frequent threats of another looming economic crisis. The university foundations, strategic approach, and organisation are discussed in Chapter 2.

Pillar 1: Programme & Curriculum Design, Teaching & Learning

The push for inclusive teaching and learning and, specifically, the move towards the Universal Design for Learning framework, is clearly shown in the results of the survey in this section, although it is clear there are areas still to

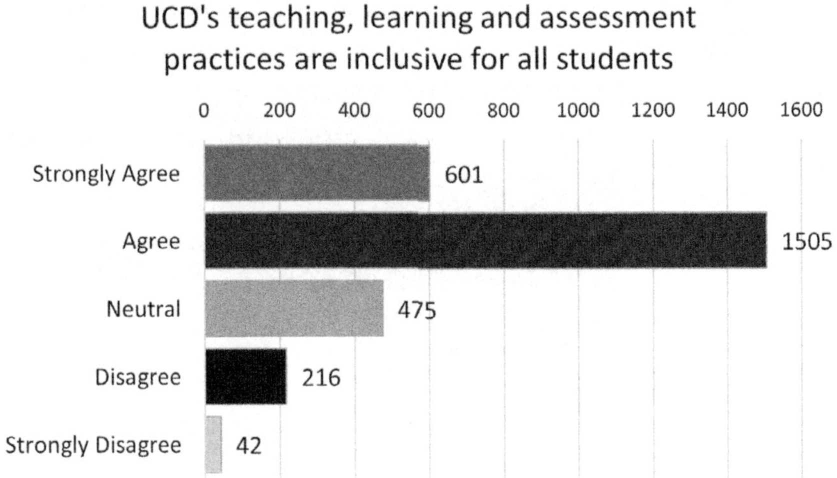

Figure 1.3 Student responses to the statement: 'In my experience UCD's Teaching, Learning and Assessment meet my needs and are inclusive for all students'

Table 1.2 Qualitative student responses on inclusion in Programme & Curriculum Design, Teaching & Learning

Positive (n = 406)	*Negative (n = 309)*
Disability supports are communicated well and provided to students who require them	Lack of understanding of diverse needs of students
Staff/Faculty are supportive and inclusive in their approach	Teaching and learning materials are not made available to students
Diversity of assessment is provided	There is an inconsistent approach to teaching, learning and assessment (some inclusive, others not)
Good communication with staff/faculty	Post Covid experiences have been negative
Flexibility is offered in teaching and learning activities	Disability supports are communicated poorly and not provided to students who require them

address. With a strong positive result in the quantitative response (see Figure 1.3) and many positive comments on disability support provision, staff and faculty approach, diversity in assessment, good communication and flexibility, the negative comments show the inconsistency that students experience in UCD. Inconsistency, in fact, is specifically called out by a number of students. The more inclusive modules within programmes become, the more obvious it is to students when these universally designed measures are absent. Continuing to foreground the student experience and address student feedback is vital in addressing these gaps, alongside a flexible professional development provision to ensure all staff have at least a grounding in Universal Design for Learning. Programme & curriculum design, as well as teaching & learning, are discussed under the umbrella of Universal Design for Learning in Chapter 5.

Pillar 2: Student Supports & Services

Again, it is clear that the majority of students feel that the student supports and services at their university are inclusive and that they meet their individual needs and the needs of the diverse student population. In qualitative responses students commented on the wide range of supports available, the welcoming and approachable nature of these services, and, importantly, the effective

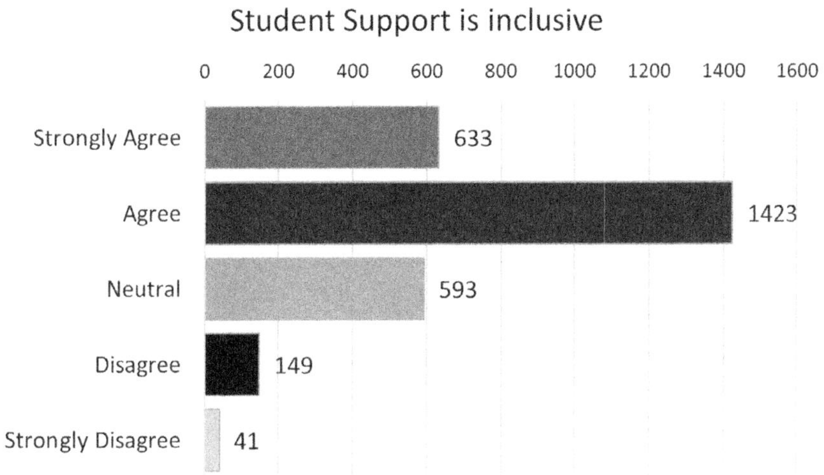

Figure 1.4 Student responses to the statement: 'In my experience UCD's Student Supports and Services meet my needs and are inclusive for all students'

Table 1.3 Qualitative student responses on inclusion in Student Supports & Services

Positive (n = 343)	*Negative (n = 185)*
Supports provided are adequate and effective	Supports provided are not adequate and are ineffective
A wide range of supports are available	The waiting times to access support services are too long
Support services are welcoming and approachable	
Supports are well advertised and communicated	

communication of these supports to students. Interestingly, the adequacy and effectiveness of the supports was the most frequent subject of both positive and negative comments. Again, the inconsistency of the student experience must be explored further to examine which areas specifically are presenting barriers to students, and where the gaps in support provision or communication may exist. Students commented specifically on the difficulties experienced because of waiting times to access services, often referring to mental health supports. The impact of Covid-19 has presented additional barriers in this area and the importance of supports and interventions for students with mental health difficulties was recently reinforced in a large-scale research survey across Irish higher education (Mahon et al., 2022). Inclusion in student supports and services is discussed in two case studies in Chapter 6.

Pillar 3: Physical Campus & the Built Environment

Inclusion in the physical campus can often be easier for people to understand, as the impact of exclusion is more immediately tangible. Again, students were very positive, with most agreeing or strongly agreeing that the campus meets individual needs and is inclusive for all students. Similar to Pillar 2, we see the same subject of most frequent positive and negative comments – the provision of sufficient facilities and amenities for students. The pace of growth and development of a campus with over 30,000 students can certainly be challenging. The University's focus on sustainable and student-centred progression is covered in Chapter 7. Provision of ramps was seen as positive by students and, in a multi-level main campus, this is one of the most visible signs of accessibility on this campus. The issue of parking raised by students points to

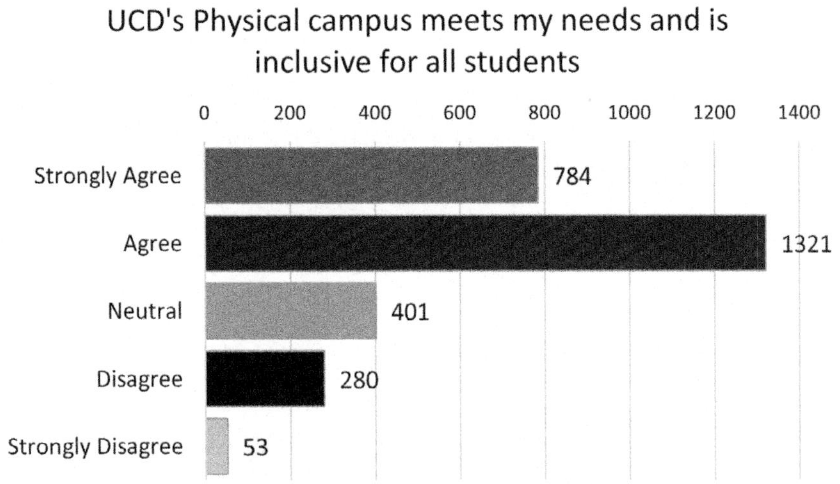

Figure 1.5 Student responses to the statement: 'In my experience UCD's physical campus meets my needs and is inclusive for all students'

Table 1.4 Qualitative student responses on inclusion in Physical Campus & the Built Environment

Positive (n = 307)	*Negative (n = 475)*
The campus provides a variety of facilities and amenities	The campus provides insufficient facilities and amenities
Equitable physical access is provided for all students on campus	Equitable physical access is not provided for all students on campus
Good provision of ramps on campus	There is insufficient parking provided on campus
	There is insufficient provision of automated doors on campus
	The size of the campus makes physical access difficult (distances between areas)

the frequency of commuting by the student population and, again, returns to the issue of affordability of accommodation raised under the foundations section above.

Pillar 4: Information Technology Systems & Infrastructure

As we move through the pillars of the inclusive institution, the general trend for the number of students choosing 'strongly agree' to inclusion in the specific area increased with each section. Again, students report inclusion in the university's technological environment, making specific positive mention of ease of use,

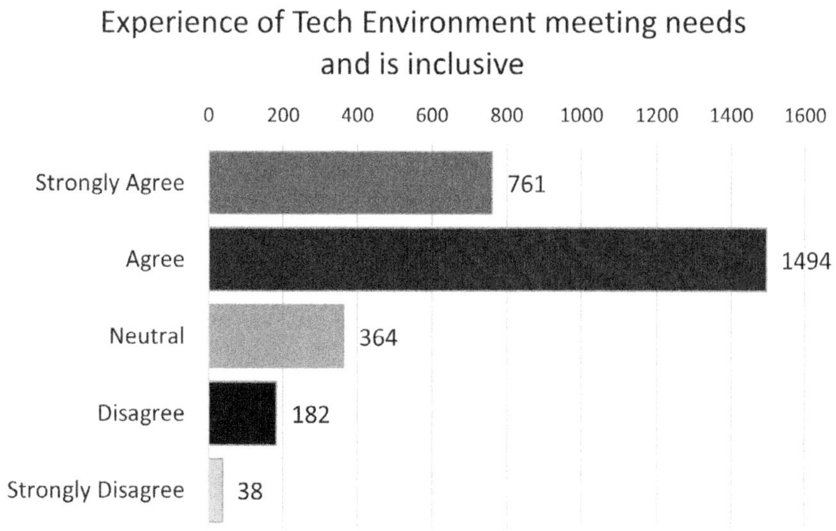

Figure 1.6 Student responses to the statement: In my experience UCD's technological environment meets my needs and is inclusive for all students

Table 1.5 Qualitative student responses on inclusion in Information Technology Systems & Infrastructure

Positive (n = 321)	*Negative (n = 339)*
Technology support and training is provided	The Virtual Learning Environment is difficult to use and/or used inconsistently
There is good technology availability and provision on campus	There is insufficient technology availability and provision on campus
The systems and technology are easy to use	There is poor information provision through systems, websites, and other university digital platforms
The Virtual Learning Environment facilitates learning	
There is good information provision through systems, websites, and other university digital platforms	

training and support, the Virtual Learning Environment, and information provision. Again, students commented most frequently, both positively and negatively, about technology availability and provision on campus, with many referring to the removal of stationary PCs on the campus as negative (see the 'technology provision on campus' in Table 1.5). However, the provision of a laptop loan scheme was a particular positive experience. The lowest number of neutral responses was seen in this area, which reflects the need for all students to engage in the use of technology and, therefore, the importance of inclusion in this pillar. Inclusion in IT Infrastructure and systems is discussed in Chapter 8, with case studies from the institution where this survey took place.

This baseline evidence has been used extensively by those leading inclusion work in UCD, having been disaggregated by discipline to aid in the implementation workshops described in Chapter 4, and to facilitate the work of change teams and other project work in the University. This baseline research survey will be repeated in the future, allowing us to measure progress against this clear benchmark. The consideration of a research and impact measurement framework is essential, alongside the other work of inclusion in higher education institutions. The ability to demonstrate impact and use evidence to assign resources is vital for long-term change projects such as the one described in this book.

Cynics and sceptics – some insight and strategies

Many of us are familiar with the film, 'As Good as It Gets' (J. Brooks, 1997), where Jack Nicholson plays Melvin Udall, the curmudgeonly character who 'knows all the angles', is suspicious and judgemental, and who is considered the epitome of the cynic or sceptic. Udall's work as a writer of romantic novels suggests a contradiction, however. During our time implementing the

University for All initiative, we often encountered Melvin Udall! Sceptical, suspicious, unconvinced, doubters who scoffed, or put up 'straw men' theories. It is important however to remember that the cynic or sceptic also plays an important role by questioning and prompting wider discussion (Baggini, 2013).

The 'inclusion leads' that we work with often say they are 'preaching to the choir' – delivering the message to those who are already invested in the idea of inclusion. As such, too often, we operate in echo chambers. 'Inclusion leads' also report 'pushback' from 'Melvin Udall types'; colleagues who are not convinced by the message of inclusion, who report being time poor, who cite their many demands, and people who see their work and responsibilities differently. Understanding the issues behind such views is important. Are they masking something else? What is prompting their views?

It is important that those leading such change initiatives in higher education anticipate the Melvin Udall's of higher education. Rogers' (2003) model of Diffusion of Innovation offers a useful way to understand and plan for encounters with Melvin Udall types. This model classifies adopters into those who are more open – the early adopters; those who come on board as momentum builds; through to those that Rogers labels as 'laggards', who tend to remain unconvinced. The implementation of the University for All initiative has mirrored this pattern of momentum. It serves to underscore the importance of communication and persuasion and reminds us not to let the perfect get in the way of the good. Organisational change studies suggest those who may be cynical about change often report being 'left in the dark'. In other words, they point to poor communications (Armenakis et al., 2007; Hammond et al., 2011; Kotter, 2012; Reichers et al., 1997). We are no longer taken by surprise when we meet cynics or sceptics; on the contrary, we are focused on developing strategies to extend ownership and buy-in, such as using the Toolkit for Inclusive Higher Education Institutions (Kelly & Padden, 2018) workshops to explore issues and find common ground (Chapter 4), presenting the data and evidence (Chapter 3). This helps to demonstrate 'what works' – such as discipline-specific case studies (Padden et al., 2021, 2019, 2017). Paying attention to communication and promotion, deploying the art of persuasion, and telling the story are central to engaging others (Chapter 4), as is including the student experience (Chapters 1 and 6).

Finally, using Communities of Practice (CoP) (Wenger, 2006, 1998) as a mechanism to share experience, knowledge, and learning proves invaluable. Our experience suggests that CoPs can be configured in myriad ways, such as being role and discipline specific. Such discussion groups can take a range of formats, including, in-person, online formats, social media platforms, and web chat tools.

Conclusion

This book lays out all the components to answer the 'how' question – 'How to make access and inclusion everybody's business – How to create a university for all'? It is informed by our experience of leading the University for

All initiative in University College Dublin (UCD) and underpinned by theory, evidence, and practice. We offer the reader the tools to translate rhetoric to reality. This is a tried, tested, and transferable model to transform higher education and create inclusive institutions, where all students feel they belong.

We have set the stage, identified the characters, described the scenes, and written the script. These are the moving parts that will build this new reality. The choreography, however, is at the discretion of the reader. It is important to remember that change is not linear but, rather, shaped by context, is iterative, incremental, and, thus, a 'big bang' or revolution is highly unusual. There is one essential component in this change journey, however: the need to begin. We urge readers to take inspiration from Horace, the Roman poet, who said, "Begin, be bold and venture to be wise". With that first step, however tentative and uncertain, the odyssey begins, and the future unfolds.

Note

1 The top five primary qualitative codes are provided where more than 20 student comments were coded with the same themed response. Many students commented that they felt the area in question was inclusive for them but didn't feel they should comment on others. Where the response was coded as this, it is removed from the top five provided in the tables.

References

Armenakis, A.A., Bernerth, J.B., Pitts, J.P., and Walker, H.J. (2007). Organizational change recipients' beliefs scale: Development of an assessment instrument. *The Journal of Applied Behavioral Science*, 43, 481–485, 487–493, 495–505.

Baggini, J. (2013). In praise of cynicism. *The Guardian*, 10 July.

Brooks, J. (1997). As Good as it Gets. Sony Pictures Releasing.

Brooks, R., Byford, K., and Sela, K. (2015). The changing role of Students' Unions within contemporary higher education. *Journal of Education Policy*, 30, 165–181.

Callaghan, P. (2000). Equality, change and institutional barriers In L. Thomas and M. Cooper (eds), *Changing the Culture of the Campus: Towards Inclusive Higher Education*. Stoke-on-Trent: Staffordshire University Press.

CFE Research (2020). *The Role of Lived Experience in Creating Systems Change: Evaluation of Fulfilling Lives: Supporting People with Multiple Needs*. Leicester, UK: CFE Research.

Czerniawski, G. and Kidd, W. (eds). (2011). *The Student Voice Handbook: Bridging the Academic/Practitioner Divide*. Bingley, UK: Emerald Group Publishing.

Greenbank, P. (2007). Introducing widening participation policies in higher education: The influence of institutional culture. *Research in Post-Compulsory Education*, 12 (2), 209–224.

Hammond, G.D., Gresch, E.B., and Vitale, D.C. (2011). Homegrown process improvement employing a change message model. *Journal of Organizational Change Management*, 24, 487–510. https://doi.org/10.1108/09534811111144638.

Hardy, T. and Ingham, P. (1895). *Jude the Obscure*. Oxford: Oxford University Press.

HEA (2015). *National Plan for Equity of Access to Higher Education, 2015–2019*. Dublin: Higher Education Authority.

HEA (2018a). *Progress Review of the National Access Plan and Priorities to 2021*. Dublin: Higher Education Authority.

HEA (2018b). *Higher Education System Performance Framework 2018–2020*. Dublin: Higher Education Authority.

Kelly, A. (2017). *An Analysis of the Implementation of National Access Policy to Integrate and Mainstream Equality of Access in Irish Universities – Through the Lens of Inclusive Design*, PhD dissertation, University College Dublin, Dublin.

Kelly, A. (2018). From the margins to mainstreaming – a universally designed and inclusive approach to access and participation in UCD. In B. Mooney (ed.), *Ireland's Yearbook of Education. Mapping the Past. Forging the Future 2017–2018*. Dublin: Education Matters.

Kelly, A.M. and Padden, L. (2018). *Toolkit for Inclusive Higher Education Institutions: From Vision to Practice*. Dublin: UCD Access & Lifelong Learning.

Kotter, J.P. (2012). *Leading Change*. Cambridge, MA: Harvard Business Press.

Mahon, C., Fitzgerald, A., O'Reilly, A., and Dooley, B. (2022). Profiling third-level student mental health: Findings from My World Survey 2. *Irish Journal of Psychological Medicine*, 1–9. doi:10.1017/ipm.2021.85.

May, H. and Bridger, K. (2010). *Developing and Embedding Inclusive Policy and Practice in Higher Education*. York: Higher Education Academy.

Padden, L., Buggy, C., and Shotton, E. (eds). (2021). *Inclusive Teaching & Learning Case Studies in Engineering, Architecture & Affiliated Disciplines*. Dublin: UCD Access & Lifelong Learning.

Padden, L., O'Connor, J., and Barrett, T. (eds). (2017). *Universal Design for Curriculum Design*. Dublin: UCD Access & Lifelong Learning.

Padden, L., Tonge, J., Moylan, T., and O'Neill, G. (eds). (2019). *Inclusive Assessment and Feedback: Case Studies from University College Dublin and Dun Laoghaire Institute of Art Design and Technology*. Dublin: UCD Access & Lifelong Learning.

Reay, D. (2020). The perils and penalties of meritocracy: Sanctioning inequalities and legitimating prejudice. *The Political Quarterly*, 91, 405–412.

Reichers, A.E., Wanous, J.P., and Austin, J.T. (1997). Understanding and managing cynicism about organizational change. *The Academy of Management Executive (1993–2005)*, 11, 48–59.

Reynolds, A. (2022). Contesting the financialization of student accommodation: Campaigns for the right to housing in Dublin, Ireland, *Housing Studies*. doi:10.1080/02673037.2021.2023731.

Thomas, L. (2011). Institutional transformation to engage a diverse student body. In L. Thomas and M. Tight (eds), *Institutional Transformation to Engage a Diverse Student Body*, International Perspectives on Higher Education Vol. 6. Bingley, UK: Emerald Group Publishing.

Thomas, L., Storan, J., Wylie, V., Berzins, K., Harley, P., Linley, R., and Rawson, A. (2009). *Review of Widening Participation Strategic Assessments*. Action on Access. The National Co-ordination Team for Widening Participation.

Tuitt, F. (2016). Making excellence inclusive in challenging times. *Liberal Education*, 102(2), 64–68.

UCD (2018). *Equality, Diversity and Inclusion (EDI) Strategy and Action Plan 2018–2020–2025*. Dublin: University College Dublin.

UCD (2020). *To the Rising Future, UCD Strategy 2020–2024*. Dublin: University College Dublin.

UCD (2021). *Education and Student Success Strategy*. Dublin: University College Dublin.

Walsh, J. (2014). The transformation of higher education in Ireland, 1945–1980. In A. Loxley, A. Seery, and J. Walsh (eds), *Higher Education in Ireland. Policies, Practices and Possibilities*. Houndmills, Basingstoke, UK: Palgrave Macmillan, pp. 5–31.

Wenger, E. (1998). *Communities of Practice: Learning, Meaning and Identity*. New York: Cambridge University Press.

Wenger, E. (2006). Communities of practice: A brief introduction. Retrieved from http://www.ewenger.com/theory/ (accessed 2 December 2010).

Chapter 2

Foundations and Scaffolding: Strategic Approach and Organisation

2.1 Adopting an institutional approach – moving from silos to mainstreaming inclusion

Anna M. Kelly

Introduction

My experience of education prompts me to think about access and widening participation in terms of 'motherhood and apple pie'! People generally believe that it is a good thing to do. Of course, there are the contrarians, but I think most people believe that everyone is entitled to a 'fair shot'. However, this belief does not easily translate into institution-wide practice and culture change, as access has remained a marginal activity in higher education. That is not to deny the work of access professionals, and committed members of the academic community, who rigorously pursue widening participation objectives. Their commitment is clear: a diverse student population continues to grow (HEA, 2018). However, this has not resulted in moving access and inclusion to centre stage in higher education. Experience suggests that an absence of know-how, confidence, and understanding has inhibited the opportunity to capitalise on progress made in widening participation. Higher education's approach to access and inclusion has been predicated on altruism, aspiration raising, and alternative entry and study options (Thomas et al., 2005). Indeed, embracing institutional transformation assumes change across the gamut of policies, procedures and processes (Kelly, 2017; Burke, 2012; Hill and Hatt, 2012; Thomas, 2011).

Almost two centuries after Newman's Idea of a University as touched on in the Foreword (Newman, 1891), UCD's University for All is shaping and informing higher education. Uniquely in Irish higher education, we have pioneered institutional transformation to create an inclusive culture and promote system change, where all students belong and are valued, and where the philosophy of 'a student is a student' underpins the development of universally designed mainstream systems, processes, and approaches. In other words, we are reimaging higher education so that it reflects the diversity of twenty-first century student populations (UCD, 2022, 2021, 2020, 2018).

University for All is our big idea for the twenty-first century, with a sustainable and supportive culture to promote and embed access and inclusion and realise institutional transformation. Its capacity-building ethos strengthens and

DOI: 10.4324/9781003253631-3

enables the entire university community to make a distinctive contribution to ensuring that the benefits of higher education are available to all in our society. Critically, implementation of this big idea generates solutions that eliminate duplication and successfully promote circularity and sustainability. We hope the legacy effect will be a culture of inclusion that will shape higher education, where university is for all. Students expect and need nothing less.

What is University for All?

University for All is a whole-institution evidence-based and systemic response to access and inclusion in higher education, which considers access and inclusion through an institutional lens (Kelly, 2018; Kelly and Padden, 2018a). University for All addresses the key components to realise the institutional transformation and culture change needed to fully embed and mainstream access and inclusion. The hallmarks of this model are as follows:

- It is a systemic response that weaves inclusion into the fabric of the university at all levels
- It engages the entire university community, academic and professional staff
- It addresses all aspects of campus life – teaching, learning, support, services, and the built and technology infrastructure
- It extends access beyond entry and admissions, to develop an inclusive educational experience for all students.

Uniquely, this model is not focussed on opening doors to higher education; instead, its focus is on the institution's ethos, values, principles, and practice. Historically, some groups of students in higher education were referred to as 'other' – they were considered differently, labelled accordingly, considered 'non-traditional', their journey to university was described as 'exceptional'; they 'beat the odds', they were 'not like the rest', 'not one of us', not a 'traditional' student. In today's diverse society, University for All challenges these assumptions and perceptions; it questions how things are done; it demands that the difference is recognised; that diversity is valued. Inclusion is placed centre-stage; student access, participation, and success migrate from the margins to the mainstream. University for All flips our thinking, transforms problems into opportunities, and develops new ways of doing. In so doing, 'how' rather than 'why' becomes the question. University for All offers a universally designed approach that values all students, recognising that 'a student is a student'. Conversations shift from theoretical arguments about the merits of inclusion, to solution-mode and the need to offer flexible responses that accommodate and include all. It replaces a siloed or bolted-on approach (Jones and Thomas, 2005) in favour of embedding and integrating access and addressing the question of how to make inclusion a collective responsibility and everyone's business.

Policy context

The University for All model was developed as an innovative response to national access policy, to widen participation to reflect the diversity of Ireland's population (HEA, 2018, 2015, 2008, 2004). Crucially, these policies also advocate the integration of access and inclusion into the "everyday life of the HEIs so that it permeates all faculties and departments and is not marginalised as the responsibility of the designated access office" (HEA, 2015, p. 25). This vision very clearly moves access and inclusion from being an institutional 'add on' to being integral to the higher education institution – becoming an institutional core belief and value that is practised and demonstrated. Significant progress has been made to widen participation of under-represented groups in higher education (HEA, 2018). However, this vision goes much further; it challenges us to move beyond opening doors, beyond the development of a pipeline of diverse students, beyond silos, beyond quotas, beyond labels, beyond the rhetoric of access. This policy calls for systemic change; it asks institutions to translate the vision for diversity and inclusion into tangible changes across all aspects of campus life.

However, the pace of implementation has remained slow. A review undertaken by the HEA observed

> Equity of access remains for the most part on the margins in higher education. It is not yet part of the day-to-day practical agenda of institutions. This slows progress in attracting and retaining students from diverse backgrounds and in introducing inclusive teaching and learning strategies into the higher education.
>
> (HEA, 2006, p. 14)

In the first study of its kind, I interviewed the Presidents/Provosts, Chief Academic Officers/Registrars, and Student Union Presidents in Ireland's seven universities. This study revealed an absence of institution-wide policies and practices to foster and inculcate inclusion and diversity (Kelly, 2017). Yet another review by the Higher Education Authority noted the "uncertainty in higher education institutions as to the meaning of mainstreaming and its operation in practice" (HEA, 2018, p. 14). Anne Rabbitte, T.D. and Minister for Disability also noted the absence of progress in the area of mainstreaming inclusion (IUA, 2020).

Throughout Europe, there is an increasing awareness of diversity, inclusion, and equity issues in higher education with migration and globalisation contributing to this growing awareness. The Bologna Process frames the enhancement of European higher education, focussing on degree structures, ECTS credits, mobility of staff and students, quality assurance, and the creation of socially inclusive higher education (EUA, 2008; Westerheijden et al., 2010). It is argued it has "transformed the face of European higher education" (European Commission et al., 2012, p. 7): however, progress is less evident in respect of equity of access (European Commission, EACEA, and Eurydice, 2015). More recently, Ministers responsible for higher education reaffirmed their commitment to developing a more inclusive, innovative, interconnected, and resilient European Higher Education Area (EHEA Rome 2020, 2020). Over the years, we have seen much discussion, reports, and, indeed, commitment at state, institutional, and personal levels. As experienced access professionals however, it became apparent to us that this belief in the merits of access and inclusion was not matched with the confidence or knowledge to realise the vison of inclusion (Unger, 2019).

Development of the University for All model

The evolution of the University for All approach was influenced by, and drew on, work in 'Universal Design' (Mace, 1998; Rose and Meyer, 2002), 'inclusive design' (Goodman, 2016; Clarkson and Coleman, 2015; Politis et al., 2014), and 'design for all' (Bendixen and Benktzon, 2015). This approach also built on my earlier research, where I developed an Inclusive Design Framework that proposed key institution-related elements to support universities to embed and mainstream access and develop an inclusive ethos and approach (Kelly, 2017). The University for All model was also influenced by practice of the University's access professionals, whose work to widen participation for specific groups highlighted the need for sustainable, long term holistic solutions. Such thinking reinforced the importance of a universal designed learning experience, where all students would feel welcome and were not considered 'other'. Rather than expecting, or indeed requiring, some students to modify or change in order to fit in, it became apparent that a change of practice was needed.

Critically, the University for All initiative, it is not a 'one size fits all' approach. Rather, this model recognises a need to offer a range of bespoke solutions to meet the requirements of particular students. Importantly however, the University for All approach ensures that such solutions are offered in an integrated mainstream way, and do not result in students being marginalised or 'othered'. The theme of Universal Design and its central place in the University for All concept is detailed in Chapter 6, while Chapter 5 elaborates upon the development and use of the Toolkit for Inclusive Higher Education Institutions (Kelly and Padden, 2018b).

From vision to practice – is there a magic answer to implementation?

We are frequently asked this implementation question – regrettably, there is no magic answer with no single action that can be taken; there in no silver bullet. However, since we began this journey, we have amassed experience, wisdom, and expertise, and through this we have developed and refined the list of ingredients necessary for implementation success.

The first of these ingredients is to **begin**! Taking a lead from George Bernard Shaw, who advised that we "don't wait for the right opportunity, create it: the critical decision is to start, to seize the day – carpe diem!" Momentum will build and there are numerous strategies that can be deployed to create interest, but not until you begin and create that opportunity. Our experience suggests that the beginning is not easy, it can be a solitary isolated space; best characterised as 'ploughing a lonely furrow'. Aristotle observed, "Men become builders by building and lyreplayers by playing the lyre; so too we become just by doing just acts, temperate by doing temperate acts, brave by doing brave acts". So too, we must act to enable the odyssey of change and transformation to commence!

Understanding of implementation challenges

Enabling institutional transformation and culture change, such as University for All, is a complex and challenging endeavour. It can be daunting, even intimidating; our access colleagues in UCD coined the word 'OBAAT' – one bite at a time! Originally, it was invented to help students withstand the deluge of information, material, and instructions as they grapple with their studies. The OBAAT strategy also serves our implementation purpose very well. Our experience confirms that translating ideas into action in a higher education institution can be equally overwhelming. As Pressman and Wildavsky (1984), considered the 'founding fathers' of implementation studies, observed:

> People appear to think that implementation should be easy: they are therefore upset when expected events do not occur or turn out badly. We consider our efforts a success if more people began with the understanding that implementation under the best of circumstances, is exceedingly difficult. They would, therefore, be pleasantly surprised when a few good things really happened.
>
> (pp. xx–xxi).

Higher education institutions are complex organisations, with different traditions, missions and structures, competing priorities, external pressures, and financial constraints. In such circumstances, implementation is intricate and multi-facetted. Van Meter and Van Horn's (1975) framework, cited by Hill and Hupe (2009, p. 47), proposed six inter-related implementation-related features:

- Standards and objectives
- Resources
- Inter-organisational relationships
- Characteristics of implementing organisations
- Environmental factors
- 'Disposition' of implementers.

Our experience of translating policy into practice reinforces the role of each of these. As the people leading the implementation of University for All in a large public university, we are what Bowen (1982) called 'hopeful implementers'. She recommended a compelling range of tactics and associated strategies, including: the importance of persistence, developing multiple implementation ideas, setting priorities and engineering a 'bandwagon effect' (pp. 18–20). This appreciation of the implementation strategy, and understanding the place of tactics, coupled with our own pragmatic and opportunistic mentality, equipped us well for our implementation odyssey.

Intangibles – essentials for this journey

On reflection, the practice of change implementation has highlighted the importance of mind-set when undertaking such a large-scale project. My experience of leading change in various large public organisations, knowing the highs and lows, has instilled in me a 'glass half full' mentality, searching for the silver lining, constantly learning how to make the best out of situations.

So, with this in mind, I consider courage and self-belief, comfort with ambiguity, and a healthy respect for imperfection, as essential ingredients in sustaining the development and implementation of a project of this scale and complexity. These intangibles helped us to make progress, propelled us forward, and strengthened our resolve in the face of headwinds.

The dictionary definition of **courage** is "the quality of mind or spirit that enables a person to face difficulty, danger, pain, etc., without fear; bravery", while self-belief is described as "confidence in your own abilities or judgment". Inspired by the oft-misquoted line "If you build it, he will come" from the film 'Field of Dreams' (1989), such courage and self-belief inspired and, indeed, sustains the development of University for All. Of course, project planning was integral to its development, but, at the start, we were breaking new ground. The blueprint for a holistic whole-institution initiative was developed in real time, in a highly regarded public university, where reputation, standing, and image are key considerations. Thus, having a courageous confident 'build and they will come' attitude was key; its role cannot be underestimated.

Being comfortable with levels of **ambiguity** is another intangible that, in my view, is invaluable to implementation. Grappling with uncertainties, and expecting the unexpected, are features of many projects, but were particularly evident at the beginning of our implementation process. As noted earlier, we were innovating; this was a first in Irish higher education, and this ground had not been mapped. As Donald Rumsfeld famously said, there are 'known knowns', 'known unknowns', and 'unknown unknowns' (Zak, 2021). Despite the best planning, scenario making, and contingency preparation, things will not always go to plan. Setbacks, unintended consequences, alongside happy coincidences and pleasant surprises, all featured in University for All implementation. Holding one's nerve, staying calm and resolute in the face of

Table 2.1 The key components of the University for All Implementation Framework as indicated in Figure 1.1 (previous chapter)

Critical components of the University for All Implementation Framework	
Component	*Action*
Institutional leadership and strategic planning	• Articulate the vision and commitment to becoming an inclusive university in the institution's strategic plan. This creates visibility, offers direction, anchors the initiative, and signals institutional commitment both internally and externally • Develop the university's access and inclusion strategy, which includes key objectives that focus on institutional components, such as teaching and learning, built and technological environments, as well as those of the student dimension, e.g. engagement, support and welfare, and measurable targets, and key performance indicators • Assign leadership and accountability responsibility to a senior institutional leader who sits on the institution's management team, and acts as senior sponsor • Seek the support of senior academic and professional staff who have a vital role in achieving buy-in and communicating the University for All message
Evidence and data (see Chapter 3)	• Use evidence and data as a key lever to guide and support institutional change • Set participation targets at institution and programme levels that include and reflect all the under-represented groups • Gather and publish student data, including entry, participation, and success at institution and programme levels
Governance & structures	• Develop institutional governance arrangements that integrate with organisational structures and process, and enable coherence, co-ordination and strategic alignment • Establish an institutional oversight committee, led by a senior leader, to guide, monitor and support institutional change. Members are nominated representatives rather than selected because of their personal interest only • Develop a hybrid structure for the management of student access, diversity and inclusion, which provides central co-ordination while dispersing responsibility and accountability to academic schools and programmes • Incorporate 'top-down' and 'bottom-up' in the implementation process to facilitate discussion and allow time and space to align implementation with 'local' factors

Critical components of the University for All Implementation Framework

Implementation planning & delivery	• Be realistic in implementation timelines; systemic change takes time, so allow for incremental change, early adopters, and develop strategies to extend ownership and buy-in (Rogers, 2003) • Assign 'local' people to lead, co-ordinate and champion implementation of University for All within their Schools, Units, Colleges • Promote the development of local alliances, such as senior leaders for Teaching & Learning, Equality, Diversity & Inclusion (and others, where appropriate) • Designate a team to provide University for All 'scaffolding', which enables and drives the process of institutional change and provides the requisite expertise and knowledge • Use the Toolkit for Inclusive Higher Education Institutions (Kelly and Padden, 2018b) to drive the implementation process, including gathering examples of good practice, identifying areas to be addressed and developing and publishing Action Plans • Ensure that the student voice is incorporated • Make local implementation plans available to all
Consultation	• Build in regular consultation arrangements, including with individuals, groups, and 'Town Hall' style meetings, to test awareness and develop understanding of mainstreaming and inclusion.
Promotion & communication	• Develop a communications strategy to articulate and represent the institution's vision, support and commitment to inclusion • Develop strategies to encourage and support buy-in, build visibility and accountability, e.g., availability of local implementation plans to the entire community, using dissemination opportunities, such as publication of reports, speeches, symposia/conferences • Identify early 'adopters' and use a variety of means to showcase good practice, such as publishing case studies; celebrate pockets of good practice as they emerge • Promote the development of Communities of Practice • Use consistent branding to ensure communication of a clear message
Staff training and development	• Promote the use of recognition and reward systems to acknowledge and encourage staff to participate and adopt inclusive practices • Develop a professional development framework for all employees (faculty, professional, support), which use a variety of ways and opportunities to develop understanding of mainstreaming and inclusion, such as an induction process for new staff and formal training such as Universal Design.

adversity, are the hallmarks of those who work in areas of social justice. Such qualities proved invaluable.

The final intangible that sustained us during the implementation of University for All was a healthy respect for **imperfection**. Voltaire is attributed with the phrase "perfection is the enemy of the good"; during the work to design and implement an inclusive university, this phrase provided solace and ensured that the project did not get bogged down. A clearer picture emerged over time, but in the early stages, there was a lot of fuzziness, with pictures not yet in focus. Being able to assess risk, make adaptions, and problem solve are significant at the projection initiation stage. However, we continue to invoke these, as momentum builds, and implementation takes root across the university.

The lasting lesson learnt during development of the University for All idea, is that incremental achievement, compromise and less than perfect solutions all generate movement in the right direction. Courageously taking that step forward demonstrates a level of seriousness and intention, conveys energy and belief, and is integral to building momentum, or as Bowen (1982) put it, creates the bandwagon effect.

Implementation Framework

Systemic change is not easily achieved. It is a not linear process and in our experience doesn't have a pre-determined starting point. The development of our implementation strategy was influenced by research in three particular domains. We drew on Bowen (1982), Hill and Hupe (2009), and Pressman and Wildavsky (1984), whose work concerns policy implementation. We also relied on studies that examined higher education access policy from an institutional perspective, specifically, Kelly (2017), Tuitt (2016), Blythman and Orr (2002), and Woodrow and Thomas (2002). This strategy was shaped by leadership research of Kotter (2001, 2014), Aguirre and Martinez (2002), Butcher et al. (2012), and the ECU (2014).

Finally, in developing our implementation approach, our access practice, knowledge, and experience of higher education, greatly enhanced and grounded it in practicability and feasibility. Relying on these research and practice sources offered important building blocks; however, it is important to also note that our approach to implementation remains iterative, amenable to adjustment, and pragmatic (Bowen, 1982).

Conclusion

Higher education institutions are increasingly reflective of society's diverse population mix and, as a result, universities and colleges are now different places, and so need to plan for this new reality. Higher education institutions in the twenty-first century are challenged to design-in more flexibilities that meet the needs of all students and offer a learning experience that takes account of the breadth of student needs. The key question is how to build on the success of 'opening doors' to higher education; how to move access and inclusion from an 'add on' or marginal activity. The answer lies in the University for All model, which offers a roadmap to transforming higher education institutions and building a culture of inclusion, where all students feel that they belong.

We initially developed University for All as a concept and now have successfully translated this vision into a tangible and workable institutional approach to inclusion. There is no magic wand sadly, but our experience has enabled us to identify a set of key ingredients necessary to navigate this change journey. We have developed an implementation strategy in real-time, in a public research-intensive highly regarded university. We have developed a sophisticated understanding of the challenges and opportunities inherent in this journey of institutional transformation and systemic culture change. Because of our experience of learning through doing, and the judgement that we applied to this complex and intricate task, we can confidently share our collective wisdom, insights, and expertise in adopting an institutional approach, moving from silos to mainstreaming inclusion.

References

Aguirre, A.J. and Martinez, R. (2002). Leadership practices and diversity in higher education: Transitional and transformational frameworks. *The Journal of Leadership Studies*, 8, 54–62.

Bendixen, K. and Benktzon, M. (2015). Design for all in Scandinavia – a strong concept. *Applied Ergonomics*, 46, 248–257. https://doi.org/10.1016/j.apergo.2013.03.004

Blythman, M. and Orr, S. (2002). A framework for institutional change. In A. Hayton and A. Pacuska (eds), *Access, Participation and Higher Education*. London: Kogan Page, pp. 165–177.

Bowen, E. (1982). The Pressman-Wildavsky Paradox: Four addenda or why models based on probability theory can predict implementation success and suggest useful tactical advice for implementers. *Journal of Public Policy*, 2, 1–2.

Butcher, J., Corfield, R., and Rose-Adams, J. (2012). Contextualised approaches to widening participation: A comparative case study of two UK universities. *Widening Participation and Lifelong Learning*, 13, 51–70. https://doi.org/10.5456/WPLL.13.S.51

Clarkson, J. and Coleman, R. (2015). History of inclusive design in the UK. *Applied Ergonomics*, 46, 235–247. https://doi.org/10.1016/j.apergo.2013.03.002

ECU (2014). *The Rationale for Equality and Diversity: How Vice-Chancellors and Principals Are Leading Change*. London: Equality Challenge Unit.

EHEA Rome 2020 (2020). Rome Ministerial Communiqué. EHEA, Bologna Process, Italian BFUG Secretariat.

EUA (2008). *Europe's New Education Landscape*. Brussels: European University Association.

European Commission, EACEA, and Eurydice (2015). *The European Higher Education Area in 2015*. Bologna Process Implementation Report. Luxemburg: Publication Office of the European Union.

European Commission, Eurydice, Eurostat, & Eurostudent.eu (2012). *The European Higher Education Area in 2012: Bologna Process Implementation Report*. Brussels: Education, Audiovisual and Culture Executive Agency (P9 Eurydice).

Goodman, L. (2016). *Generation touch: Hippocratic innovation, empathetic education and creative technology – innovation for real social change.* Paper presented at the ISSAConference on Early Childhood in Times of Rapid Change, 11–13 October, Vilnius, Lithuania.

HEA (2018). *Progress Review of the National Access Plan and Priorities to 2021.* Dublin: Higher Education Authority.

HEA (2015). *National Plan for Equity of Access to Higher Education, 2015–2019.* Dublin: Higher Education Authority.

HEA (2008). *National Plan for Equity of Access to Higher Education: 2008–2013.* Dublin: Higher Education Authority.

HEA (2006). *Annual Report 2005 and Outline Plans 2007.* Dublin: National Office for Equity of Access to Higher Education, Higher Education Authority.

HEA (2004). *Achieving Equity of Access to Higher Education in Ireland: Action Plan 2005–2007.* Dublin: National Office for Equity of Access to Higher Education.

Hill, M. (2012). *The Public Policy Process*, 6th edn. New York: Pearson.

Hill, M. and Hupe, P. (2009). *Implementing Public Policy*, 2nd edn. London: Sage.

IUA (2020). IUA Future of Ireland Webinar: The Inclusive University: Moving access, inclusion and diversity from the margins in higher education. Available at: https://www.iua.ie/events/iua-future-of-ireland-webinar-the-inclusive-university-moving-access-inclusion-and-diversity-from-the-margins-in-higher-education-26-nov-1230/ (accessed 29 July 2021).

Jones, R. and Thomas, L. (2005). The 2003 UK Government Higher Education White Paper: A critical assessment of its implications for the access and widening participation agenda. *Journal of Education Policy, 20*, 615–630.

Kelly, A. (2018). From the margins to mainstreaming – a universally designed and inclusive approach to access and participation in UCD. In B. Mooney (ed.), *Ireland's Yearbook of Education. Mapping the Past. Forging the Future 2017–2018.* Dublin: Education Matters.

Kelly, A. (2017). *An Analysis of the Implementation of National Access Policy to Integrate and Mainstream Equality of Access in Irish Universities – Through the Lens of Inclusive Design*, PhD Dissertation, University College Dublin, Dublin.

Kelly, A. and Padden, L. (2018a). University for All: Embedding equality of access, participation and success in higher education. In *Universal Design & Higher Education in Transformation Congress: Conference Proceedings.* Dublin: Centre for Universal Design/IOS Publications.

Kelly, A.M. and Padden, L. (2018b). *Toolkit for Inclusive Higher Education Institutions – From Vision to Practice*, University for All Publication Series. Dublin: UCD Access & Lifelong Learning, Dublin.

Kotter, J. (2001). What leaders really do. *Harvard Business Review*, December, pp. 3–11.

Kotter, J.P. (2014). *Accelerate: Building Strategic Agility for a Faster-Moving World*, 1st edn. Boston, MA: Harvard Business Review Press.

Mace, R. (1985). Universal design: Barrier free environments for everyone. *Designers West*, 33(1), 147–152.

Newman, J. (1891). *Historical Sketches.* Volume 3 of *Rise and Progress of Universities; Northmen and Normans in England and Ireland; Medieval Oxford Convocation of Canterbury.* London: Longmans, Green, and Co, New York.

Politis, Y., Deveril, D., Baldiris Navarro, S., Avila, C., de Lera, E., Monjo, T., & Goodman, L. (2014). *Introducing the Inclusive Learning Handbook: An OER for teachers and policy makers.* Paper presented at the 6th Annual International

Conference on Education and New Learning Technologies (Edulearn'14), International Association of Technology, Education and Development (IATED), Barcelona, Spain.

Pressman, J.L. and Wildavsky, A.B. (1984). *Implementation*. Berkeley, CA: University of California Press.

Robinson, P.A. (1989). Field of Dreams. Universal Pictures.

Rogers, E. (2003). *Diffusion of Innovations*, 5th edn. New York: Free Press.

Rose, D.H. and Meyer, A. (2002). *Teaching Every Student in the Digital Age: Universal Design for Learning*. Alexandria, VA: Association for Supervision and Curriculum Development.

Thomas, L. (2011). *Institutional Transformation to Engage a Diverse Student Body*. Institutional Transformation to Engage a Diverse Student Body, Vol. 6. Bingley, UK: Emerald Group Publishing.

Thomas, L., May, H., Harrop, H., Houston, M., Knox, H., Lee, M., … Trotman, C. (2005). *From the Margins to Mainstream: Embedding Widening Participation in Higher Education*. Universities UK and the Standing Conference of Principals. Available at: http://www.universitiesuk.ac.uk/Publications/Documents/margins_fullreport.pdf

Tuitt, F. (2016). Making excellence inclusive in challenging times. *Liberal Education*, 102(2), 64–68.

UCD (2022). *Submission to the HEA National Access Plan 2022–2026 Public Consultation Process*. Dublin: University College Dublin.

UCD (2021). *Education and Student Success Strategy*. Dublin: University College Dublin.

UCD (2020). *To the Rising Future, UCD Strategy 2020–2024*. Dublin: University College Dublin.

UCD (2018). *Equality, Diversity and Inclusion (EDI) Strategy and Action Plan 2018–2020–2025*. Dublin: University College Dublin.

Unger, M. (2019). *Why is there so little progress on the social dimension in the Bologna Process? Some hypotheses*. Paper presented at the Erasmus+ Project "SIDERAL – Social and International Dimension of Education and Recognition of Acquired Learning" Kick-off Conference, 2 July, Zadar, Croatia.

Van Meter, D. and Van Horn, C. (1975). The policy implementation process: A conceptual framework. *Administration & Society*, 6, 445–488. https://doi.org/10.1177/009539977500600404

Westerheijden, D., Beerkens, E., Cremonini, L., Huisman, J., Kehm, B., Kovac, A., … and Yaggi, Y. (2010). *The Bologna Process Independent Assessment. The First Decade of Working on the European Higher Education Area. Executive Summary, Overview and Conclusions*. CHEPS, Incher-Kassel, ECOTEC. Brussels: European Commission, Directorate-General for Education and Culture.

Woodrow, M. and Thomas, L. (2002). Pyramids or spiders? Cross-sector collaboration to widen participation. Learning from international perspectives. In L. Thomas, M. Cooper, and J. Quinn (eds), *Collaboration to Widen Participation in Higher Education*. Stoke-on-Trent: Trentham Books, pp. 3–28.

Zak, D. (2021). 'Nothing ever ends': Sorting through Rumsfeld's knowns and unknowns. *Washington Post*, 1 July.

2.2 Creating universities for all

30 top public research universities in the US respond to anti-Black violence

Leslie A. Williams, Patrick Kent Russell and Frank Tuitt

Background/introduction

The 25th May 2020 murder of George Floyd by Minneapolis police catalysed national and international movements challenging anti-Black racism, which had been building following the killings of Ahmaud Arbery, Breonna Taylor, and many other African Americans by law enforcement officials and vigilantes. Across the United States (US), this new wave of state sanctioned anti-Black violence led to intensified demands for Historically White institutions (HWIs) to dismantle systems of race-based oppression, igniting a renewed sense of urgency to diversity, equity, inclusion, and justice (DEIJ) efforts (Wesley, Dunlap, and Russell, 2021). Inspired by the Black Lives Matter movement, students, faculty, and staff mobilized to press HWIs to address deeply rooted racist practices that have persisted since many of these institutions were integrated six decades ago, such as the underrepresentation of Black students, faculty and staff; exclusion and or marginalization of Blacks in the curriculum; and hostile campus climates including anti-Black violence, hate speech and over-aggressive policing (Jenkins, Tichavakunda, and Coles, 2021; Mustaffa, 2017; Nelson, 2019; Nichols, 2020; Smith et al., 2016).

Within this context and under the auspices of the University of Connecticut Office for Diversity and Inclusion (ODI), we launched a study to examine whether highly ranked public research universities in the US were responding to the current wave of anti-Blackness and, if so, how. More specifically, we investigated whether there was a publicly articulated plan of action such as statements from presidents, provosts, boards of trustees or other senior leaders available on public-facing websites at 30 of the 50 highest ranked public universities and, if so, what were the main features. Utilizing a conceptual framework synthesizing conflict, institutional, and critical race theories we analysed our findings by focusing on the external contexts, which featured group conflict, internal implementations, and the pervasive ideology of White supremacy, which have influenced the development and outcomes of race-based educational equity policies (L. Williams, 2017).

DOI: 10.4324/9781003253631-4

Methodology

We selected 30 of the highest ranked public research universities in the United States based on the 2020 Top Public Colleges and Universities: U.S. News Rankings, which we cross-referenced with the *Wall Street Journal/Times Higher Education* US College Rankings best public universities in the United States 2020. We focused on institutions that are similar to the University of Connecticut, thus excluding military academies or technical institutes. We also sought geographic diversity and factored in Association of American Universities membership and conference affiliation. We then collected data from each university's publicly accessible website using a structured protocol, which sought to identify whether institutional leaders had issued a public response to the wave of anti-Black violence, including an action plan. We analysed our findings to identify patterns and themes.

Key findings

Our data suggest that 27 of the 30 universities we investigated showed clear evidence of responding to the current wave of state-sanctioned anti-Black violence. In general, these institutional responses included many familiar promises from the past 50 years such as increasing the structural diversity of faculty, students and staff; creating a more inclusive curriculum; and improving mental health services to better meet the needs of students of colour. While focused broadly, these commitments were also often explicit about addressing the specific needs of Blacks/African Americans. Several institutions also pledged to reform campus policing and rename buildings and remove statues to purge campuses of individuals tied to legacies of anti-Black racism. These issues had been raised by Black, Indigenous and other peoples of colour (BIPOC) for decades but had not previously gained much traction until recently (Platt, Foster, and Bradshaw, 2021).

All 27 of these universities began reviewing or implementing changes to their institutional policies, practices, and structures. Among the actions undertaken were:

- Assessing, revising or transforming campus policing policies, practices, and structures
- Establishing bodies such as advisory boards, commissions, councils, task forces, and working groups to examine and revise DEIJ policies, practices, and structures
- Planning or launching DEIJ assessments such as climate surveys and diversity audits, and establishing accountability measures
- Creating new offices and/or staff positions to design, implement, and assess DEIJ efforts
- Reviewing and reorganizing counselling centres to better serve BIPOC students.

Almost all universities sought to increase structural diversity through new efforts to recruit, hire or enrol, and retain more BIPOC faculty, staff, and students, both undergraduate and graduate, by launching or expanding cluster hiring and pipeline programs. A significant majority of these universities engaged in efforts to improve the climate for DEIJ. Among the actions undertaken were:

- Instituting co-curricular programs such as book clubs, conferences, dialogues, lectures, seminars, and town halls to explore and enhance knowledge about DEIJ issues on campus and in society
- Offering DEIJ trainings and workshops for faculty, students, staff, and administrative leaders
- Reviewing and revising policies on buildings and monuments on their campuses to ensure that those structures met standards and values of equity, inclusion, and justice.

Several of these universities sought to enhance or expand academic opportunities to learn about and engage with issues on DEIJ. Among the actions undertaken were:

- Offering new courses on DEIJ, including courses on anti-Blackness
- Assessing DEIJ general education requirements with the goal of enhancing or expanding them
- Establishing new institutes and research centres to focus on racial equity and justice.

Finally, a little more than half of these universities identified funding or established fundraising efforts to support the initiatives outlined above. Among the actions undertaken were:

- Offering general funding or establishing fundraising efforts for DEIJ initiatives
- Providing grants for research on DEIJ issues
- Offering funding for fellowships and scholarships to attract and retain BIPOC students.

Discussion

In the wake of the racial reckoning following George Floyd's murder, the vast majority of the highly ranked public HWIs in our study made commitments to addressing and dismantling systems of race-based oppression. Leaders at HWIs pledged new policies, practices, administrative structures, human and financial resources, implementation plans, and accountability mechanisms in order to create universities where everyone, particularly Black students, faculty, and staff, can thrive. These commitments mirror many of the promises made following previous mobilizations by Blacks and allies demanding greater access to and inclusion in HWIs (e.g. Biondi, 2012; Bradley, 2018; Duster, 2009; B. Williams and Tuitt, 2021).

Examining this long history of the struggle for equity, inclusion, and justice for Blacks in American higher education reveals evidence of incremental progress in increasing the structural diversity of students, faculty, and staff (Espinosa, Turk, Taylor, and Chessman, 2019; Karen, 2002; Stewart and Bridges, 2011; Wilson, 1994), enhancing support for students (Patton, 2010), and curricular transformation (Biondi, 2011). However, that same history also demonstrates that the rhetoric and visions of meaningfully inclusive HEIs are extremely difficult to realise (Harper, Patton, and Wooden, 2009; L. Williams and Grande, 2021). Scholars have convincingly documented how mobilizations by subordinated groups for greater opportunity in higher education have inevitably been met by counter-mobilisations from dominant groups that seek to preserve the status quo through legal and political challenges (Duster, 1995; Karen, 1991; Mikcsh, 2008; L. Williams and Grande, 2021). Furthermore, HWI pledges to create more racially diverse, equitable, inclusive, and just campuses often conflict with other deeply held institutional interests and ideals such as academic excellence, free speech, autonomy, and stability, which inhibit progress (Chang, 2000), or are scaled back during national and state economic downturns (Bowen and Bok, 1998; Elfman, 2021; Mitchell et al., 2018).

Given the evidence above, the HWIs in our study will need to exhibit an unwavering commitment and persistent sense of urgency in their efforts to create universities that are truly for all. They must develop strategic plans that comprehensively incorporate the elements we have identified in this study such as:

- Reviewing, assessing, and implementing changes to their institutional policies, practices and structures
- Increasing the structural diversity of faculty, students and staff
- Improving the climate for diversity, equity, inclusion and justice
- Enhancing and expanding academic opportunities to learn about and engage with issues on diversity, equity, inclusion, and justice
- Securing funding to support DEIJ efforts.

Finally, anticipating and strategically preparing for the inevitable counter-mobilization will be crucial for overcoming the enduring challenges to creating diverse, equitable, inclusive, and just higher education institutions.

Conclusion

Overall, the findings of our study suggest that HWIs, seeking to make excellence inclusive and anti-racist, must commit to moving beyond superficial performative DEIJ pretences and engage in the hard work of transforming their institutions. Specifically, HWIs must avoid becoming stuck in a diversity loop that often starts with a DEIJ statement, moves to DEIJ strategic planning, only to stall until another racist incident occurs, beginning the cycle over again (Kennedy, 2020). Accordingly, the implications of our study for institutional transformation point to the need for HWIs to identify a set of concrete substantial remedies that will directly address persistent racial inequities. Specifically, HWIs will need to:

- Avoid minimalist actions that only serve to conceal systemic and institutional racism, and, instead, identify strategies to dismantle the policies and practices that allow racism and anti-Blackness to remain (Kennedy, 2020; Tuitt, 2022).
- Connect anti-racism efforts to the systems and structures that drive day-to-day operations and avoid leaving intact the vestiges of coloniality that produced the oppressive environments in the first place (Tuitt, 2016; Tuitt and Stewart, 2021).
- Engage in professional development opportunities, accountability practices, and overall infrastructure that build individual and institutional capacity, to create anti-racist institutions (Tuitt, 2022).
- Incentivise and reward efforts to utilise anti-racist practices and hold accountable those who resist efforts to create inclusive, affirming, and equitable institutional environments (Tuitt, 2022).

In conclusion, HWIs will not be able to achieve the goal of becoming an anti-racist institution without centring the lived experiences of the racially minoritized communities in their midst. HWIs must also keep in mind that they do not exist in isolation; therefore, an understanding of the impact of the racialized contexts external to their institutions is vital (Tuitt, 2022). HWIs' willingness to embrace these considerations as essential components of their anti-racism efforts will determine whether or not they are successful in transforming their institutions into vibrant inclusive, affirming, and equitable learning environments.

References

2020 Top Public Colleges and Universities: U.S. News Rankings. Available at: https://www.usnews.com/best-colleges/rankings/national-universities/top-public (accessed 28 February 2022).

Biondi, M. (2011). Controversial blackness: The historical development & future trajectory of African American studies. *Daedalus*, 140(2), 226–237.

Biondi, M. (2012). *The Black Revolution on Campus*. Berkeley, CA: University of California Press.

Bowen, W.G. and Bok, D. (1998). *The Shape of the River: Long-term Consequences of Considering Race in College and University Admissions*. Princeton, NJ: Princeton University Press.

Bradley, S.M. (2018). *Upending the Ivory Tower*. New York: New York University Press.

Chang, M.J. (2000). Improving campus racial dynamics: A balancing act among competing interests. *The Review of Higher Education*, 23(2), 153–175.

Duster, T. (1995). They're taking over! And other myths about race on campus. In M. Berube and C. Nelson (eds), *Higher Education Under Fire: Politics, Economics, and the Crisis of the Humanities*. New York: Routledge, pp. 276–283.

Duster, T. (2009). The long path to higher education for African Americans. *Thought & Action*, Fall, 99–110.

Elfman, L. (2021). Institutions adjust faculty diversity strategies amid COVID-19 pandemic. *Diverse Issues in Higher Education*, 13 October. Available at: https://www.diverseeducation.com/covid-19/article/15279536/institutions-adjust-faculty-diversity-strategies-amid-covid19-pandemic (accessed 28 February 2022).

Espinosa, L.L., Turk, J.M., Taylor, M., and Chessman, H.M. (2019). *Race and Ethnicity in Higher Education: A Status Report*. Washington, DC: American Council on Education. Available at: https://www.equityinhighered.org/resources/report-downloads/race-and-ethnicity-in-higher-education-a-status-report/ (accessed 28 February 2022).

Harper, S.R., Patton, L.D., and Wooden, O.S. (2009). Access and equity for African American students in higher education: A critical race historical analysis of policy efforts. *The Journal of Higher Education*, 80(4), 389–414.

Jenkins, D.A., Tichavakunda, A.A., and Coles, J.A. (2021). The second ID: Critical race counterstories of campus police interactions with Black men at historically white institutions. *Race Ethnicity and Education*, 24(2), 149–166.

Karen, D. (1991). The politics of class, race, and gender: Access to higher education in the United States, 1960–1986. *American Journal of Education*, 99(2), 208–237.

Karen, D. (2002). Changes in access to higher education in the United States: 1980–1992. *Sociology of Education*, 75(3), 191–210.

Kennedy, D. (2020). Moving beyond 'performative' diversity commitments. Presidian Blog, 7 December. Available at: https://www.presidio.edu/blog/moving-beyond-performative-diversity-commitments/ (accessed 28 February 2022).

Miksch, K.L. (2008). Institutional decision-making and the politics of fear: 30 years after Bakke: Affirmative action, equal opportunity, and access. In P. Marin and C. L. Horn (eds), *Realizing Bakke's Legacy: Affirmative Action, Equal Opportunity, and Access*. Sterling, VA: Stylus, pp. 198–218.

Mitchell, M., Leachman, M., Masterson, K., and Waxman, S. (2018). Unkept promises: State cuts to higher education threaten access and equity. Center on Budget and Policy Priorities, 4 October. Available at: https://www.cbpp.org/research/state-budget-and-tax/unkept-promises-state-cuts-to-higher-education-threaten-access-and (accessed 28 February 2022).

Mustaffa, J.B. (2017). Mapping violence, naming life: A history of anti-Black oppression in the higher education system. *International Journal of Qualitative Studies in Education*, 30(8), 711–727.

Nelson, V. (2019). Addressing racial trauma and hate crimes on college campuses. Center for American Progress, 9 August. Available at: https://www.americanprogress.org/article/addressing-racial-trauma-hate-crimes-college-campuses/ (accessed 28 February 2022).

Nichols, A.H. (2020). 'Segregation forever'? The continued underrepresentation of Black and Latino undergraduates at the nation's 101 most selective public colleges and universities. Education Trust. Available at: https://eric.ed.gov/?id=ED607325 (accessed 28 February 2022).

Patton, L.D. (2010). *Culture Centers in Higher Education: Perspectives on Identity, Theory, and Practice*. Herndon, VA: Stylus Publishing.

Platt, R., Foster, H., and Bradshaw, L. (2021). Repurposing the Confederacy: Understanding issues surrounding the removal and contextualization of lost cause iconography at southern colleges and universities. In B. Williams, D. Squire, and F. Tuitt (eds), *Plantation Politics and Campus Rebellions: Power, Diversity, and the Emancipatory Struggle in Higher Education*. Albany, NY: SUNY Press.

Smith, W.A., Mustaffa, J.B., Jones, C.M., Curry, T.J., and Allen, W.R. (2016). You make me wanna holler and throw up both my hands! Campus culture, Black misandric microaggressions, and racial battle fatigue. *International Journal of Qualitative Studies in Education*, 29(9), 1189–1209.

Stewart, D.L. and Bridges, B. (2011). A demographic profile of multicultural student services. In D.L. Stewart (ed.), *Multicultural Student Services on Campus: Building Bridges, Re-visioning Community*. Herndon, VA: Stylus Publishing.

Tuitt, F. (2016). Making excellence inclusive in challenging times. *Liberal Education*, 102(2), 64–68.

Tuitt, F. (2022). More than a hashtag: Nurturing Black excellence in traditionally white institutions. *Journal of Minority Achievement, Creativity, and Leadership*, 1(2), 274–300.

Tuitt, F. and Stewart, S. (2021). Decolonizing academic spaces: Moving beyond diversity to promote racial equity in postsecondary education. In D. Thomas (ed.), *Doing Diversity for Success in Higher Education: Redressing Structural Inequalities in the Academy*. London: Palgrave Macmillan, pp. 99–116.

Wall Street Journal/Times Higher Education US College Rankings. Available at: https://www.timeshighereducation.com/rankings/united-states/2020#!/page/0/length/25/sort_by/rank/sort_order/asc/cols/stats (accessed 28 February 2022).

U.S. News (2020). 2020 Top Public Colleges and Universities: U.S. News Rankings. Available at: https://www.usnews.com/best-colleges/rankings/national-universities/top-public (accessed 28 February 2022).

Wesley, A., Dunlap, J., and Russell, P.G. (2021). *Moving from Words to Action: The Influence of Racial Justice Statements on Campus Equity Efforts*. Washington, DC: NASPA. Available at: https://www.naspa.org/report/moving-from-words-to-action-the-influence-of-racial-justice-statements-on-campus-equity-efforts (accessed 28 February 2022).

Williams, B. and Tuitt, F. (2021). Carving out a humanity: Campus rebellions and the legacy of plantation politics on college campuses. In B. Williams, D. Squire, and F. Tuitt (eds), *Plantation Politics and Campus Rebellions: Power, Diversity, and the Emancipatory Struggle in Higher Education*. Albany, NY: SUNY Press.

Williams, L.A. (2017). *Towards a critical conceptual analysis of race-based educational equity policies: Assessing the impact of affirmative action on higher education admissions*. Paper presented at the Association for the Study of Higher Education Annual Meeting, Houston, TX, 1–3 November.

Williams, L.A. and Grande, S. (2021). Trumpocalypse and the historical limits of higher education policy: Making the case for study/struggle. *Qualitative Inquiry*. Available at: https://journals.sagepub.com/doi/abs/10.1177/10778004211014615 (accessed 10 March 2022).

Wilson, R. (1994). The participation of African Americans in American higher education. In M. Justiz, R. Wilson, and L. Bjork (eds), *Minorities in Higher Education*. Phoenix, AZ: The Oryx Press, pp. 195–209.

2.3 Inclusive post-secondary education

Is there such a thing?

Vianne Timmons

Equity, diversity, and inclusion (EDI) was a major focus in Canadian universities in 2021. There are many approaches being taken to ensure our campuses better reflect the society we live in. Concrete initiatives focus on what is often described as "more inclusive campuses". In particular, there is a movement to Indigenize our post-secondary institutions. Since the release of the Truth and Reconciliation Report in 2015 (nctr.ca/records/reports/#trc-reports), these efforts have intensified. In every strategic plan, you can find reference to Indigenization of the academy. Universities are developing EDI policies, hiring senior leaders to lead EDI initiatives, developing policies and rolling out anti-bias training, and looking at cluster hires, comprised of a group of faculty with similar lived experiences. These reflect just a few areas of focus.

Universities have provided services to students with disabilities for decades. There now is a more targeted effort to accommodate faculty and staff. Accessibility is also seen as an important focus as EDI efforts on campuses ramp up. In addition, the federal government has released new guidelines on accessibility, which require institutions to invest in physical structures. All these efforts are making an impact on how institutions support students, faculty, and staff who have unique lived experiences and contribute to more welcoming campuses. At the same time, there is the reality that universities are elitist, many with exclusive admission requirements and still proud to weed out those who cannot make it.

How then, do young people with intellectual disabilities fit into this inclusive movement? The answer is they do not. In the programmes and policies that have been introduced, there is little, if any, reference to people with intellectual disabilities. There have been some pioneer programmes, such as the On Campus programme at the University of Alberta (www.ualberta.ca/admissions-programs/inclusive-education/index.html) that have been operating since 1987. There are a handful of others in Canada that are successful, such as the University of Calgary (https://www.ucalgary.ca/student-services/services/ipse) and the University of Regina (www.uregina.ca/student/accessibility/campus-for-all/). These programmes have proven to be sustainable and successful. However, they are seen as separate from the EDI movements that are sweeping Canadian universities, if they are seen at all.

DOI: 10.4324/9781003253631-5

So how can we ensure that an academy's inclusive efforts are truly all-inclusive? Being involved in two programmes, one at the University of Prince Edward Island, and one at the University of Regina, I learned that there are some key factors for success. I will use programmes for students with intellectual disabilities as examples, but these factors are critical for the success of many EDI initiatives.

The first component is to ensure there is a champion, ideally in the senior ranks. Many universities have created senior positions with an EDI and/or Indigenous focus, but there are few with a specific disability focus. In the EDI movement, disability often garners less attention and focus. It is, therefore, important that a champion keeps it on the agenda. The challenge is that if this person leaves the institution, the focus can be lost, therefore the champion needs to recruit others who see the value and will advocate for these students and programmes. As a senior leader, one has to ensure that the programmes become institutionalised, part of the fabric of the campus.

How does one do that? Providing core funding for programmes is essential. Programmes that run on soft or one-time monies are always vulnerable. The staff have little job security and spend their time continually looking for funding when they could be focused on programming. Institutions put money where they identify priorities.

Communities are connected to these programmes. These connections need to be fostered and cultivated. Programmes should work with and maintain communication with local associations that support people with intellectual disabilities and their families. These relationships ensure that there are community advocates for post-secondary programmes, also serving as recruitment agents for universities.

There also needs to be attention paid to celebrating successes. Programmes for young people with intellectual disabilities are full of potential stories that touch people's hearts. The impact on their peers can also be transformational. For programmes to be embedded in the academy, they need to be visible and promote pride. There needs to be a concerted effort to highlight the benefits of these programmes. Students in these programmes should have experiences that mirror as closely as possible those of other students. There should be tuition charged, though maybe at a differentiated rate and the university needs to look at raising funds for scholarships and bursaries. The students need to fully participate in all the university's signature events, such as convocation. Students with intellectual disabilities need to be seen as students and have access to all student experiences.

As we see post-secondary institutions attempt to transform the sector into more inclusive communities, we need to ensure that 'all' truly means 'all'. We have a number of successful programmes that support students with intellectual disabilities in Canada, and there are lessons to be learned from them. We need to ensure that the programmes and voices of students and advocates of people with intellectual disabilities are considered as part of EDI.

In many institutions, there are competing challenges for resources. We are seeing this materialize in the EDI movement. Are the resources focused on racialized individuals and Indigenization? What about the LGBTQ+ and the disability communities? Are our efforts making our campuses more inclusive for some, but not all? We need to promote inclusive programmes that make our campuses better for everyone. This is often disruptive and challenging. The whole idea of who is eligible to attend university becomes a question. The many supports necessary can be costly. There can be competing priorities even within EDI efforts.

It is important to ensure our efforts are not selective. Leaders need to ensure that there are conversations held on campuses and resources allocated that serve all groups. If done properly, this will transform the academy. It takes commitment, conversations, resources, and leadership. Are we up for this? Will it make a difference? Time will tell. I know I am up for the challenge. Are you?

2.4 Applying the values and principles that underpin Universal Design at a national level

Gerald Craddock

> The only important thing about design is how it relates to people.
>
> Victor Papenek (1971)

Ireland is unique internationally in having Universal Design defined in primary legislation. Universal Design is an approach to the design of environments, products, and services to be accessible, understandable, and usable by the widest range of people, in particular by people of any age, size, ability, or disability. Ireland has recognised the importance of Universal Design with the establishment of the Centre for Excellence in Universal Design (CEUD) in 2007 as part of the National Disability Authority through national legislation (Disability Act 2005). Universal Design for Learning (UDL) is an extension of, and is underpinned by, Universal Design in Education (UDE). UDE focuses on a whole-systems design so that the physical and digital environments, the educational services, and the teaching and learning can be easily accessed, understood, and used by the widest range of learners and all stakeholders, in a more inclusive environment. A foundational publication for the centre is the United Nations Convention on the Rights of People with Disabilities (UNCRPD; United Nations, 2006) which endorses Universal Design as the preferred approach to inclusion and advocates that it should frame national policies on the design of environments, products, services, and information communication technologies (ICT).

The CEUD statutory functions are to contribute to the development of Universal Design standards and promote their adoption in practice by the relevant public bodies, industry, and professions. It also has a role to assist in the integration of Universal Design and UDL in education curricula and examinations for relevant professions and occupations; and general awareness-raising of Universal Design such as through national awards schemes. The Centre advances these areas through ongoing engagement and involvement of a wide range of stakeholders such as disability groups including Disabled Persons Organisations (DPO), government agencies, professional bodies, and educational institutions. At a European level, Universal Design has been recognised as encapsulating and expanding the promise of accessible

DOI: 10.4324/9781003253631-6

design. The most recent examples are the new European Accessibility Act (EAA) 2019, which states:

> accessibility should be achieved by the systematic removal and prevention of barriers, preferably through a Universal Design approach, which contributes to ensuring access for persons with disabilities on an equal basis with others.

Also, the European Association of Service Providers for People with Disabilities (EASPD) has endorsed Universal Design in their 2021 Lisbon Declaration on Inclusive Education based on the UNCRPD (Article 4 on Universal Design and Article 24 on Education and General Comment No.4 on Inclusive Education). At a national level, SOLAS (state body for further education and training provision in Ireland) in its FET (Further Education & Training) strategy (2020–2024), states that the strategic priority "Fostering Inclusion" must be met through applying a Universal Design approach.

However, in Ireland, we have a considerable way to go to create the environment that enables persons with disabilities to fully participate on an equal level with the rest of society. The latest OECD report "Disability, Work and Inclusion in Ireland", funded by the National Disability Authority (NDA, 2021), states that barriers continue to exist in education with four out of ten working-age individuals with a disability having only primary or lower secondary education, twice the rate of the rest of the Irish population. It goes on to state that lower levels of education, skills, and adult learning participation act as a major impediment to the labour force participation of persons with disabilities in Ireland.

Removing barriers within society requires more than a focus on accessibility and accommodation. Mitigating these inequalities requires the systematic removal and prevention of barriers, preferably through a Universal Design approach. This will ensure access for persons with disabilities on equal bases with all others. Within the current educational system, a paradigm shift is needed to achieve this ambition, which necessitates moving beyond minimal compliance with accessibility standards, basic access, and usability of facilities to a Universal Design approach which considers the needs of the whole person.

It is widely acknowledged that education is key in mitigating many of the inequalities in our society. Central to implementing this system, a core message of CEUD is that a Universal Design approach can enable the transformation of education, from an inequitable learning environment for many students to a more holistic, human-centric experience at all levels of education, including pre-school services, further and higher education, and lifelong learning (CEUD, 2022).

UDE has seen the addition of UDL as a key driver in advancing a more inclusive educational experience for a wide range of students, including students with disabilities. UDL can enable many schools, colleges, and universities to move from simply 'doing inclusion' or 'doing diversity' to providing an inclusive learning experience that benefits all students, reducing barriers to learning, while maintaining academic rigour (Tobin and Behling 2019).

The CEUD applies an ecological systems approach to ensure that these areas are interlinked and interconnected and enables a person to participate in such domains as home, community education, training, transportation, and work. An ecological systems model of human development recognises the many layers of our environment that influence our development (Bronfenbrenner, 1979). This model is closely aligned with the UN Sustainable Development Goals (SDGs), in that having well designed environments that are inclusive are also more sustainable over the longer term.

Based on a human ecological framework, Universal Design recognises the multiple layers within the educational ecosystem as follows:

- Macro level – national level – establishing directives, passing legislative acts, developing standards, promoting awareness, ensuring the diffusion of Universal Design and its adoption at national and regional educational levels.
- Meso level – institutional level – covering governance, policies and procedures as well as linking families and the community-based initiatives, which is now known to be critical for growing and sustaining innovative learning.
- Micro level – individual level – ensuring needs and abilities are recognised and catered for through teaching practices; classroom design and layout; technologies including assistive technologies; learning resources and spaces.

An example of this approach that specifically looked at the built environment pillar was the funded research on Universal Design of Shared Educational Campuses in Ireland (Universaldesign.ie, 2015).

This whole-system framework shifts the focus of education from institutional to individual learners, re-orienting it towards the user; and ensuring user involvement in the co-design of their own education. It proposes a transformation of the whole of the education and training ecosystem.

This was clearly articulated at two international conferences co-hosted by the CEUD and Technological University Dublin in 2015 (Universal Design in Education, 2015) and 2018 (UDHEIT, 2018) that were specifically focused on transforming further and higher education.

To advance the systems model, the CEUD has concentrated on the seven elements and developed a range of resources, guides, and standards in order to create a more inclusive equitable environment and society (Figure 2.1). It is only when these elements are in place that it is possible to advance a more holistic approach to our educational ecosystem.

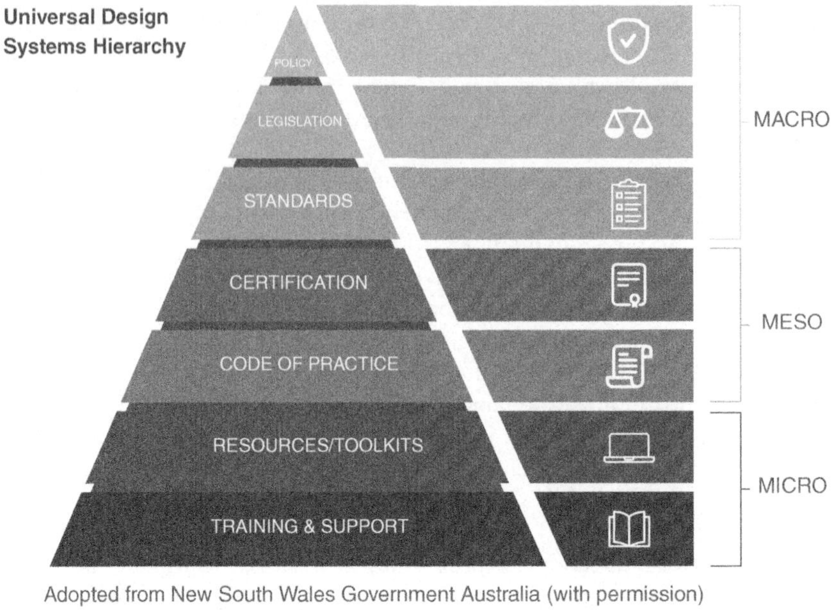

Figure 2.1 The seven element Universal Design system within a human ecological framework

These seven elements support learner-centred approaches to education and environments that maximally support learners with diverse physical, linguistic, cognitive, and learning styles, while at the same time meeting national education standards. Mitigating these inequalities demands the systematic removal and prevention of barriers through a Universal Design systems approach which contributes to ensuring access for all on an equal basis.

Universal Design presents a comprehensive blueprint for our profession as educators, for our practice as teachers, providing a framework that encompasses the values and beliefs that have been the hallmark of good education over the decades. However, it is important to embody these core values and principles in teaching and learning curriculum (McNutt and Murphy, 2011, p. 112).

References

Bronfenbrenner, U. (1979). *The Ecology of Human Development*. Cambridge, MA: Harvard University Press.

Centre for Excellence in Universal Design (CEUD) (2015). Universal Design in Education Conference. Available at: https://universaldesign.ie/news-events/events/universal-design-in-education-conference.html

Centre for Excellence in Universal Design (2022). *Universal Design in Education and Training – Policy Landscape in Ireland*. Briefing paper. Available at: https://universaldesign.ie/web-content-/universal-design-in-education-nd-training-policy-landscape-in-ireland-2022.pdf

Disability Act 2005. Available at: https://www.irishstatutebook.ie/eli/2005/act/14/enacted/en/html

European Accessibility Act (2019). Available at: https://eur-lex.europa.eu/legal-content/EN/TXT/PDF/?uri=CELEX:32019L0882&from=EN

European Association of Service Providers for Persons with Disabilities (EASPD) (2021). Available at: https://easpd.eu/press-releases-detail/easpd-launches-lisbon-declaration-for-inclusive-education/

McNutt, L. and Murphy, D. (2011). Sharing innovative practice / managing diversity. In N. Fitzpatrick and J. Harvey (eds), *Designing Together: Effective Strategies for Creating a Collaborative Curriculum to Support Academic Development*, pp. 106–114. Available at: https://eprints.teachingandlearning.ie/id/eprint/1813/1/Fitzpatrick%20and%20Harvey%202011%20Designing%20Together.pdf

National Disability Authority (NDA) (2021). *Disability, Work and Inclusion in Ireland. Report*. Available at: https://nda.ie/publications/disability-work-and-inclusion-in-ireland-engaging-and-supporting-employers

Papanek, V. (1971). *Design for the Real World*, 1st edn. London: Thames & Hudson.

SOLAS (2020). *Future FET: Transforming Learning – The National Further Education and Training (FET) Strategy* [online]. Available at: https://www.solas.ie/f/70398/x/64d0718c9e/solas_fet_strategy_web.pdf

United Nations (2006). *Convention on the Rights of Persons with Disabilities (UNCRPD)*. Available at: https://www.un.org/development/desa/disabilities/convention-on-the-rights-of-persons-with-disabilities/convention-on-the-rights-of-persons-with-disabilities-2.html

Universal Design & Higher Education in Transformation Congress (UDHEIT) 2018. Available at: https://www.udheit2018.org/

Universaldesign.ie. (2015). *Research on Universal Design of Shared Educational Campuses in Ireland | Centre for Excellence in Universal Design* [online]. Available at: http://universaldesign.ie/Built-Environment/Shared-Education-Campuses/

Chapter 3

Data as a driver of change

3.1 Driving change – using data to tell the story of inclusion

Bairbre Fleming

Imagine you are standing on a familiar platform, one that you have been standing on for years. Then consider the sudden and compelling urgency to act as you realise what you are standing on is burning. This metaphor is offered by Kotter to convey the challenge and importance of creating a sense of urgency to prompt change. Standing on a 'burning platform' is an evocative and tangible way to prompt us to act (Kotter, 2008, p. 120).

Data can be considered that platform. Those who stand happily on that data platform "will begin to act differently if a fire starts on the floor beneath their feet" (Kotter, 2008). The clear, transparent, and democratic use of access data to record the proportions of all access students can offer us that platform and may have the impact of inciting enough urgency to generate change. In that context, performance metrics are an increasingly important factor in higher education decision making, particularly at public institutions (Felten and Hrabwski, 2016).

> Inclusion of a WP [Widening Participation] metric … has the effect of reducing some of the differences … somewhat levelling the playing field between universities with different institutional priorities.
>
> (Hubbard et al., 2021, p. 295)

The use of Widening Participation (WP) data in capturing, reporting, and shaping an institution's mission is a particularly compelling concept. In fostering an inclusive university environment, "using the institution's data is a useful way to begin a conversation on student participation, progression, engagement, and success" (Kelly and Padden, 2018, p. 35).

The University for All Toolkit offers a series of prompts, self-assessment statements, and case studies on the effective use of data gathering, metrics, and dissemination (Kelly and Padden, 2018, p. 84). This chapter on data, and how they can be used in a University for All, offers an additional perspective. It will not discuss the merits of gathering WP, or the methods and approaches that could be used (Fleming et al., 2022), as this is well documented (Gorard et al., 2019; HEPI, 2018; Holland et al., 2017). This chapter will, instead, focus on storytelling, and its role in gathering, sharing, and reporting on data metrics in access and inclusion.

DOI: 10.4324/9781003253631-8

Telling the story

The outbreak of cholera in London in 1854 is an unexpected but fascinating place to start an exploration of data in the context of a University for All. Johnson's *The Ghost Map* gives an account of how one map, or visualisation, perpetually altered perceptions, attitudes, and behaviours (Johnson, 2006). Johnson depicts London as a city where "civilisation and barbarism walked this boastful island together" (Johnson, 2006, p. 14). It is an account of a deadly outbreak, of unknown origin, that swept through the densely populated streets of SoHo. At the time, it was believed that cholera spread through the air, and was connected to foul smells and unsanitary housing conditions. This assumption was incorrect, as the disease is a bacterium that is spread through the water supply. In this contested space where civilisation and barbarism walked, one man, a medical doctor called John Snow, began drawing a map by hand. His map accounted for each death and showed the source was one well. However, in spite of his work, the incorrect theory of transmission persisted for several more years. The hero of this story, Dr Snow, persisted with his data collection and his data depiction. Eventually, sanitation practices were changed to eliminate the source and conditions in which cholera spread (Ball, 2009).

This story is often cited in the context of data visualisation, as it is one of the earliest accounts of how a visual representation of data can be used to demonstrate critical patterns. This map was clearly more effective than any other way of documenting the deaths of more than 10 per cent of the inhabitants on one street in two weeks.

By extension, the 'Ghost Map' of Johnson's account illustrates how progress, theories, ideas, and scientific discoveries can evolve, even in the context of resistance or antipathy. The Ghost Map reminds us of the importance of evidence in promoting and driving change.

Data storytelling

> There is a story in your data. But your tools don't know what that story is. That's where it takes you—the analyst or communicator of the information—to bring that story visually and contextually to life.
>
> (Knaflic, 2015, p. 3)

In Bruner's *Act of Meaning*, he illustrates how narrative helps us find ways of understanding the unusual – "The function of story is to find an intentional state that mitigates or at least makes comprehensible a deviation from a canonical cultural pattern" (Bruner, 1990, pp. 49–50). Bruner's description of the value of narrative has become synonymous with a suggestion that we are 22 times more likely to remember a story than a fact.

The challenge of telling that story, and knowing what that story is, was particularly relevant in developing our data for a University for All. While we had established some of the tools, the definitions and the Key Performance

Indicators, we struggled to find a way to tell our story. We had established a pattern of presenting a range of data at Widening Participation Committee meetings. However, the data presentations were dense and unremarkable. Critically, the data tables were highlighting patterns of low participation among equity groups and "deviations from canonical cultural patterns", which showed a homogeneity in student population that differed from the diversity of our Irish communities. However, the tabular nature of the depiction clearly failed to tell that story. There was no urgency as there was no sense of a 'burning platform'. The lack of engagement was evident from the absence of discussion or reaction to the several presentations and WP data reports. It resonated with the Irish Higher Education Authority's earlier comments in its review of Targeted Initiatives as being ineffective in understanding what was being depicted, and, by inference, what its value was (Higher Education Authority, 2004).

The lack of engagement prompted a rethink on how to 'tell the data story'. While there was a lot of data to share, their relative value was hard to interpret. We considered how we could 'scaffold' the data to allow us to narrate a relatable story (Mutonyi, 2016). Access and Lifelong Learning (ALL) trialled an alternative concept and set the challenge – 'If UCD was a village of 100 people'. In this village scenario, both the university and separate academic programme areas could be understood as villages of 100. Each target group could then be described relative to that village. Basic visualisations were shared with the WP committee to immediate interest and debate. We showed them what the university looked like as a village of 100 people – and what proportions of those 100 were on low income, or had a disability, for example. We also showed what a specific programme looked like, using the same village analogy.

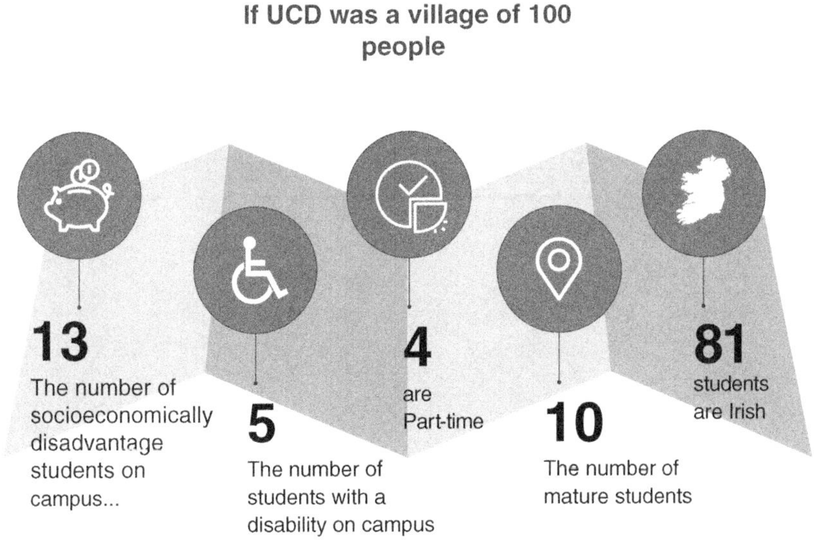

Figure 3.1 Sample of the university as a village of 100, used to convey the relative proportions of under-represented cohorts in the university c. 2015

This simple change in how we shared the data – and how we told that story – had a remarkable impact the next time we presented data. Suddenly, we had colleagues sit up and react forcefully to what we were showing. There was general disbelief at the remarkably low levels of participation among some student groups and in particular programme areas. The depiction prompted colleagues to ask more questions, for some to doubt or challenge the evidence, and for many to suggest some drivers for change.

There was now a sense of urgency in our collective drive to be inclusive. The outcome of this narrative approach informed our practice. For us to use data effectively, we needed to find a way to make the data relatable. The data helped us tell a story to trigger action.

The story scaffold

The first step in establishing how to use whatever data you have, is to set your scene. Cole Nussbaumer Knaflic outlines key stages in using data to tell a story (Knaflic, 2015). She offers a framework of understanding the context, then choosing an effective visual, eliminating the clutter, and then focusing attention on the critical detail. This allows the data to tell the story. This approach can be expanded further to consider what elements there are in storytelling, and how these can relate to telling a story through data. The following framework in Figure 3.2 outlines what the steps can be using the context of one university's process in developing data metrics to drive systemic change.

Step 1: Set the scene – exposition

The first and most important step in telling any story is to establish the context. The context for our university coincided with Irish policy and the

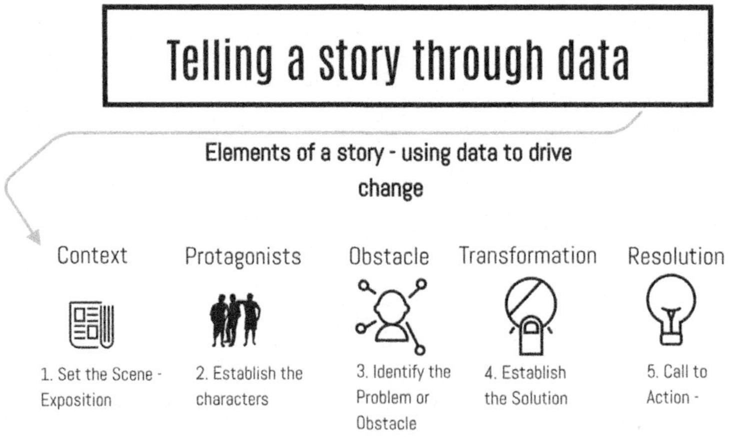

Figure 3.2 Elements of storytelling using data

establishment of a national equity policy unit. The articulation of Ireland's ambition to ensure equity of access to higher education had its origin in a Government Green Paper – Education for a Changing World (Department of Education Ireland, 1992). This ambition prompted the establishment of, almost two decades ago, a National Office for Equity of Access to Higher Education to facilitate educational access and opportunity for groups who are under-represented in higher education. Different European countries target different groups (Wasserman and Berkovich, 2022), with a focus, for example, on first generation entrants (Flanders), male students (Finland), and those from lower socio-economic groups and living in areas of multiple deprivation (United Kingdom). The context for your story will, therefore, depend on what you wish to highlight or depict.

Step 2: Establish the characters – protagonists

In this Irish context, the protagonists of this data review are equity groups. These groups were defined in 2004 and were defined as people with a disability, mature students, young people from socio-economically disadvantaged backgrounds, and members of the travelling and refugee communities. The equity groups have been adapted during the course of the various national access plans to reflect the increasing diversification of Irish society. The protagonists will vary by country, sector, and context.

Step 3: Identify the problem or obstacle

There are a number of challenges in telling an access data story. The first challenge lies in the data itself. Data, or the lack of appropriate and adequate data in the original targeted initiatives, were evident in a range of reviews (Osborne and Leith, 2000). The earliest reports of access relied disproportionately on narrative or qualitative data, rather than offering robust quantitative data on various access initiatives. This process has taken over 10 years in our university, and is described elsewhere (Fleming et al., 2022) and summarised below.

The first and critical action in establishing our challenge was the consideration of KPIs for participation of underrepresented students. UCD developed these KPIs, which committed the university to achieving 33 per cent of undergraduates being drawn from target equity groups by 2020. A robust data system was developed to identify and track the participation of underrepresented student cohorts in the University. The process required significant collaboration and coordination with the Director of Institutional Data. The key datasets are outlined in Figure 3.4 and are subject to ongoing enhancement and additions.

Step 4: Establishing a solution – transformation

The penultimate step involves moving the narrative from problem focus to a solution focus. In our context, our University re-established a new WP

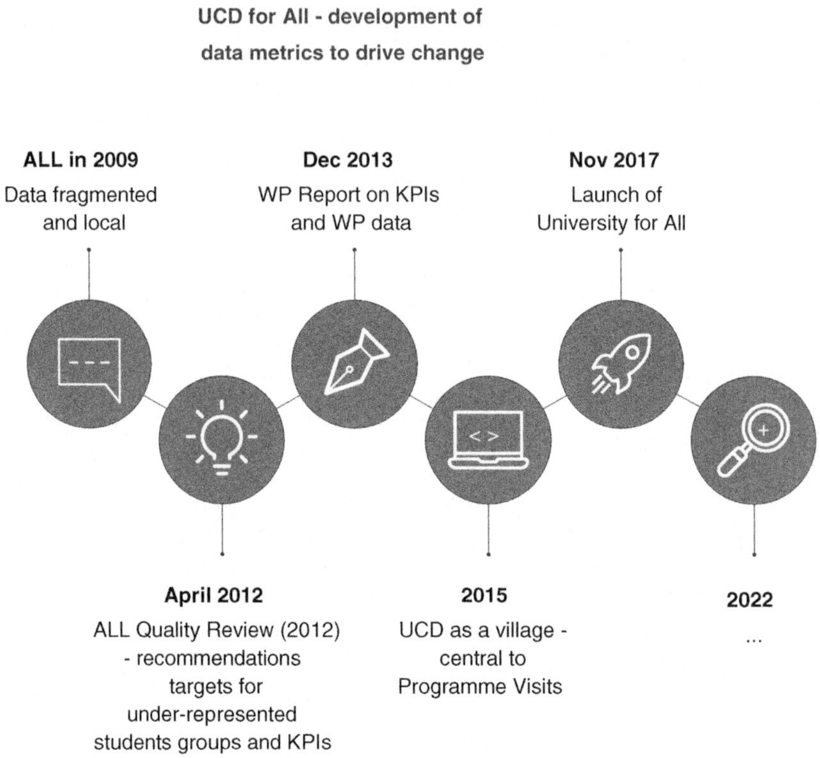

Figure 3.3 Key moments in identifying the 'data problem'

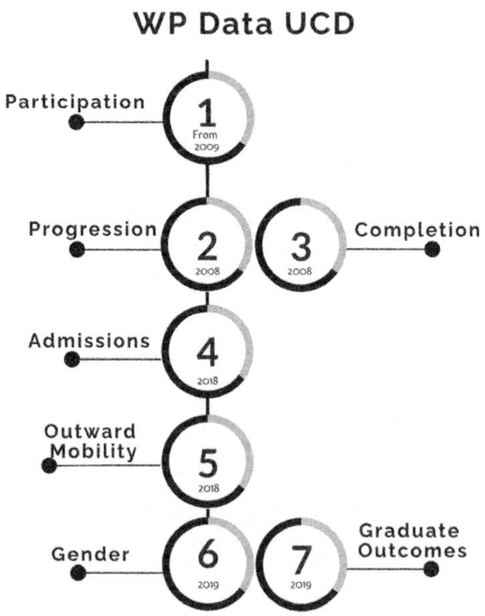

Figure 3.4 Timeline and rollout of Quantitative Data Measures

Committee in 2016, with new Terms of Reference. This new WP Committee reviewed progress made towards the achievement of recommendations made in the Institutional Barriers report (UCD, 2015). Each University Programme Board was invited to provide a report on progress towards meeting targets for under-represented student groups and on actions taken to promote inclusion, participation, and student engagement (UCD, 2017). The following year, the University's Governing Authority discussed access developments. A comprehensive briefing was provided on the systemic approach to building a mainstream inclusive university community. Actions and progress across key institutional dimensions, including infrastructure, academic integration, student support, data, and research, as well as engagement and outreach were discussed. The Governing Authority commended and endorsed the approach taken. This offered a roadmap for the quantitative data metrics that is now used to report on access and inclusion.

The rollout of the University for All offered an additional perspective.

Step 5: Call to action – resolution

The collation, reporting, and dissemination of data became the Call to Action or resolution to the Data Story. A decision to democratise and share all available anonymised data within the university has acted as a 'call to action' as the various threads and arcs of the various stories become evident.

The launch of UCD's University for All initiative has given further impetus to the data process as we explore and share other ways of visualising and displaying our data with programme areas. When the University for All initiative was introduced to programme boards by the project team, colleagues requested data disaggregated by programme in order to get greater visibility of the diversity within their programmes and to make informed implementation and action plans. As a result of this, a data visualisation project was started in April 2018 to provide institutional and programme level data on our widening participation student profiles. These data were benchmarked against our 33 per cent target and provided to members of the Widening Participation Committee in UCD. The provision of programme level data is key to the implementation of University for All, and the dissemination of these disaggregated data through programme boards and University for All programme workshops has created a significant lever for change. This democratisation of data is critical in empowering and fostering a sense of ownership of the University for All initiative.

> You can't be what you can't see.
>
> Marian Wright Edelman

The singular use of data metrics to tell the story of inclusion is not sufficient. As the process of the University for All developed, it was clear that the voice of students would have to be one of the key ingredients. Students are catalysts for change and finding ways to capture their experience and weave their contribution into the implementation process became crucial, as is described elsewhere. Consequently, the capacity and freedom for students to tell their stories has become integral to our own data story.

The student voice in the data story

We have an active cohort of student leaders who are trained to lead fellow students and to be 'what others can see' as role models. Students are encouraged to consider what they wish to share and, critically, what they will not disclose. The narrative is theirs to shape and tell. Their stories are particularly powerful as a context for staff to hear a first-hand experience of aspects of inclusion in their programme or unit. For example, a programme-based student may share the experience of hearing a student welcome message that inadvertently alienates them by assuming that they come from a position of privilege or are progressing to university directly from school. Their stories are powerful and provocative in challenging our assumptions, critiquing our approach, and offering an alternative narrative or experience that offers a more inclusive message.

Mixed methods

The data we use to drive change in fostering a University for All are mixed, with an outline of the key processes shown in Figure 3.5 below.

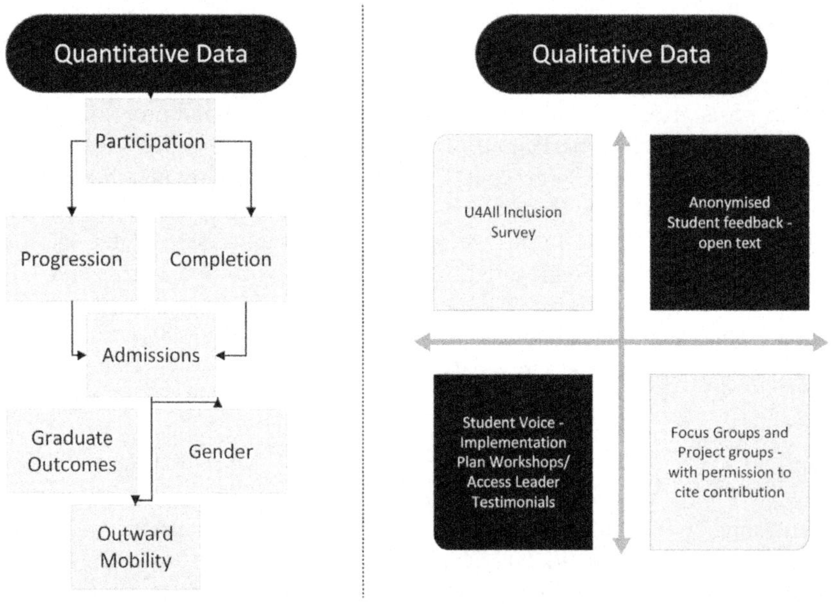

Figure 3.5 Mixed data options to inform a University for All – the elements required to tell the story

So, where to start?

Telling any story requires an audience, and this is particularly relevant in telling a data story. The key is to know your audience and recognise that there will be a range of audiences who will want different data and will respond differently. By segmenting your audience, you can develop and offer different perspectives and insights, as illustrated in Figure 3.6.

1 Policy Makers and Funders will need to see data around compliance and KPIs. Being clear at the start of every project and initiative around the data requirements will make the implementation and reporting manageable. It will also address any data compliance concerns by identifying them at the outset.
2 HE Institutions and Programmes will be interested in internal performance, and how those measures compare across the institution. The capacity to share data with colleagues should inform and prompt action. However, it is also important to establish anonymity around the data so that individual cases in smaller programmes are not identified. Where programmes have a small number of students (in our case we defined this as less than 50), we did not share any reports on the programme. Data can have particular impact on those who are guarded or cynical about change.
3 Access Staff and Outreach Practitioners can use data to illustrate success to date, and targets for the future. The data give those who are seeking to influence the appropriate evidence to reassure, inspire, or provoke debate and action.
4 University for All; Researchers and Communities of Practice – the data, both quantitative and qualitative, move the compelling case of inclusion and diversity from one of persuasion to evidence. The voice and presence

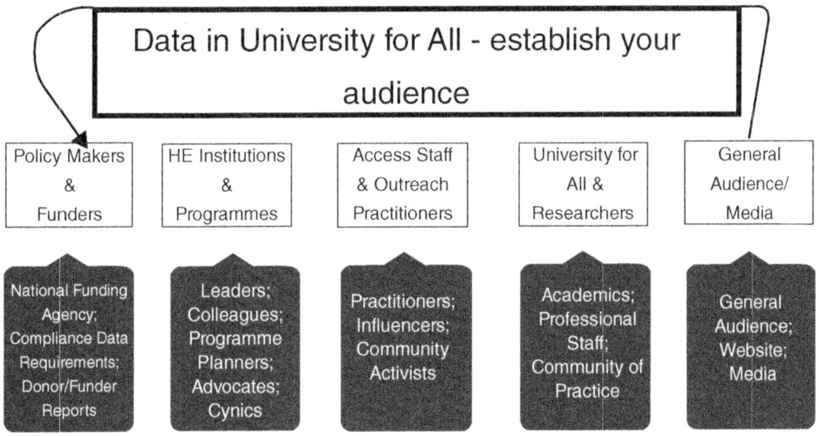

Figure 3.6 Knowing your audience – segmentation allows different data approaches

of the student in the data moves the narrative from rhetorical to factual and is a significant resource in delivering an inclusive message.

5 General Audience & Media. Your university or institution is most likely regularly asked to comment or share data on access and inclusion. The metrics around access will be of interest to a general audience. Journalists and other media outlets regularly look for responses or stories about students who have 'triumphed' or 'beaten the odds'. The data you can share move the focus away from individual 'zero to hero' stories to the more objective and anonymised platform that will allow the university to share its success and contribution, without compromising the anonymity or integrity of a single student narrative.

The impact of sharing data with such a broad audience should enhance the institution's reputation for access and inclusion. Critically, this could have the impact of attracting more under-represented students in the future.

What next?

Once you have established who your audience is, you need to consider what story you wish to tell them. Depending on who your audience is, you will need to adapt your story. This is illustrated in Figure 3.7. In this example, the audience is an internal university cohort and the data were developed to prompt and drive action

Conclusion

The reality is that there is no perfect dataset and no single 'button' that we can press that will generate the evidence and pictures we need to demonstrate our work and illustrate our impact. This is illustrated in the Holness and Mozaffari case study in the next section. Many practitioners can be frustrated by the fragmented data available, and the extent to which those fragments are scattered and hosted in various places across the institution. Similarly, there may be the inevitable promises of a future perfect dataset, which will require patience as the utopian scene is developed. The aphorism, 'don't let the perfect be the enemy of the good', is particularly appropriate here (see Figure 3.8). The reality for most is that there will be gaps in the data and it will not be perfect, but, in Holness and Mozaffari's words, it may be 'good enough', and that's a good place to start.

> … institutions are advised to 'measure what we value, not value what we measure.
>
> (O'Farrell, 2019)

The value of data in driving change is incontrovertible. This chapter has focused on the power of data, and the particular impact of visual representation

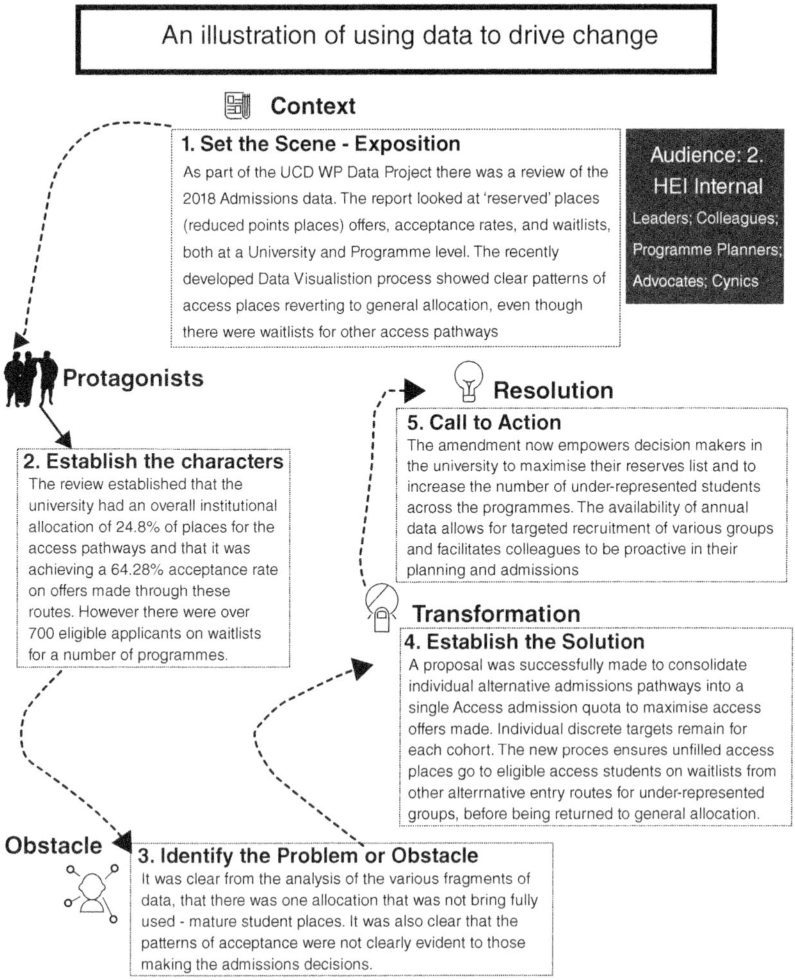
An illustration of using data to drive change
Context
1. Set the Scene - Exposition
As part of the UCD WP Data Project there was a review of the 2018 Admissions data. The report looked at 'reserved' places (reduced points places) offers, acceptance rates, and waitlists, both at a University and Programme level. The recently developed Data Visualistion process showed clear patterns of access places reverting to general allocation, even though there were waitlists for other access pathways
Audience: 2. HEI Internal
Leaders; Colleagues; Programme Planners; Advocates; Cynics
Protagonists
2. Establish the characters
The review established that the university had an overall institutional allocation of 24.8% of places for the access pathways and that it was achieving a 64.28% acceptance rate on offers made through these routes. However there were over 700 eligible applicants on waitlists for a number of programmes.
Resolution
5. Call to Action
The amendment now empowers decision makers in the university to maximise their reserves list and to increase the number of under-represented students across the programmes. The availability of annual data allows for targeted recruitment of various groups and facilitates colleagues to be proactive in their planning and admissions
Transformation
4. Establish the Solution
A proposal was successfully made to consolidate individual alternative admissions pathways into a single Access admission quota to maximise access offers made. Individual discrete targets remain for each cohort. The new proces ensures unfilled access places go to eligible access students on waitlists from other alterrnative entry routes for under-represented groups, before being returned to general allocation.
Obstacle
3. Identify the Problem or Obstacle
It was clear from the analysis of the various fragments of data, that there was one allocation that was not bring fully used - mature student places. It was also clear that the patterns of acceptance were not clearly evident to those making the admissions decisions.

Figure 3.7 Illustration of use of data to identify and prompt action to drive change

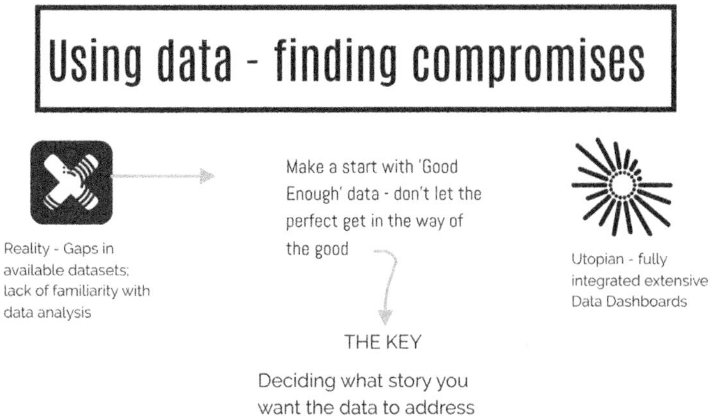
Using data - finding compromises
Reality - Gaps in available datasets; lack of familiarity with data analysis
Make a start with 'Good Enough' data - don't let the perfect get in the way of the good
Utopian - fully integrated extensive Data Dashboards
THE KEY
Deciding what story you want the data to address

Figure 3.8 Using data and finding compromises

and a clear narrative in telling the data story. The metrics institutions use, and how they share their data stories, can suggest the value placed on diversity. We treasure what we measure. The potential value of WP data can be in conflict with the competing demands imposed on, and perpetuated by, the higher education system. As an illustration, the increasingly popular use of University League Tables reflects the current value systems of our higher education sector. Typically, the current league tables do not reflect the extent to which an institution has been successful in widening participation (Hubbard et al., 2021).

However, this chapter has focused on what is possible, irrespective of the context. Data have the capacity to act as the 'burning platform' that conveys real urgency and confers authority and credibility on the narrator. They move us from the language of persuasion and idealism to evidence-based practice. This shift in approach has moved us from telling that one story of that one student who was an outlier, to narrating a different story, with evidence of patterns and progress that allows a reflective look at systems and practices.

This chapter illustrates the benefits of creating that bigger picture, through data. It illustrates how using the correct media, and knowing your audience, will allow the data to tell your story. This will, in turn, allow the many elements of data, the micro points, to become a much bigger picture that offers a compelling tale. This was illustrated in showing what happened when the fragments of admissions data were collated to show lower patterns of acceptance in some groups that could benefit other access cohorts.

In the spirit of recognising the value of the student voice, we leave you with the view of one of our access leaders on the power of data:

> I believe that … data … is an essential part to achieving a University for All. Without such data students similar to me from disadvantaged backgrounds are overlooked and unseen, this is not what we want. The system cannot and will not improve unless change is encouraged. This data allows all students to be represented in an equal manner. It means that any barriers or blockers, which are detrimental to the overall college experience, will be assessed and changed in order to allow all students a fair opportunity at their academic studies.
>
> … I believe data is not only crucial to incite change for students but it will also promote awareness, awareness that not all students are equal, we did not all run the same race for our spot in university, however with change and with adaptation we can all finish the race at the same pace.
>
> – Lorraine Dunster, UCD Access Leader BA Student

The following case study in 3.2 offers additional perspective on how data can become a lever for change

References

Ball, L. (2009). Cholera and the pump on Broad Street: The life and legacy of John Snow. *The History Teacher (Long Beach, Calif.)*, 43, 105–119.

Bruner, J.S. (1990). *Acts of Meaning*. London and Cambridge, MA: Harvard University Press.

Department of Education Ireland (1992). *Education for a Changing World: Green Paper on Education (Green Paper)*. Dublin: The Stationery Office.

Felten, P. and Hrabwski, F.A. (2016). *The Undergraduate Experience: Focusing Institutions on What Matters Most*. San Francisco, CA: Jossey-Bass.

Fleming, B., Padden, L., and Kelly, A.M. (2022). *Who Counts? University for All Data, Metrics, and Evidence 2020–2021*. Dublin: UCD Access & Lifelong Learning.

Gorard, S., Boliver, V., Siddiqui, N., and Banerjee, P. (2019). Which are the most suitable contextual indicators for use in widening participation to HE? *Research Papers in Education*, 34, 99–129.

HEPI (2018). Benchmarking widening participation: How should we measure and report progress? In I. Martin (ed.), *HEPI Policy Note 6*. Oxford: Higher Education Policy Institute.

Higher Education Authority (2004). *Towards a National Strategy: Initial Review of HEA Targeted Initiatives to Widen Access to Higher Education*. Dublin: National Office for Equity of Access to Higher Education, Higher Education Authority.

Holland, N., Houghton, A.-M., Armstrong, J., and Mashiter, C. (2017). Accessing and assessing appropriate widening participation data: An exploration of how data are used and by whom. *Studies in Continuing Education*, 39, 214–233.

Hubbard, K., O'Neill, M., and Nattrass, S. (2021). Levelling the playing field: The effect of including widening participation in university league tables. *International Review of Education*, 67, 273–304.

Johnson, S. (2006). *The Ghost Map: The Story of London's Most Terrifying Epidemic – And How It Changed Science, Cities, and the Modern World*. New York: Riverhead Books.

Kelly, A.M. and Padden, L. (2018). *Toolkit for Inclusive Higher Education Institutions: From Vision to Practice*. Dublin: UCD Access & Lifelong Learning.

Knaflic, C.N. (2015). *Storytelling with Data: A Data Visualization Guide for Business Professionals*. Hoboken, NJ: Wiley.

Kotter, J. (2008). *A Sense of Urgency*. Cambridge, MA: Harvard Business Press.

Mutonyi, H. (2016). Stories, proverbs, and anecdotes as scaffolds for learning science concepts: Stories, proverbs, and anecdotes as scaffolds. *Journal of Research in Science Teaching*, 53, 943–971.

O'Farrell, L. (2019). Understanding and enabling student success in Irish higher education. National Forum for the Enhancement of Teaching and Learning in Higher Education. Available at: https://www.teachingandlearning.ie/our-priorities/student-success/defining-student-success

Osborne, R.D. and Leith, H. (2000). *Evaluation of the Targeted Initiative on Widening Access for Young People from Socio-Economically Disadvantaged Backgrounds: Report to the Higher Education Authority*. Dublin: Higher Education Authority.

UCD (2017). *Widening Participation Committee Annual Report 2016/17*. Available at: https://www.ucd.ie/t4cms/Widening%20Participation%20Committee%20Annual%20Report%202016-17.pdf

UCD Widening Participation Committee (2013). *Institutional Barriers to Full Participation by Students Constrained by Personal or Professional Circumstances, or Economic or Social Disadvantage.* Dublin: UCD Widening Participation Committee.

Wasserman, V. and Berkovich, I. (2022). Higher education professionals in the age of NPM and digital knowledge: Distinction strategies for forming new occupational capital. *Studies in Higher Education (Dorchester-on-Thames)*, 47, 146–158.

3.2 Student engagement and retention through a data driven approach in higher education

A case study of developing inclusive practice addressing the attainment gap

Marilyn Holness and Hameed Mozaffari

Higher education has seen a growth in the use of, and reliance on, performance metrics to inform decision-making and strategy, elevating the role of data to one of the fundamental drivers for institutional change. Universities are rich in datasets, local intelligence, and growing expertise in deploying learner analytics to identify insights and key indicators to inform actions demanded by regulators like the Office for Students (OfS). Against this backdrop, data should be treated as evidence that is a lever for moving conversations beyond just the operational to creating inclusive and accessible environments.

In institutional contexts, data, in the day-to-day operation, can be misunderstood, especially if there is a lack of guidance for educators and practitioners on how to use data effectively (Elliot and Sammons, 2001; Goldstein, 2001). Broader research in the education sector has revealed that data can be effective in developing more inclusive practices in teaching and learning through areas such as more effective allocation of staff and resources, monitoring the effectiveness of initiatives and strategies, and evidence-based discussions, which can lead to institutional change (Kirkup et al., 2005). The shift towards moving conversations about data beyond the operational towards the strategic is crucial when it comes to programme and curriculum design, and the development of existing teaching and learning practices.

When it comes to adapting student support and services in response to data, it is important to start somewhere, noting the gap between the ambition to work with deep, broad datasets and the reality of gaps in available datasets. Thus, how we build the data picture becomes key. There is never a perfect dataset and holding out for such is detrimental when it comes to supporting students. Instead, available data should be utilised and organised in a proactive manner in order to implement change. 'Good enough' data, which tell enough of a story to trigger action, can be used to make things happen in impactful ways, and so they should be the starting point to engage in discussion of, for example, pedagogical practices.

'Good enough' data should be diverse; they should be reflective of real life and representative of the environment within which you are exploring. On the

DOI: 10.4324/9781003253631-9

macro and micro level, data inform the work we do, and they inform our approach to the interventions which we deliver as part of a growing package of support offered to students. The RAFA2 (Re-imagining Attainment for All) project was an evidence-informed approach to addressing the attainment gap which exists in the landscape of higher education (RAFA2, 2019). While data existed which demonstrated that Black and Asian students statistically achieved lower overall degree classifications than their white counterparts, what did not exist were data which revealed the contributing factors for such a problem. Rather than waiting for these data, we proactively began discussions about this attainment gap, to move the focus beyond operations to the strategic; all the while collecting additional data which became evidence that became a driver of institutional change through a series of interventions.

RAFA2 emerged from two previous research enquiries led by the Learning and Teaching Enhancement Unit (LTEU) at the University of Roehampton. In 2009, we began 'Journey to Success', to explore, understand, and work to reduce our attainment gap. Starting with this small research project, the LTEU examined the work conducted in the schools' sector, examining how it had successfully begun to raise the attainment of Black and Asian pupils to see if lessons could be learnt for higher education. As a result, in 2011, RAFA was born. RAFA narrowed the focus to provide greater transparency in the process of assessment and the communication of high expectations to all students. This was the first step in using data to drive change, becoming a lever through which we reconfigured and redefined teaching, learning, and assessment, and the overall academic culture at Roehampton. In 2017, aided by the Catalyst Fund, RAFA2 was launched. This phase built on existing data and aimed to extend the knowledge base and develop practical solutions by working towards overcoming the Black and Asian attainment gap as part of a sector-wide approach.

The data from RAFA, which subsequently led to the need for new data which emerged from RAFA2, were implemented. However, they showed that little changed. Systematic differences existed in undergraduate degree attainment between certain student cohorts at UK universities and beyond. Perhaps most conspicuously, white students continued to achieve higher overall awards than Black and Asian students. The data from RAFA2 became a driver of institutional change through a scaffolding technique which led to programme development, adaption in curriculum design, changes in methods of teaching and learning, development in student services and support, and additional training and awareness for staff (Pillars 1 and 2 of the Toolkit for Inclusive Higher Education Institutions).

It is important to note though that the RAFA2 data were one of the starting points of institutional change. There was no sense in waiting for the perfect data to be developed but rather, given the context of the attainment gap which RAFA sought to address, we acknowledged that we just needed to start.

> We ran CPD sessions presenting academics with the attainment data for their students across the institution, department, and at programme level

> and asked them to explore the issues behind the data, to consider where the responsibility lies and the actions they could take. In every CPD session, questions of the data's robustness, reliability and credibility were raised as an explanation for the disparity. Academics also challenged the validity of the construct of race and ethnicity, preferring to foreground the debate by social class and socioeconomic status instead. Intersectional factors, such as attendance, students' commute and family and caregiving responsibilities, were also raised as explanations for the disparity. Additionally, issues pertaining to the sample size, power size as well as reference to the types of statistical analysis conducted and what this might mean for the integrity of the data e.g., cumulative error, were also voiced.
>
> (RAFA2.org)

Rather than be side-tracked by discussions about 'the data are wrong!', we made data a central focus, investigating the gathering, creation, analysis, interpretation, and use of data, including how to come up with a plan of what to do, in parallel with ongoing work with staff and students on addressing the barriers to the awarding gap. Alongside this, further data were collected that explored additional factors which had not been previously explored; for example, the entry qualification pathways (see Figure 3.9). This

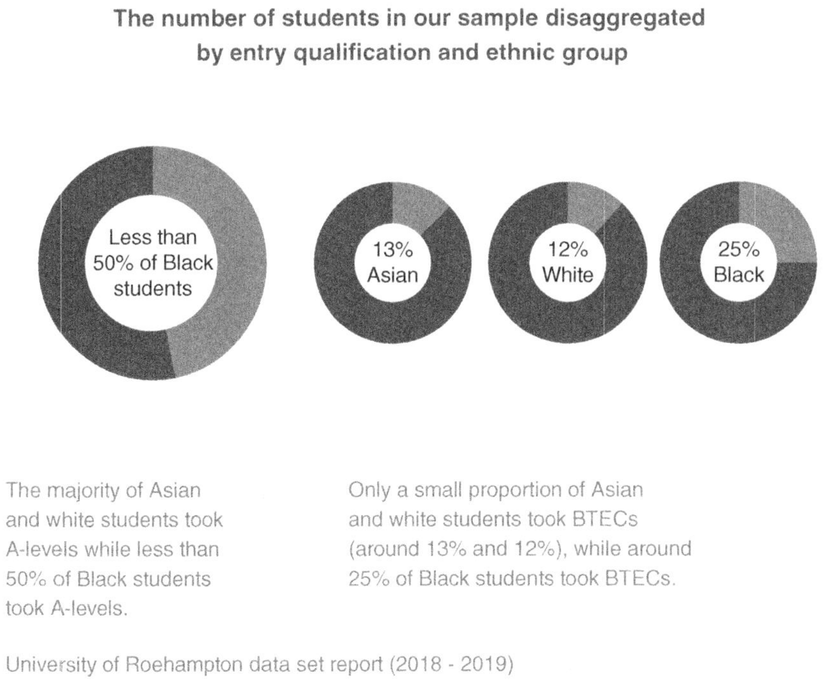
The number of students in our sample disaggregated by entry qualification and ethnic group
Less than 50% of Black students
13% Asian
12% White
25% Black
The majority of Asian and white students took A-levels while less than 50% of Black students took A-levels.
Only a small proportion of Asian and white students took BTECs (around 13% and 12%), while around 25% of Black students took BTECs.
University of Roehampton data set report (2018 - 2019)

Figure 3.9 RAFA2 data entry qualifications

THE RAFA WAY

The RAFA WAY is a 10 step approach developed by the RAFA team as a practical tool which can be adopted by academics as a way of engaging more and understanding the needs of BAME students

1. Keep under review BAME attainment data.
2. Talk to students.
3. Talk to staff.
4. Create spaces and opportunities for staff and students to work in partnership.
5. Facilitate local discussions, activities, interventions and make them routine.
6. Embed local action plans, that feed into institutional approach.
7. Continue to identify areas for further development as part of ongoing learning.
8. Embed and incorporate priorities into institutional strategies.
9. Update processes and procedures - keep policies updated to reflect developments.
10. Review as part of ongoing monitoring and evaluation and close the feedback loop with staff and students.

Figure 3.10 The RAFA Way

illustrates that, while certain characteristics can be overrepresented in certain groups, which should not have an impact on student outcomes, evidence showed they do.

In this instance, we argued that the cause of the discrepancy was not down to BTECs or Black students. Instead, we attributed it to structural and institutional processes manifested in the organisation and delivery of teaching, learning, assessment and support, lack of knowledge about our learners and their prior learning experiences, in the dynamics of our classrooms and in our processes to induct and onboard learners into their studies; simply put, how we work with students. With respect to Pillar 4 of the Toolkit, our data contributed to implementing a change in the way digital learning environments and information technology systems went on to be structured. Our data also played a role in the use of formative assessments, through Moodle, online forum opportunities to encourage student voice, the development of more relevant content, requiring students to use a diverse range of theorists in their work and more participatory learning approaches. Deliberate steps were taken to create a community of inclusion whereby students developed a sense of belonging but also increased access to their degrees.

There is great value and importance in knowing micro and macro data, as they are the evidence necessary to create institutional change and progress access and inclusion in education. The data generated through RAFA2 led to the creation of the 'RAFA Way' (see Figure 3.10), a practical e-toolkit which could be adopted by academics as a way of engaging more and understanding the needs of Black and Asian students. This was the first of many practical steps taken in direct response to the data to further develop inclusive practices.

The bigger picture among all this is the way data can be effectively used to drive student success and improvements in outcomes across access, engagement, retention, continuation, completion, and progression of all students. Without data, there is no driver. This can lead to student interventions for students at risk of non-completion or provide data for students positioned on grade boundaries or offer the challenge and stretch required for our most able students. Data are important, but they must be fit for purpose and produced in ways that staff can fully engage with them. Reporting must require more than just 'knowing' the gaps, but focus on how it improves better decision making, accountability, and in measuring impact. To achieve this, universities need to be agile in their use of data analytics, using it to gain early, real-time alerts and metrics that matter to inform change and impact on successful outcomes for all students.

References

Elliot, K. and Sammons, P. (2001). Using pupil performance data: Three steps to heaven?. *Improving Schools*, 4(1), 54–65.

Goldstein, H. (2001). Using pupil performance data for judging schools and teachers: Scope and limitations. *British Educational Research Journal*, 27(4), 433–442.
Kirkup, C., Sizmur, J., Sturman, L., and Lewis, K. (2005). *Schools' Use of Data in Teaching and Learning*. DfES Research Report 671. London: DFES.
RAFA2 (2019). *Re-imagining Attainment For All* [online]. Available at: https://rafa2.org/homepage/

Chapter 4

From vision to practice: A Toolkit for Inclusive Higher Education Institutions

4.1 Tell me how! Development, methodology, and use of the Toolkit for Inclusive Higher Education Institutions

Lisa Padden

If the road to hell is paved with good intentions, then higher education institutions that have failed to implement inclusion are built, brick by brick, with belief and vision that has never become reality. Shown in Figure 4.1, The Toolkit for Inclusive Higher Education Institutions (Kelly and Padden, 2018a) was developed for use in the higher education sector in response to the need for a whole-institution response to access, participation, and success of under-represented students. It was developed as a tool to assist universities and colleges to progress mainstreaming and inclusion for all students. The Toolkit offers a strategic institution-wide lens to assess progress, identify opportunities for improvement, and create a bespoke action plan to develop a whole-institution approach to inclusion, where every student feels welcome, that they belong, and are valued. The Toolkit helps turn rhetoric into action, converting intentions into actions and, therefore, creating positive institutional change.

The University for All initiative (described in Chapter 1 of this book) was launched in November 2017, and this launch was accompanied by a targeted institutional promotional campaign. In the following months, the project team visited the University's programme boards and policy/support units to provide an overview of the goals of the initiative, share access and widening participation data and, most importantly, to ask what colleagues needed to progress this initiative locally (Kelly and Padden, 2018a; 2018b). During and following these meetings, colleagues asked for two specific supports to progress inclusion: 1) a how-to guide, which translated the vision for inclusion into clear and achievable actions; and 2) disaggregated and easily accessible data on access and widening participation, showing the full student journey in our institution. We got to work on both of these requests – our data journey is outlined in Chapter 3 of this book. We searched for a guide or a toolkit which we could offer our colleagues as the practical guide they requested but found nothing which offered a comprehensive view of an inclusive institution. We established then that there was a gap – that there were several examples of mission and vision statements on inclusion, but no practical resources to illustrate how the process could be actioned. We then began the development of our own Toolkit for Inclusive Higher Education Institutions.

DOI: 10.4324/9781003253631-11

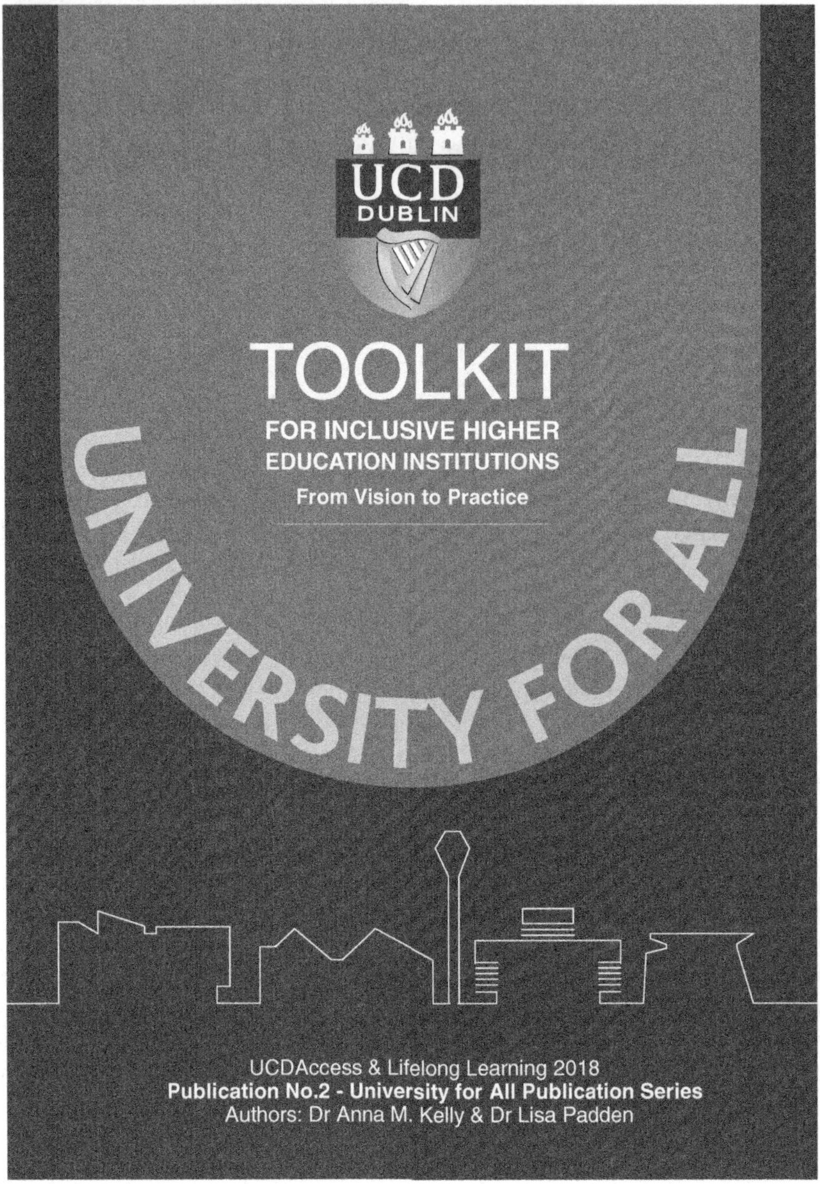

Figure 4.1 Toolkit for Inclusive Higher Education Institutions (Kelly and Padden, 2018a)

Development of the Toolkit

The development of the Toolkit was influenced by the literature in a number of research areas focused on inclusion: Universal Design (Mace, 1998; Rose and Meyer, 2002) inclusive design (Goodman, 2016; Politis et al., 2014), and design for all (Bendixen and Benktzon, 2015). Colleagues can become mired or overwhelmed because of what might be considered competing or non-aligned frameworks (Bianchin and Heylighen, 2017; Persson et al., 2015). We, therefore, approached the Toolkit development in a practical sense, taking what is most applicable, most important, and ultimately most necessary in the creation of an inclusive higher education institution (HEI). The development of this Toolkit was fundamentally informed by the work of Kelly (2017a, 2017b), Padden (2016), and Padden, O'Connor, and Barrett (2017).

Structure of the Toolkit

The Toolkit is divided into five sections – the four pillars and the foundations and scaffolding (see Figure 4.2) – with each section containing the following components:

Self-Assessment Statements. These statements present a state of inclusion for all students, which must then be scored 0–5 – from not addressed at all to fully addressed and leading internationally in the field. Sample scoring is provided in the Toolkit, with clear instructions on how to score. However, it should be noted that the scores here are far less important than the dialogue and the recording of good practice and decision on priorities and project planning for those areas where a low score is evident. In total, the Toolkit currently has over 140 self-assessment statements, so it spans the full range of activity within a HEI. As will be described below, we continue to adapt and add to these statements as we develop and refine our use of the Toolkit. We also encourage others to do the same in their own contexts as the landscape we work in continually evolves.

Actions to Consider. The Toolkit gathers some of the pivotal actions which can create positive change in an institution. These draw on various areas of inclusion research, as well as best practice across the sector. While many examples are drawn from our own institution, we also ensure that international examples are used wherever possible. We continue to gather these examples and, again, encourage adaptation of these sections by other institutions using the Toolkit to ensure that they can see themselves and their good practice reflected.

Possible Challenges and Suggested Solutions. The challenges and barriers to implementing system change for inclusion are widely discussed and reported, and so we would have been remiss not to acknowledge these. We note the challenges but, vitally, also offer suggestions as to how they may be overcome or addressed. The challenges we cover are often the well-rehearsed reasons for lack of progression in access and inclusion, including a focus on research output and lack of time and resources. It is vital not to shy away from these challenges but rather to face them and plan for how they will be addressed in the immediate and long-term future.

Examples of Good Practice. These examples are from HEIs internationally and provide inspiration for readers who are at all stages of their journey to inclusion. The examples are provided briefly, with links and references for further exploration. These examples include specific inclusion-focused initiatives in each section e.g. provision of reduced cost childcare on campus for full-time students (Kelly and Padden, 2018a, p. 62), as well as reference to specific policies which support inclusion e.g. institutional policy on inclusion for content creation (Kelly and Padden, 2018a, p. 85).

Resources. A curated list of resources is provided for each section, drawing together key pieces of research and links to guides and sources which can be used in practical implementation activities.

The Toolkit focuses on the four institutional pillars of a typical HEI, as well as the foundation and scaffolding components necessary to develop a whole-institution approach to mainstreaming and inclusion. The sections are designed to reflect the structure of typical HEIs, focusing on the functions of the university and keeping the student journey at the centre. The sections are shown in Figure 4.2 and described below. This structure is also reflected in the delineation of the chapters of this book.

Foundations and Scaffolding: Strategic Approach and Organisation

Scaffolding elements are typically those units or committees that support the development or work of inclusion, access, and widening participation within the institution. These are usually the units working to translate national or institutional access and inclusion policy into practice. This section covers institutional strategy and approach, as well as policies. Here, we ask users of

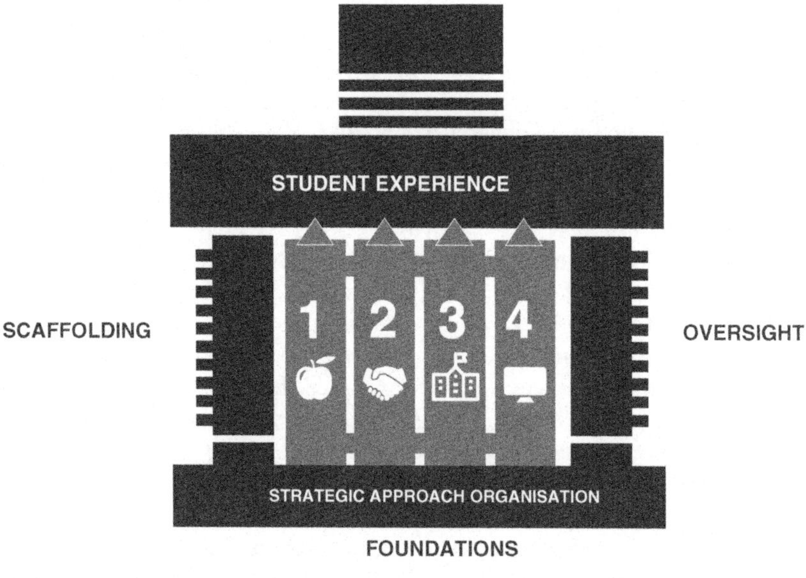

Figure 4.2 University for All components

the Toolkit to assess many institutional interventions and practices which provide a foundation for inclusion, including the institutional vision and mission, admissions policies, outreach practices, key performance indicators, designated responsibility and governance for equitable access and inclusion, professional development provision, and quality assurance processes. This section, even more than the pillars to follow, speaks to senior management and leadership in an institution.

Pillar 1: Programme & Curriculum Design, Teaching & Learning

This section refers to the academic programmes of study offered by an institution and how they are taught and assessed. Self-assessment statements in this area are delineated under three categories: general principles, assessment, and teaching materials/classroom practices. In general principles, a number of areas are examined, such as the inclusion of Universal Design for teaching and learning in institutional strategy, consideration of students with commitments beyond their study, the requirement for inclusion-focused work to be evidenced in academic promotion pathways, and the provision of Reasonable Accommodations (referred to as Reasonable Adjustments in some contexts) for students with disabilities. In the area of assessment, statements cover immediate needs for change, such as elimination of the 100 per cent terminal exam and other long-term changes such as development or co-development of rubrics, marking criteria, and grade descriptors. Accessibility is a focus in the section on teaching materials and classroom practices, as well as other embedded inclusion approaches such as visibility of Equality, Diversity, and Inclusion in the programme content through work such as decolonising the curriculum.

Pillar 2: Student Supports & Services

This section covers supports and services provided to students in the HEI and covers general support principles, careers services, IT support, Library services, and student mental health services. The section on general principles can be applied to all support areas, with some additional considerations given for some areas. Considering the student journey, this section covers advertisement and encouraging engagement, cross referral systems, staff training, flexible provision of services, and types of supports available. Accessible and inclusive student supports and services are vital for the success of a diverse student population and, the more integrated these supports are to the student's educational journey, the more positive their experience is likely to be.

Pillar 3: Physical Campus & the Built Environment

This section covers the physical campus infrastructure of a HEI, including external and internal considerations as well as student accommodation. A whole-institution approach to physical accessibility is necessary to provide a fully inclusive experience for all students. Most jurisdictions now have legislation which covers building accessibility, but in this section we break down the notion of overall access and inclusion in the physical space to self-assessment statements which most employees can comment on including signage, wayfinding, building entrances, provision of equipment in teaching spaces, and provision of respite spaces. The student accommodation section speaks to physical accessibility but also affordability of accommodation and the need to provide for all students, including those who commute long distances to engage in their programme of study.

Pillar 4: Information Technology Systems & Infrastructure

This section covers websites, Virtual Learning Environments, application, fees and registration systems, data-gathering, mining and visualisation, and social media platforms. In the development of this section, we considered the varying size and scope of institutional information technology infrastructures and associated services. Responsibility for IT systems is not always clear in large organisations, and universities are the same. Ultimately, all university employees have at least some degree of responsibility for inclusion in systems, whether we aid in the design of those systems, create policies for the procurement of them, or guide students in their use. This section points towards international standards and guidance, while also considering areas which most employees can relate to, such as document creation, training provision and engagement, data protection, and use of materials on social media.

As the Toolkit was developed, it was drafted and tested a number of times with higher education professionals in our own institution. This resulted in a number of changes to statements which were refined over a series of revisions and rewrites. Using a workshop format, a draft iteration of the Toolkit was trialled by a broad range of academic and professional staff from another HEI over a half day on site visit by the developers. This testing process assisted in ensuring the Toolkit could be used by other HEIs at different stages of embedding inclusion. The Toolkit allows for the identification of progress already made, which offers reassurance and a platform on which to build. The goal is to help identify any levers of change, potential resources available, and, ultimately, enable the development of an action plan for the creation of an inclusive higher education environment.

In summary, the Toolkit is intended to:

- Assist in creating an action plan
- Recognise the progress already achieved
- Identify areas of priority
- Offer practical steps to implement and embed inclusive practice
- Facilitate dialogue between faculty, professional staff, technical staff etc. on the importance of inclusive higher education practice.

(Kelly and Padden, 2018a, p. 23)

Who should use the Toolkit?

The Toolkit is intended for use by all university and college leaders, faculty members, and professional and administrative staff. Application of the Toolkit will depend on the size of your institution. In a large university, we recommend an overarching steering committee maintain oversight of its use in the implementation of inclusive practice, with representatives on the committee leading on the use of the Toolkit in local workshops – this might be individual professional, administrative or support units or Colleges, Schools or Disciplines. While it can be used at various levels and departments throughout the organisation, use of the Toolkit should be collaborative, and the discussion should include individuals with some responsibility for the organisational strategy, as well as each of the four pillars. In our University, to date, the Toolkit has been used to facilitate workshops across the institution in all programme areas, led by our Widening Participation Leads and their local change teams.

As we note many times in this book, support and commitment of senior management is vital when attempting to create whole-institution system change for inclusion. The self-assessment statements are many and varied, and it will take considerable time and effort to work through all of them. We suggest starting with a small number (five or six) and expanding from there. You will see exactly how this Toolkit is being used and what kind of changes have been achieved as a result in the case studies from those who are leading this work in the developer's University. The completion of the self-assessment exercise with as many colleagues as possible is highly effective in creating awareness of inclusive practice. Undertaking this exercise collaboratively also acknowledges and respects domain expertise and demonstrates inclusion in practice. In highly complex educational organisations, considering the perspective and standpoint of all stakeholders, including students, results in more creative problem solving and effective solutions (Page, 2007).

How is the Toolkit used in University for All implementation?

Our impetus to develop the Toolkit was to support the implementation of the University for All initiative, and it is now central to that process. Our Widening Participation Leads, who have designated responsibility for progressing inclusion and widening participation in specific areas of UCD, use the Toolkit to tailor their approach to University for All implementation. The overall goal of this implementation is to make access and inclusion the core work of each individual in the university, with the Toolkit helping all employees of the University to understand how their work can impact the experience of students. This implementation strategy was approved by our institution's senior management team through formal channels. This formal approval is advisable, as this process helps to ensure buy-in and accountability across the institution.

Figure 4.3 University for All implementation process including workshop

The four steps to implementation are shown in Figure 4.3 and include:

1 **Senior Leadership Buy-in**. Getting support from the academic or administrative senior leader e.g. College Principal, Dean, Director.
2 **Form Change Team**. Establishing a change team to drive the project locally, including key colleagues e.g. leaders and staff with responsibility

for Equality Diversity & Inclusion, Teaching & Learning and other relevant areas.

3 **Plan and Deliver Workshop**. Planning an initial University for All workshop (with support of the senior leader and change team). Previous experience has shown that attendance can be maximised when the invitation is disseminated by the local senior leader. The workshop is planned with consideration of local needs, and we recommend using the structure below; although this can vary depending on time available and some elements may be presented in separate sessions:

a Exploration of Widening Participation data to include admissions, participation, progression, completion, outward mobility and graduate outcomes. Change teams determine which data are most useful and how they should be presented (e.g. intersectionality of access groups, gender balance etc.). These data are shared through external and internal reports (Fleming, Padden, and Kelly, 2022) but having the data shared and explained by a local colleague usually produces more interest in the figures and eventually more action to address the gaps identified.

b Engagement with the student voice. Student ambassadors can offer their perspective on inclusion, providing personal insight into the good practice currently ongoing and exploring how local areas can improve their practice. These students should be trained and rewarded for their time and expertise, but it is important not to stray into 'coaching' students for these sessions, to ensure their authentic voice and experience is shared. Training of these students should include disclosure techniques and understanding how to share their experience. We cannot ignore the toll that student advocacy can take and students should not be called upon repeatedly for this type of work – a large and well-supported team of student ambassadors is important. More on the student voice and their role in implementation is outlined below.

c Universal Design/Inclusive Practice training and development. Local leaders in the area can provide training in Universal Design and Inclusive Practice. Areas for development should be determined by the Widening Participation Lead and their change team. Opportunities for expanded training should be showcased, and engagement with this training should be encouraged by senior management. Engagement in training should be tracked and reported to ensure transparency, and impact can then be tracked using this metric.

d Toolkit Self-Assessment. This is the most important element of the University for All workshop. The self-assessment exercise assists with identification of areas of good practice and areas which should be prioritised for immediate or short/long term action. The selection of the statements is done by the local change team to ensure focused and productive discussion, as it isn't possible to use the full Toolkit in one session

4 **Create, Agree, Publish Inclusion Action Plan (with senior leadership sign off).** Following the workshop, an action plan is created, identifying local University for All projects to be progressed. This action plan can then be workshopped with the University for All project team before being presented to the local senior leader for approval and publication. Again, this promotes visibility of this inclusion work and accountability when plans are not actioned.

The student voice in University for All implementation

The voice of the student is central to University for All implementation; from the inception of the University for All initiative, to the detailed workings of the workshop, the student must be foregrounded and their experience must shape the plans created in disciplines and units in a HEI. At the outset, we asked students to define for us what a University for All might be and, from then on, we have continued to be steered by the experiences of our students. Students from under-represented, or under-served, groups (referred to as access students in our institution) provide powerful student contributions in our workshops, but this is not their only role. We undertake a programme of regular focus groups with students from various disciplines and from different access groups, with questions designed in collaboration with Widening Participation Leads who have designated responsibility for inclusion in their discipline or area of the institution. These focus groups are conducted by access professionals, with anonymised transcripts then provided to local change teams afterwards.

Time and again, we have found access students to be generous with their time, and in these focus groups they openly share their experience with the clear goal of making the university a more inclusive place for their fellow students and those who will be in their position in the future. One of the key questions we ask in these focus groups is what inclusion means to students and we are always struck by the simplicity and clarity of the answers we receive. For students in our institution, inclusion means: meaningful representation of diversity in the student and staff/faculty population and in communication materials; a sense of belonging for all students fostered by faculty and staff who are expecting them; clear, open, and frequent two-way communication not hindered by hierarchical barriers or fear of asking a question; and provision of integrated, timely, and tailored supports for those student groups that require them.

The creation of action plans, as described above, is always informed by the student experience. The use of the Toolkit for Inclusive Higher Education Institutions would lack impact without this focus on foregrounding students.

Reimagining as a digital interactive toolkit

In 2020, along with most of the world, Irish higher education moved online and remote as the impact of COVID-19 was experienced in all aspects of our lives. In our University, we quickly pivoted and looked at how we could continue our University for All implementation and how the Toolkit could facilitate this. In the original development of the Toolkit, we considered creating an online version and we offered a spreadsheet tool to be used alongside the document. We had always hoped to create an interactive tool and the impetus of online and hybrid working made the need for this more immediate. We worked with a development team to realise this vision and now we have a fully adaptable online toolkit which has been used in all implementation workshops since June 2020. This online toolkit allows for scoring of the self-assessment statements, as shown in Figure 4.4. Once a score is selected, it allows for the capture of examples of good practice (Figure 4.5) and ideas for possible actions (Figure 4.6). As you can see in Figures 4.5 and 4.6, we can add prompts to the "good practice" and "possible actions" response captures. These are fully customisable and so can be agreed in advance with the local change team. The tool has a multi-faceted reporting function, allowing for instant download of workshop outputs and sharing with Widening Participation Leads and their

Figure 4.4 The scoring mechanism of the digital toolkit

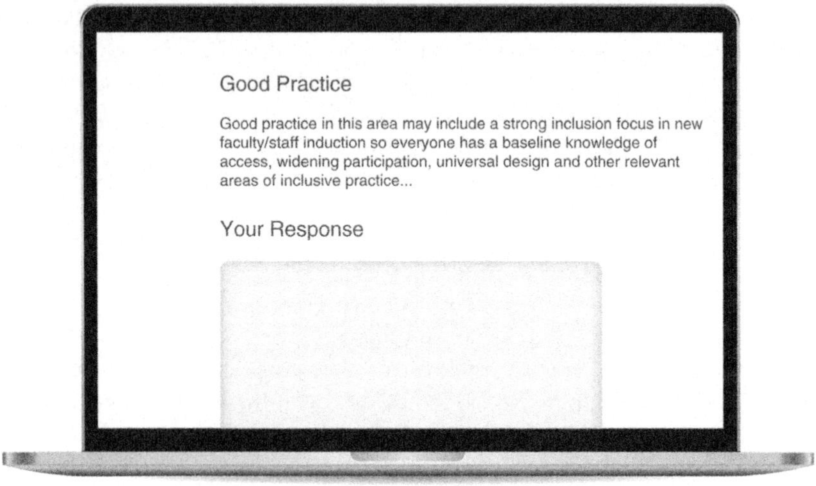

Figure 4.5 Capturing good practice in the digital toolkit

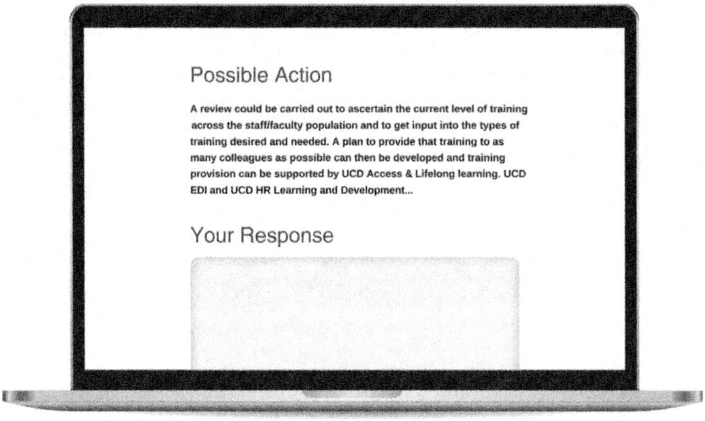

Figure 4.6 Capturing participant ideas for possible actions in the digital toolkit

local change teams. This output then forms the basis of planning and development of inclusion projects.

Through this digital toolkit, statements can be amended and added easily. Also, prompts can be provided for each workshop and developed with specific relevance to the discipline or unit in which the workshop is taking place. For example, when asking participants to score the diversity represented on the HEI website, a link can be shared to the website and examined in real time during the workshop. The digital toolkit can easily be amended to include local institutional branding and be used elsewhere, with, again, the functionality to offer bespoke prompts as desired.

Next steps – the Toolkit as a living document

We have now been using the Toolkit for four years to assist in our work to progress a whole-institution approach to inclusion. We have, throughout this time, been looking for opportunities to further enhance and develop the Toolkit and ensure its ongoing relevance and usefulness for the higher education sector, both nationally and internationally. We have presented the Toolkit at various conferences (e.g. European Access Network annual conference, Ghent, Belgium 2019; AHEAD annual conference, Dublin, Ireland, 2019; ECIO Congress, the Netherlands (online) 2021). From this work, we have developed an international Community of Practice which brings together colleagues from across the globe who are planning to use or are already using the Toolkit in their own contexts.

The Toolkit has been published under creative commons licence, allowing for adaptation with attribution, and we are aware of at least two jurisdictions where the Toolkit is being adapted and used in Canada and the Netherlands. We also continue to discover and address areas we had not previously included in the Toolkit e.g. the role of the Students' Union and now the need to address the desire for continued aspects of remote or hybrid learning. We will continue to see and use the Toolkit as a living document which will evolve and adapt to the ever-changing higher education landscape. In line with the overall approach in creating an inclusive HEI, this Toolkit is not a one size fits all solution but one which is flexible, adaptable, and offers choice in engagement for participating institutions. In short, if you are stuck on that road paved with good intentions, you can use this Toolkit to turn your institution's journey into one of inclusion and action.

References

Bendixen, K. and Benktzon, M. (2015). Design for all in Scandinavia: A strong concept. *Applied Ergonomics*, 46(1), 248–257.

Bianchin, M. and Heylighen, A. (2017). Fair by design. Addressing the paradox of inclusive design approaches. *The Design Journal*, 20(1), S3162–S3170.

Fleming, B., Padden, L., and Kelly, A.M. (2022). *Who Counts? University for All Data, Metrics, and Evidence 2020–2021*. Dublin: UCD Access & Lifelong Learning.

Goodman, L. (2016). *Generation touch: Hippocratic innovation, empathetic education and creative technology – innovation for real social change*. Paper presented at the Early Childhood in Times of Radio Change conference, Vilnius, Lithuania.

Kelly, A.M. (2017a). *An Analysis of the Implementation of National Access Policy to Integrate and Mainstream Equality of Access in Irish Universities – through the Lens of Inclusive Design*. Dublin: University College Dublin.

Kelly, A.M. (2017b). From the margins to mainstreaming – a universally designed and inclusive approach to access and participation in UCD. In *Ireland's Yearbook of Education. Mapping the Past. Forging the Future. 2017–2018* (pp. 377–384). Dublin: Education Matters.

Kelly, A.M. and Padden, L. (2018a). *Toolkit for Inclusive Higher Education Institutions: From Vision to Practice*. Dublin: UCD Access & Lifelong Learning.

Kelly, A.M. and Padden, L. (2018b).University for All: Embedding equality of access, participation and success in higher education. In G. Craddock, C. Doran, L. McNutt, and D. Rice (eds), *Transforming our World Through Design, Diversity and Education: Proceedings of the Universal Design & Higher Education in Transformation Congress.* Dublin: Centre for Universal Design/IOS Publications.

Mace, R. (June, 1998). *Designing for the 21st century: An International Conference on Universal Design.* Paper presented at the International Conference on Universal Design, Hofstra University, Hempstead, New York.

Padden, L. (2016). Universal Design for curriculum design. *The AHEAD Journal,* issue 3, 52–61.

Padden, L., O'Connor, J., and Barrett, T. (eds). (2017). *Universal Design for Curriculum Design.* Dublin: UCD Access & Lifelong Learning.

Page, S.E. (2007). *The Difference. How the Power of Diversity Creates Better Groups, Firms, Schools, and Societies.* Princeton, NJ: Princeton University Press.

Persson, H., Åhman, H., Yngling, A.A., and Gulliksen, J. (2015). Universal design, inclusive design, accessible design, design for all: different concepts – one goal? On the concept of accessibility – historical, methodological and philosophical aspects. *Universal Access Information Society,* 14, 505–526.

Politis, Y., Deveril, D., Baldiris Navarro, S., Avila, C., de Lera, E., Monjo, T., and Goodman, L. (2014). *Introducing the Inclusive Learning Handbook: An OER for teachers and policy makers.* Paper presented at the 6th Annual International Conference on Education and New Learning Technologies (Edulearn'14), International Association of Technology, Education and Development (IATED), Barcelona, Spain.

Rose, D. H. and Meyer, A. (2002). *Teaching Every Student in the Digital Age: Universal Design for Learning.* Alexandria, VA: Association for Supervision and Curriculum Development.

4.2 Who 'does' inclusion? Using the Toolkit to create change from the margins

Mary Farrelly

It is a truth nearly universally ignored (at least among university managers) that the students' learning environment is the staff's working environment, and that inclusive classrooms cannot exist without inclusive workplaces, where everyone in the university community is valued and their voices can be heard. However, while universities tout inclusivity policies, resources, and facilities for students, these purported values are often not reflected in employment and promotion practices (Olsen et al., 2020; Dupree and Boykin, 2021; Wagner et al., 2022). Accessibility and inclusion problems for staff and students do not only exist in parallel but also feed into and perpetuate one another. Too often, the day-to-day work of making inclusive higher education a reality for students reproduces structures of exclusion and marginalisation for academic staff, undermining from the start the impact of those very initiatives in the classroom. For me, as a female, early career academic, on a chain of fixed-term contracts before becoming permanent, the value of the Toolkit for Inclusive Higher Education Institutions (Kelly and Padden, 2018) has been in empowering me to take concrete, positive actions within an institution that has often felt overwhelming and unwieldy. Through the growth mindset of 'Plus-One' thinking (Tobin and Behling, 2018), the Toolkit empowers Early Career Academics and other marginalised colleagues to take a lead in creating inclusive universities while also safeguarding against overwork, exploitation, and anxiety. By ensuring visibility and recognition for this work, the Toolkit also contributes to fairer workloads and supports professional development that will make inclusion sustainable into the future.

Too many of us share the experience of attending Equality, Diversity & Inclusion (EDI) committee meetings, workshops on accessibility, symposia on inclusive education etc., only to look around the room and see a space dominated by women, colleagues of colour, colleagues on precarious contracts, and other marginalised and underrepresented groups. While these spaces are enriching and useful, the predominance of these groups within them underlines how the work of making higher education inclusive disproportionately falls on marginalised faculty and staff already falling prey to 'the minority tax', whereby "faculty members from underrepresented groups (URGs), especially early-career faculty, thus risk becoming overburdened with

DOI: 10.4324/9781003253631-12

providing service at the expense of working on other scholarly activities required for promotion and tenure (i.e. conducting research, publishing)" (Carson et al., 2019, p. 2). While the term 'minority tax' is useful in articulating this dynamic of unequal engagement with inclusion and accessibility work, as well as the strain it puts on the colleagues affected, terms like 'tax' and 'service' do not do justice to the passion, love, and care that drives this work and hence the 'emotional labour' that comes with it. Rickett and Morris have clearly illustrated how this overlooked emotional work is also "devalued, unaccounted for and potentially harmful to those who do engage in it, therefore shoring up/reinforcing a class and gender stratified UK academy" (2021, p. 87) – although this dynamic is also at play in Ireland and beyond.

Combatting this inequality, the Toolkit offers a structured map for transforming the invisible, diffuse, and mundane tasks needed to make the university accessible into meaningful leadership work that can progress careers and find its place at the very highest levels of the university. The 'Plus-One' mindset promoted by the Toolkit not only breaks down the big-picture goal of the University for All initiative into individually achievable tasks but also situates each 'Plus-One' within the bigger picture, empowering us to make change at all levels, from the personal to the institutional. Like many ECAs, I first became involved with inclusion work as a PhD student, organising outreach and widening participation activities. I loved this work, but as my career progressed the individual tasks involved (making alien masks, inventing learning games, comforting a child overwhelmed to be on a huge university campus for the first time etc.) became incongruent with my long-term ambitions. The expectation arose that progression in academia necessitates leaving behind work with access and inclusion to engage with more 'serious' aspects of university life. Through the Toolkit, however, I saw the small things I had been doing in the context of the bigger picture and the Toolkit also provided a framework to navigate institutional structures and use my experiences to take on bigger roles so that my work for inclusion can continue changing and growing with my career.

Central to the Toolkit's goals, and key to preventing the reduction of inclusion work to a 'minority tax', is the aphorism that 'inclusion is everyone's business'. Indeed, the uneven workloads in access and inclusion across the university are often perpetuated by the 'preaching to the choir' dynamic illustrated above. The Toolkit challenges this by offering a springboard for discussion and development that engages every aspect of university life in a meaningful way. There can be no more complaints that 'this isn't my area' and 'this doesn't apply to me' when there is something for everyone. The language and structure of the Toolkit also lends even the most marginalised voices the authority of the institutional mandate when advocating for change. In this way, the Toolkit is an invaluable support for onboarding senior staff and other disengaged faculty, shifting pressure away from the junior, female, and minority faculty on whom this work often falls by default.

For marginalised and underrepresented university staff, the Toolkit can become both a sword and a shield in combating exclusion in all areas of the university. In order to best make visible the work and share the workload:

- Embrace the language of the Toolkit and use it to shout about your current inclusion work and dreams of the future to anyone who will listen
- Share the Toolkit in formal and informal spaces – workshops are great but one-to-one hallway discussions are also an effective way to spread the word
- Use the self-assessment exercises as a reason to celebrate achievements big and small, individually and with colleagues.

References

Carson, T.L., Aguilera, A., Brown, S.D., Peña, J., Butler, A., Dulin, A., … Cené, C.W. (2019). A seat at the table: Strategic engagement in service activities for early career faculty from underrepresented groups in the academy. *Academic Medicine: Journal of the Association of American Medical Colleges*, 94(8), 1089–1093.

Dupree, C.H. and Boykin, C.M. (2021). Racial inequality in academia: Systemic origins, modern challenges, and policy recommendations. *Policy Insights from the Behavioral and Brain Sciences*, 8(1), 11–18.

Kelly, A.M. and Padden, L. (2018). *Toolkit for Inclusive Higher Education Institutions: From Vision to Practice*. Dublin: UCD Access & Lifelong Learning.

Olsen, J., Griffiths, M., Soorenian, A., and Porter, R. (2020). Reporting from the margins: Disabled academics reflections on higher education. *Scandinavian Journal of Disability Research*, 22(1), 265–274.

Rickett, B. and Morris, A. (2021). "Mopping up tears in the academy" – working-class academics, belonging, and the necessity for emotional labour in UK academia. *Discourse: Studies in the Cultural Politics of Education*, 42(1), 87–101.

Tobin, T. and Behling, K. (2018). *Reach Everyone, Teach Everyone: Universal Design for Learning in Higher Education*. Morgantown, WV: West Virginia University Press.

Wagner, K., Pennell, S.M., Eilert, M., and Lim, S.R. (2022) Academic mothers with disabilities: Navigating academia and parenthood during COVID-19. *Gender, Work & Organization*, 29(1), 342–352.

4.3 "It has to come from the top!"

Using the Toolkit for bottom-up planning for inclusion

Graham Finlay

We used the Toolkit for Inclusive Higher Education Institutions (Kelly and Padden, 2018) to develop our Implementation Plan for Widening Participation for the College of Social Sciences and Law at University College Dublin. There were a number of ways in which the Toolkit helped us frame the questions for our workshop. It also helped to focus the discussion in the workshop and informed the resulting plan. Some interesting dynamics emerged, however, that others doing this work may also experience.

The Toolkit has a large number of self-assessment statements that can be used to assess current practice and to identify possible improvements. We selected seventeen of these to discuss in a trial run of the workshop, with the goal of reducing them to six. We focused on goals that were under our control, as a college, and added goals that were particularly relevant to the work of both teaching and professional staff: staff development and training, student supports, diversity in assessments, provision of student feedback, and fostering a community of learners. The trial run, held with senior officers of the College, helped us identify priorities for different Vice Principals' roles, especially Teaching and Learning. The actual workshop began with a panel of student representatives called 'Access Leaders' in this institution and was attended by almost 50 professional and teaching staff. The Access Leaders very much helped to focus discussions, as well as inform them with their lived experience. Participants were divided into small groups and responded to the self-assessment statements drawn from the Toolkit. They were free to focus on one or two of these and to record local good practice, as well as ideas for potential actions.

The results reflected diverse views and were in keeping with a bottom-up approach; many of the participants were not members of the Widening Participation (WP) committee and had not previously engaged with WP. There was less focus on assessing our current practice and, when this occurred, participants tended to underrate current practice. Despite being a 'bottom-up' rather than 'top-down' event, a number of participants suggested that change has to come to a considerable extent from the top, so that practice matched the University's rhetoric and the necessary resources were provided to achieve the goals agreed upon. Accordingly, some recommended actions are outside

DOI: 10.4324/9781003253631-13

of the College's power, requiring changes to university systems (e.g. requiring module coordinators to sign-off that reasonable accommodations have been provided) or training to be developed by the University Teaching and Learning unit.[1] Much of the existing work of widening participation is being developed by interested members of individual schools in a spontaneous and organic way that embeds the programming in specific disciplines. It is very important that these spontaneous initiatives are also supported by the implementation of College- or University-wide actions and policies.

Most of these recommendations were incorporated into the draft Implementation Plan which is, at the time of writing, the subject of consultation first with the WP committee of the College and then online with the entire College. Professional staff in the College made a significant contribution to the plan, both by emphasising their particular needs for training and the development of good ways of communicating supports to students. Many of the actions involved setting up short training and development opportunities that could be availed of by all staff, not just teaching staff and not just staff heavily engaged with WP. Although colleagues have been very good at recommending actions – some of which may be controversial (e.g. WP as a standing item on School agendas) – there were concerns that the way the goals appear in the draft plan may provoke resistance. The most obvious one was "Students always have a choice or variety of assessment e.g. a module isn't assessed using only one method such as a mid-term essay followed by essay-style exam questions/answers". While the action points emphasised making training available in how to develop a variety of assessments and incorporate Universal Design for Learning (Rose and Meyer, 2002) into your modules, presenting the goal before indicating the action points seemed to require that module coordinators change their assessment strategies rather than making training available for them to consider doing so. We are going with a solution-focused approach and the flexibility of the Toolkit allows for us to add to and amend some of the self-assessment statements so that the wider community of the College feels comfortable engaging with our inclusion planning.

While we currently do not have our final draft, the process of adding new actions and refining the original suggestions has begun in earnest. Actions are specific, doable, and have clear dates by which they should be achieved. Much of the work of implementation will involve working across the College and University with other WP leaders. Ultimately, however, the goal will be to harness the agency of all staff by giving them as much input into the concrete actions as possible.

Note

1 College here refers to a group of Schools or Disciplines in a wider University. University College Dublin has six Colleges.

References

Kelly, A.M. and Padden, L. (2018). *Toolkit for Inclusive Higher Education Institutions: From Vision to Practice.* Dublin: UCD Access & Lifelong Learning.

Rose, D.H. and Meyer, A. (2002). *Teaching Every Student in the Digital Age: Universal Design for Learning.* Alexandria, VA: Association for Supervision and Curriculum Development.

4.4 Embedding inclusion in the Engineering discipline

Using the Toolkit for Inclusive Higher Education Institutions both online and in person

Mark Flanagan

The Toolkit for Inclusive Higher Education Institutions (Kelly and Padden, 2018) has been used to enhance inclusive practice within the Engineering discipline at this institution since 2019. Toolkit sessions were held at two Widening Participation (WP) workshops, which took place in October 2019 and January 2021. In each case, the Toolkit session was preceded by a presentation on the WP data and on principles and practice of inclusive teaching; these presentations were found to be very beneficial in providing a clear context for the discussions that ensued from using the Toolkit. The first Toolkit session was a face-to-face session, while the second (due to COVID-19-related restrictions) was an online session. In both cases, in order to provoke meaningful discussion, self-assessment statements were pre-selected; where the statement was deemed to be important to the session's participants, but where the corresponding institutional score was anticipated to be relatively low.

Interestingly, the online format led to a number of advantages. One issue with our first Toolkit session was that, while it led to constructive discussions regarding the inclusivity of our teaching and assessment practices, it was not easy to record the specific points made in real time, and thus afterwards to summarise our collective thoughts and create corresponding actions. However, in the online session, the online interactive tool was used, containing some sample self-assessment statements from the Toolkit. The Toolkit session was then based on joint discussion of, and individual completion of, this online tool, thus capturing individual responses. The online format also allowed for our full discussions to be captured via audio and video recording (with the prior consent of the attendees). This was very valuable, as it meant that all issues and recommendations which arose could be considered carefully afterwards.

Securing buy-in from academic staff is particularly important to progress the inclusive teaching agenda within the discipline. Therefore, our first two Toolkit events focused mainly on Pillar 1 "Programme & Curriculum Design, Teaching & Learning", and these sessions were well attended by many academic staff who were interested in improving their teaching and student

DOI: 10.4324/9781003253631-14

support practices. More recently, we have run a Toolkit session focusing on (but not limited to) Pillar 4 "Information Technology Systems & Infrastructure", involving stakeholders in the College aside from academic staff. This session included representatives from the Engineering Programme Office and Marketing Office, as well as a representative from the institutional WP Outreach Coordinating Network. This session was useful in identifying areas of improvement outside of module delivery and student supports (e.g. in addressing barriers that students may face before even arriving at the university).

In order to ensure appropriate engagement of academic staff, we found it to be very beneficial if communications to colleagues regarding Toolkit sessions are made through the most senior College-level representative (i.e. Dean or College Principal). This also helps to ensure that key stakeholders in Schools (Heads of Discipline, Heads of Teaching and Learning, Vice-Principal for Teaching and Learning, Programme Directors, and the EDI representative) are strongly encouraged to attend and participate in these sessions. This approach also sends a strong message to staff regarding the importance of the event and of the WP agenda, in general. In the case of our 2021 Engineering WP workshop, this event was organised through the office of the College Principal and Dean, Prof. Aoife Ahern. We also found that engagement with WP representatives from other units in the university was very beneficial in order to share experience and ideas before and after the Toolkit sessions.

The Toolkit has impacted very positively on our inclusive practice in Engineering. Our experience is that the specific self-assessment statements therein provoke debate and engagement among colleagues in a way that "opening the floor" without creating context for discussion cannot efficiently do. Preselecting self-assessment statements from the Toolkit that are judged to be particularly pertinent to the session's participants, and where institutional or disciplinary weaknesses are already perceived, was found to be very effective, as the discussion time per session is limited. Since our first Toolkit sessions began, our discipline has recruited three University for All Faculty Partners (discussed in Chapter 5 of this book) who act as agents of change in the area of WP, and Inclusive Teaching is now a standing item on the agenda of our discipline-wide Teaching and Learning Committee. These Toolkit sessions also acted as a primer for a pilot study on Inclusive Teaching in Engineering which successfully redesigned a selection of modules across Engineering based on inclusive design principles (Padden et al., 2021). A message is also now broadcast every Trimester to academic staff which provides details regarding how to support students with disabilities in online and locally arranged exams. Feedback from the Toolkit sessions was also used to inform the University for All Implementation Plan for our discipline, which was prepared in consultation with the College Principal in July 2021, and which is now published on the institution's staff intranet along with the plans from all disciplines across the institution. Finally, the Toolkit sessions have also helped to identify key areas of improvement within our discipline,

Engineering, including widening the pathways for admission of more mature students and part-time learners.

References

Kelly, A. M. and Padden, L. (2018). *Toolkit for Inclusive Higher Education Institutions: From Vision to Practice*. Dublin: UCD Access & Lifelong Learning.

Padden, L., Buggy, C., and Shotton, E. (eds). (2021). *Inclusive Teaching & Learning Case Studies in Engineering, Architecture & Affiliated Disciplines*. Dublin: UCD Access & Lifelong Learning.

Chapter 5

Programme & Curriculum Design, Teaching & Learning

5.1 From national collaboration to grassroots implementation

Achieving widespread inclusion through Universal Design for Learning

Lisa Padden

> A University for All is … a place where everyone is comfortable enough to talk in class … where all the slides and materials are available on the Virtual Learning Environment … where everyone has what they need to do well … where the lecturers know we are all different.
>
> Collated student responses in answer to the question: What is a university for all?
>
> – University College Dublin (UCD), 2017

What is inclusive higher education? For students, as seen in the quote above, the answer is simple and clear. However, in higher education institutions and their policies, the answer to this question often addresses admissions and not the everyday experience of the student. Ultimately, the student experience in their academic programme is central to their higher education journey. Therefore, an inclusive university must foreground inclusion in teaching, learning, and assessment practices. While a number of frameworks can be used to promote and embed inclusion in the teaching, learning, and assessment space, Universal Design for Learning (UDL) is the framework central in the University for All approach (CAST, 2018). Universal Design is a broader umbrella term which began in physical building design and now has application across systems, environments, and products. The more specific term of Universal Design for Learning refers to an approach that seeks to offer flexibility to remove barriers which disadvantage learners in an educational setting through provision of multiple means of engagement, representation, and action and expression (Meyer, Rose, and Gordon, 2014; CAST, 2018). This framework has grown in recognition and practice globally over the past ten years (Tobin and Behling, 2018; Kennette and Wilson, 2019; Rao, Torres, and Smith, 2021). UDL is a mindset rather than a list of instructions or a checklist, with the UDL mindset helping faculty to embrace the need for change and, ultimately, to provide an equitable experience to the increasingly diverse student population across all disciplines (Fovet, 2021).

While UDL has historically been framed in terms of its benefits for students with disabilities, more recently there has been an increase in framing UDL in terms of its benefits for all students in higher education (Padden,

DOI: 10.4324/9781003253631-16

O'Connor, and Barrett, 2017; Heelan and Tobin, 2021). Within the University for All initiative, our broad interpretation of UDL focuses on understanding the diversity of the students in the classroom and, ultimately, reducing the need for students to raise their hand and be labelled because of a need for support or Reasonable Accommodation due to a barrier being in place (AHEAD, 2017). UDL is not a set of rules but rather a framework which prompts a change in thinking and practice, encouraging faculty to consider the diversity of their students before they even begin to design or redesign their programme. UDL espouses the development of flexibility to provide students with multiple means of engaging with their learning, accessing learning materials, and demonstrating their learning through assessment and other activities.

Changes in higher education can be challenging to implement due to long-acknowledged competing priorities within the higher education landscape – research, teaching, and, more recently, a shift towards academic capitalism and managerialism (Vican, Friedman, and Andreason, 2020). In light of this complex context, we have developed a multi-faceted approach to promoting UDL and embedding inclusion in all areas of teaching, learning, and assessment, with a strong focus on empowerment and encouragement, rather than enforcement. This chapter will provide practical guidance on how UDL can be embedded across a complex organisation using a multi-pronged and multi-directional leadership and development strategy. This chapter will outline a number of strategic initiatives which encourage widespread adoption of UDL for the benefit of a diverse student population.

Although Universal Design has its origins in the area of disability, the promotion of UDL requires a broader vision to encourage educators to change their mindset and make the necessary adjustments to their practice. UDL benefits all students in education, especially those who are under-represented, or those who traditionally may require additional support in an educational environment. In Ireland, UDL is included in the National Forum's 'Embedding Student Success' guiding framework (2021), as well as the National Access Policy (HEA, 2015). In our institution, like others in Ireland, UDL is promoted as beneficial to all students. In training and development, we provide examples of the benefits to students from equity groups (low-income, disability, part-time, further education award holders, mature, ethnic minority, refugee/asylum seekers etc.), international students, and those who may not fit into any of these 'boxes'. UDL has been embraced internationally as a framework which can offer embedded equity to all students (Al-Azawei, Serenelli, and Lundqvist, 2016; Bracken and Novak, 2019; Burgstahler, 2015; Hockings, 2010; LaRocco and Wilken, 2013).

The case studies in this chapter outline the UDL practices which can embed inclusion through interventions which move action beyond the individual to create systemic change, as summarised in Figure 5.1.

Dr Linda Yang expertly outlines a framework which links UDL and intercultural learning and can be implemented across an institution. Dr Mustapha

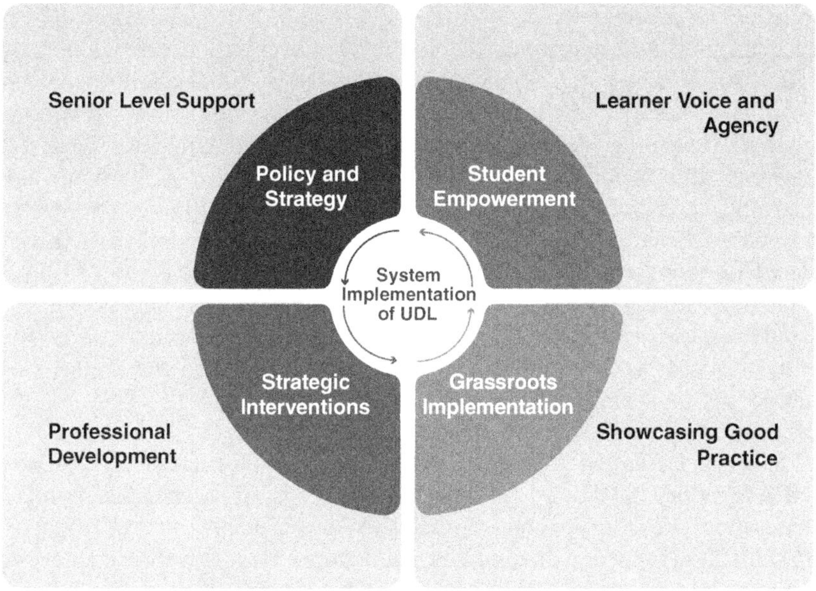

Figure 5.1 System implementation of UDL

Aabi and Dr Sean Bracken move the UDL discussion beyond the Global North to outline how UDL is being embraced in Morocco through a student-centred approach, which can easily be replicated elsewhere. This introductory section outlines some of the transferable strategic initiatives which have been implemented in an institution in Ireland and which can easily be adopted elsewhere. The contexts of the initiatives differ, from jurisdictions at different stages in embedding inclusion across an institution. However, the message remains universal in how UDL can be introduced and implemented strategically.

UDL professional development as strategic intervention

In Ireland, there is currently no requirement for those teaching in higher education institutions to hold a teaching qualification. This is not the case in the further education sector in Ireland; Further Education and Training, or FET, includes apprenticeships, traineeships, level 5–7 programmes, community and adult education, as well as literacy and numeracy programmes. Research conducted in the UK by Nurunnabi et al. (2019) shows a correlation between student satisfaction and formal teaching qualifications. Despite this requirement not being in place in Ireland, higher education institutions have developed advanced teaching and learning programmes for their teaching staff. The Irish National Forum has developed a Professional Development Framework and a suite of micro-credentials which support training and development while also accommodating the time-poor nature of most academics (National Forum, 2021; HEA, 2015). In 2016, the National Forum began scoping and developing a plan for a constellation of digital badges (Ryder, 2017). These digital badges were created by the sector for the sector, drawing on expertise in a range of teaching and learning areas – Technology Enhanced Learning, Assessment and Feedback, and Universal Design for Learning, among many others. The development process of these digital badges was collaborative and iterative, including opportunities for feedback and redevelopment. A key element to these micro-credentials was the concurrent development of a 'facilitator pack', which would allow institutions to facilitate these digital badges locally. The goal was, and is, for these digital badges to be simple for colleagues to facilitate without the requirement for local expertise, since this is already included in the digital badge materials.

Following an expression of interest, a development team for a Digital Badge in Universal Design for Teaching and Learning was formed in 2017 – led by AHEAD, with UCD as co-developer (AHEAD is an independent non-profit organisation working to create inclusive environments in education and employment for people with disabilities in Ireland). Having worked on a number of sectoral projects together previously, this development team was able to work together seamlessly, allowing for a creative and collaborative approach to the development. Over a number of months, the badge was formed – five online self-paced modules, with a half-day workshop and a redesign task (this is a light-touch assessment). Following the initial launch of the badges, the National Forum sought to ensure increased peer learning opportunities and, in 2019, peer groups were introduced as an alternative to the workshop peer engagement.

While some HEIs did embrace local facilitation (notably University College Dublin and University College Cork), most were reluctant to take on the task of running the Badge locally. To address this, the badge creators and coordinators proposed a MOOC-style (Massive Open Online Courses) national roll out of the badge in 2020, to maximise opportunities for learning and increase the number of facilitators (Ryder et al., 2021). Facilitators from around the country were invited to attend an information session, where we proposed they work with us as Peer Group Facilitators – a local facilitator working with participants from their local college, where possible. To support this role, we developed a series of training materials, including an extensive handbook. This supported role allowed for confidence building of the facilitators while also allowing us to open up the course to hundreds, or thousands, of participants simultaneously. Despite offering this rollout in the first year of the COVID-19 pandemic when most of the world was in lockdown, the interest in the programme was exceptionally high. The delivery as a free fully online programme certainly helped with this. Almost 1,000 participants from higher education and FET signed up for this innovative and ambitious roll out. Offering this national approach again in 2021 saw over 1200 participants register for the course and a further national roll out in Autumn 2022 again saw more than 1200 participants take part.

Feedback and outcomes from this digital badge show clearly that this micro-credential approach works. A short course with relevant and engaging materials from across the sector offers significant return on investment of time, both for the course authors and participants, with students being those who ultimately benefit from a programme which facilitates immediate adoption of UDL and future planning for long-term UDL implementation. Some of the key lessons we have learned from this type of UDL training and dissemination are included in Figure 5.2. The inclusion of Universal Design and

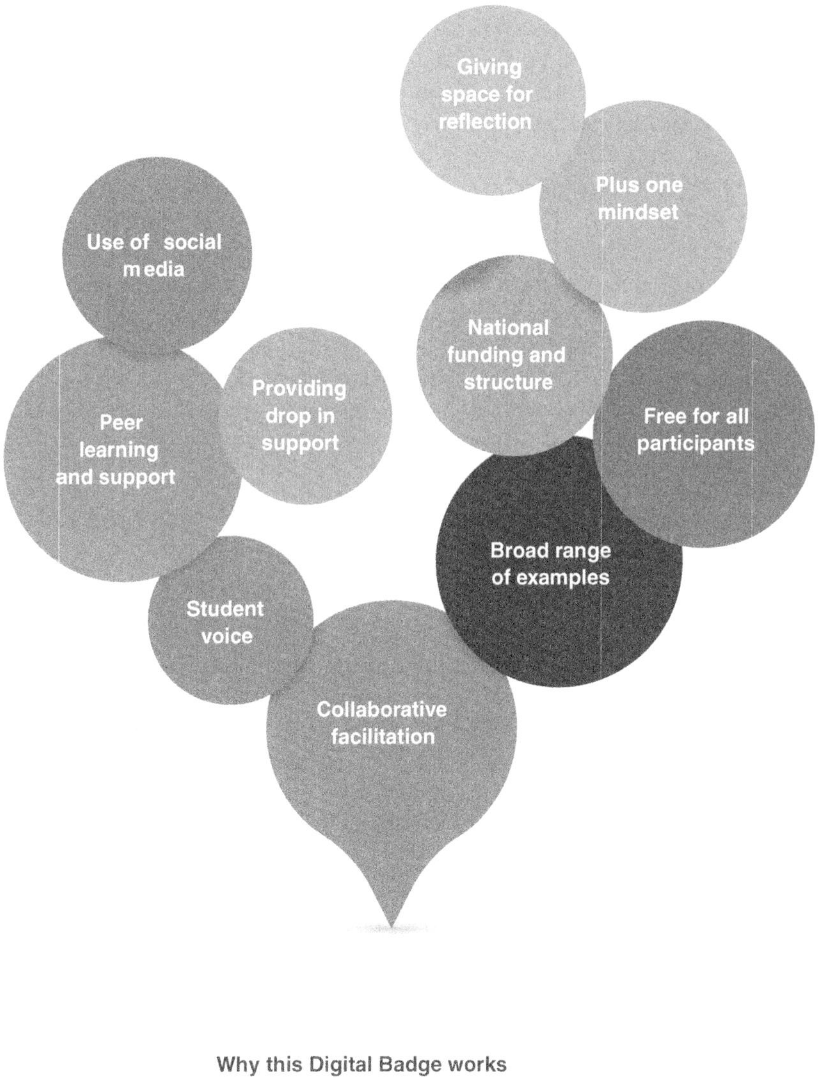

Figure 5.2 Lessons learned on why this digital badge model works for UDL training, based on feedback from participants, facilitators, and coordinators

UDL in national policies and planning has resulted in a ripple effect across the sector with widespread familiarity (Centre for Excellence in Universal Design, 2020; HEA, 2015, 2018; National Forum, 2021). The national funding of this digital badge programme has facilitated not only the badge's development but also the large-scale national roll outs. It was important for this badge programme to be free for all participants to ensure equitable opportunities for all those teaching in the sector. The national funding allowed for this. With regard to the content of the badge, we have further developed the materials each year and some of the key learning has included the importance of diverse representation in UDL examples and the inclusion of the student voice. The collaborative approach to facilitation has further increased buy-in from all areas of the sector.

Peer support and learning have been the most popular aspect of the badge in recent years. In fact, we have seen a number of local communities of practice form in institutions among those who have completed this digital badge (e.g. University of Galway, and University of Limerick). This element was added following direction from the National Forum during the first major redevelopment of the programme. As the programme is fully online, the provision of drop-in support and the focus on connection through social media visibility were also key enablers in further deepening the UDL learning of participants. In the verification of the badge, we have maintained a 'light touch' approach, considering the workload of participants. This has worked well, with a focus on providing space for reflection and ensuring a 'plus one' mindset to avoid becoming overwhelmed.

From grassroots implementation to showcasing UDL good practice and facilitating disciplinary change

For a number of years, UDL literature and events focused on persuading people that UDL should be adopted, and yet practical examples of implementation were not readily available. Through the provision of examples of good practice in case studies, we have attempted to address this gap. Provision of practical examples is an important enabler when attempting to foster any change in pedagogical practice and is one of the most common practices in higher education teaching and learning research (Harland, 2014). A common thread in all of our work to embed UDL is the importance of collaboration, ensuring that access and inclusion is not only seen as the job of the Access office but also as the responsibility of each and every individual. We have created three case study publications to date, focusing on curriculum design, assessment and feedback, and disciplinary implementation of UDL in Engineering and Architecture (Padden, Buggy, and Shotton, 2021). Our approach in all three of these publications was collaborative. The first collection of case studies emerged as vital following the first UDL workshops delivered collaboratively between the institution's Access and Teaching & Learning services. We needed to have clear contextualised examples with evidence of impact, in order to give not only the practical 'how to' but also to demonstrate the positive impact of UDL which could be achieved through just a small investment of time by the educator.

Having these case studies to use in training and development workshops, and being able to share them as a free resource with colleagues within and outside of our institution, moved the dial for us in embedding UDL. Colleagues seek out easy to understand examples of inclusion in action which can be picked up and implemented quickly and without the need for additional resources. The call for case studies was simple and collaboration with our Teaching & Learning, as well as academic, colleagues ensured we were able to share the call widely and get significant interest. Through the preparation and editing of the first collection of case studies, we were able to hone our approach, and this has been further tailored through our other collections. We now have a simple yet effective approach to sharing case studies, which are easy for those writing the case studies, and, crucially, it creates a 'plug and play' case study for others to take the idea, adapt it, and implement it in their own practice. Our second collection focused on assessment and feedback and we collaborated with another HEI, the Institute of Art, Design and Technology Dun Laoghaire (Padden et al., 2019). This further diversified our offering, including new disciplines and highly creative and replicable examples of good practice.

When disciplines do not see themselves represented in the examples of UDL or inclusive practice, they can make the assumption that it does not apply to them or that implementation will be excessively challenging or difficult. The 'Inclusive Teaching Pilot' run with the disciplines of Engineering and Architecture demonstrated the power of a disciplinary approach and collaboration among colleagues (Padden, Buggy, and Shotton, 2021). Arguments for a disciplinary, rather than institutional, teaching and learning approach and expertise (Healey, 2000) demonstrates the need for research into the application of UDL in various disciplines. While, of course, the framework is flexible and can be used widely, specific research on what UDL looks like in various disciplines can increase implementation uptake. In this programme, academics came forward and nominated modules they wanted to prioritise for inclusive change in their teaching, learning, and assessment approaches. Feedback was gathered by the project team in person at the start of the pilot within classes towards the end of the teaching term, without the teacher present, to ensure students felt comfortable providing full and frank feedback. Feedback was collected by asking students to write down commentary on notes placed next to one of the five key questions asked. Training was then provided in UDL and the feedback was anonymised and provided back to module coordinators at a one-to-one coaching session where potential UDL-based changes were discussed. Feedback was then gathered from students again after the changes had been implemented (this had to be done online due to COVID-19 related remote teaching). There has been a significant increase in the focus on inclusion in these disciplines since the beginning of the pilot study.

Recognition, reward and responsibilities – Faculty Partnership and Communities of Practice

When trying to implement systemic change in a field where professionals are almost entirely autonomous, you need an army. Kotter (2012) notes that to successfully embed change you need a large number of people to come onboard and push forward. Our institutional UDL change army is led by our University for All Faculty Partners. The Faculty Partnership Programme is designed to support and accelerate the implementation of UDL throughout the institution. It offers a structured opportunity to undertake the UDL training, to qualify as a UDL Facilitator, and to become a role model who will persuade and influence others as to the merits of inclusion for all students. When the opportunity arose to create a strategic project with additional funding from Ireland's Fund for Students with Disabilities, we immediately looked at how we could use this funding to support the embedding of a UDL approach across all disciplines in the institution to the benefit of the entire student population.

Again, in the development of this programme, we took a necessary collaborative approach, working with our colleagues in the institutional Teaching & Learning and Equality, Diversity and Inclusion units. We shaped a proposal for a programme which progressed our shared vision for an inclusive university. The success of this programme hinged on it having a competitive recruitment process, high-level visibility and recognition, and a structured programme of development and support. The application was relatively simple but required support from local senior leadership, e.g. Dean or College Principal. We launched with 17 Faculty Partners in June 2020, with two targeted recruitment campaigns early in the next academic year to ensure sufficient distribution of Faculty Partners across all disciplines, for a total in 2022 of 26 Faculty Partners.

Provision of one-to-one coaching to the Faculty Partners has allowed for their continued development as UDL practitioners and leaders. Using the model developed as part of the Inclusive Teaching Pilot outlined above, Faculty Partners were provided with access to various resources, as well as one-to-one coaching, as required. Development of leadership skills and ability to lead colleagues in the implementation of UDL were vital, with coaching offering a methodology to ensure that the individual can maximise their potential (Robertson, 2016; van Nieuwerburgh and Barr, 2016). Coaching provided to the Faculty Partners has expanded beyond the programme coordination team to include experts from other institutions offering input on innovative practice which could be adopted locally. Coaching was also evident in the interactions between Faculty Partners who supported each other through various means.

One of the most significant levers for change we have witnessed in this programme is the successful Community of Practice created among the Faculty Partners. Through simple but high impact mechanisms for casual communication, we have facilitated the sharing of ideas, resources, and support among this group of academics. The terms of the programme require a commitment to the role for three academic years following recruitment; although funding is provided only in the first year. The funding, although a relatively small amount, is vital in ensuring that the programme is viewed with esteem. We initially envisioned that this funding might be used to buy out time by academics to free them up to engage in UDL development work. However, the funding is being more commonly used to develop resources, attend training and conferences, and, in some cases, to fund equipment or a researcher for discipline-specific projects. The outputs for this programme will be shared using the case study model outlined above, but we have also hosted a well-attended symposium in May 2022, the first in a series, to disseminate the results of the programme. Our Faculty Partners are also locally continuing to share their experiences and learnings as UDL leaders in their respective disciplines.

Some of the key catalysts for change they have already shared are the importance of high-level support from Head of School/Discipline, Dean or College Principal, in assisting with recruitment for UDL training; the importance of emphasising the Plus One approach to UDL (Tobin and Behling, 2018) as time commitment is one of the most significant reasons for reluctance from colleagues; and also the importance of creating positive visibility and sustaining momentum through structured support. As the programme developers, our most important takeaway from this change initiative is the phenomenal impact it can have when you lift up your colleagues, providing them with a platform and resources – our Faculty Partners have gone above and beyond the scope we presented to them. The programme has already been far more impactful than we could have anticipated at the start. One tangible example is the year on year growth of the UDL Badge engagement from colleagues in the institution; although this is likely also in part due to the MOOC roll out increasing visibility of UDL. Our Faculty Partners engaged in a significant recruitment drive for the second national rollout and this resulted in a more than doubling of badges awarded. They have also begun their local rollouts of the badge which they are facilitating for their colleagues.

Universal Design for Learning – removing barriers

We started this chapter by asking: what is inclusive higher education? While in the past decades, access and inclusion have often been imagined as building bridges or providing ladders to overcome systemic or institutional barriers, embracing UDL, in the ways outlined here and in the following sections, provides a means through which we can remove the barriers higher education has historically presented to diverse student populations. Through a combined top-down and bottom-up approach, the implementation of UDL in institutions, disciplines, programmes, modules, and individual classes allows diverse student populations to thrive. Crucially, this approach moves away from the deficit model, asking what is missing in our students and, in fact, turns this around completely, asking instead what is missing in higher education and what we, as educators, need to change.

References

AHEAD (2017). *UDL & the Continuum of Supports.* Available at: https://www.ahead.ie/udl-pyramid

Al-Azawei, A., Serenelli, F., and Lundqvist, K. (2016). Universal Design for Learning (UDL): A content analysis of peer reviewed journals from 2012 to 2015. *Journal of the Scholarship of Teaching and Learning*, 16(3), 39–56.

Bracken, S. and Novak, K. (eds). (2019). *Transforming Higher Education Through Universal Design for Learning: An International Perspective.* Abingdon, UK: Routledge.

Burgstahler, S.E. (2015). Universal design in higher education. In S.E. Burgstahler (ed.), *Universal Design in Higher Education*, 2nd edn. Cambridge, MA: Harvard Education Press, pp. 3–28.

CAST (2018). *Universal Design for Learning Guidelines version 2.2.* CAST Professional Publishing. Available at: http://udlguidelines.cast.org

Centre for Excellence in Universal Design (2020). *Universal Design in Education and Training – Policy Landscape in Ireland.* Dublin: National Disability Authority. Available at: https://universaldesign.ie/Awards/Education/Universal%20Design%20in%20Education%20and%20Training%20%E2%80%93%20policy%20landscape%20in%20Ireland.pdf

Fovet, F. (2021). *Handbook of Research on Applying Universal Design for Learning Across Disciplines: Concepts, Case Studies, and Practical Implementation.* Hershey, PA: IGI Global.

Harland, T. (2014). Learning about case study methodology to research higher education. *Higher Education Research & Development*, 33(6), 1113–1122.

HEA (2015). *National Plan for Equity of Access to Higher Education, 2015–2019.* Dublin: Higher Education Authority.

HEA (2018). *Progress Review of the National Access Plan and Priorities to 2021.* Dublin: Higher Education Authority.

Healey, M. (2000). Developing the scholarship of teaching in higher education: A discipline-based approach. *Higher Education Research & Development*, 19(2), 169–189.

Heelan, A. and Tobin, T.J. (2021). *UDL for FET Practitioners: Guidance for Implementing Universal Design for Learning in Irish Further Education and Training.* Dublin: SOLAS.

Hockings, C. (2010). *Inclusive Learning and Teaching in Higher Education: A Synthesis of Research.* York: Higher Education Academy.

Kennette, L.N. and Wilson, N.A. (2019). Universal Design for Learning (UDL): What is it and how do I implement it? *Transformative Dialogues: Teaching & Learning Journal*, 12(1), 1–6.

Kotter, J.P. (2012). *Leading Change.* Boston, MA: Harvard Business Review Press.

LaRocco, D.J. and Wilken, D.S. (2013). Universal Design for Learning: University faculty stages of concerns and levels of use. *Current Issues in Education*, 16(1).

Meyer, A., Rose, D.H., and Gordon, D.T. (2014). *Universal Design for Learning: Theory and Practice*. Wakefield, MA: CAST Professional Publishing.

National Forum (2021). *Embedding Student Success: A Guiding Framework*. Dublin: National Forum Publications.

Nurunnabi, M., Abdelhadi, A.Aburas, R., and Fallatah, S. (2019). Does teaching qualification matter in higher education in the UK? An analysis of National Student Survey data. *MethodsX*, 6, 788–799. Available at: https://doi.org/10.1016/j.mex.2019.04.001

Padden, L., O'Connor, J., and Barrett, T. (eds). (2017). *Universal Design for Curriculum Design*. Dublin: UCD Access & Lifelong Learning.

Padden, L., Buggy, C., and Shotton, E. (eds). (2021). *Inclusive Teaching & Learning Case Studies in Engineering, Architecture & Affiliated Disciplines*. Dublin: UCD Access & Lifelong Learning.

Padden, L., Tonge, J., Moylan, T., and O'Neill, G. (eds). (2019). *Inclusive Assessment and Feedback: Case Studies from University College Dublin and Dun Laoghaire Institute of Art Design and Technology*. Dublin: UCD Access & Lifelong Learning.

Rao, K., Torres, C., and Smith, S. (2021). Digital tools and UDL-based instructional strategies to support students with disabilities online. *Journal of Special Education Technology*, 36(2), 105–112.

Robertson, J. (2016). *Coaching Educational Leadership: Building Leadership Capacity Through Partnership*, 2nd edn. London: Sage.

Ryder, D. (2017). Earn your UDL stripes with the Digital Badge for Universal Design in Teaching and Learning. *The AHEAD Journal*, issue 6. Available at: https://ahead.ie/journal/Earn-Your-UDL-Stripes-with-the-Digital-Badge-for-Universal-Design-in-Teaching-and-Learning

Ryder, D., Maguire, T., Padden, L., and Boland, T. (2021). *Pennies dropping everywhere – how engagement with UDL changes educator behaviours & attitudes*. Presentation at the UDL Implementation and Research Network Conference [online video]. Available at: https://youtu.be/P_3q1aKbpVI (accessed 25 June 2022).

Tobin, T.J. and Behling, K.T. (2018). *Reach Everyone, Teach Everyone: Universal Design for Learning in Higher Education*. Morgantown, WV: West Virginia University Press.

van Nieuwerburgh, C. and Barr, M. (2016). Coaching in education. In T. Bachkirova, G. Spence, and D. Drake (eds), *The SAGE Handbook of Coaching*. London: SAGE Publications.

Vican, S., Friedman A., and Andreasen, R. (2020). Metrics, money, and managerialism: Faculty experiences of competing logics in higher education. *The Journal of Higher Education*, 91(1), 139–164.

5.2 Drawing from the global to act local: How Universal Design for Learning lends itself to facilitating inclusion in Moroccan higher education

Mustapha Aabi and Seán Bracken

In Morocco, as enshrined in the constitution, any student who successfully completes their secondary school Baccaluaréat has the right to access a place in higher education (HE). Because large public universities, such as the University of Ibn Zohr (UIZ), operate on a non-selective 'open access' basis, they invariably encounter significant diversity in the nature of student learning requirements. While there are no panaceas on offer, educators are eager to identify ways in which their professional practices will challenge learners, while also providing them with the pathways to access the curriculum. The following chapter illustrates how the case university, UIZ, has adopted and adapted global insights of inclusive policy and practice, as shared by the International Collaboratory for Leadership in Universally Designed Education (INCLUDE) to inform emerging whole organisational approaches designed to realise the potential inherent in a 'University for All'. Increasingly, educators in UIZ are inspired by Universal Design for Learning (UDL), which provides a conceptual framework for pedagogical design, planning, and action. The case study begins by providing an overview of policy and practice within Morocco; it then shares how UDL has been championed by lecturers and learners who are keen to bring about positive change in inclusive practices. The case study then provides a tentative roadmap for sustaining changes that will better enable all learners to benefit from their experiences in HE.

Policy and practice: An overview of the context

Morocco has made considerable progress in promoting inclusive education by ratifying relevant international conventions and passing laws and reforms. For example, since its inception in 2009, the country has been a committed signatory of the UN Convention on the Rights of Persons with Disabilities, Article 24, which stipulates that all persons with disabilities will be enabled to participate in a mainstream education, with appropriate support being provided. In relation to the widening participation agenda in further and higher education, between 2010 and 2020 the percentage of young people attending post-secondary education rose, from an estimated 15 per cent, to 36 per cent

DOI: 10.4324/9781003253631-17

(UNESCO, 2020a, p. 27). There is no doubt, therefore, that, in terms of policy, significant advancements have been made; however, as in many other jurisdictions, it is in the shift from theory and policy into practice that Morocco has encountered challenges for the development of truly inclusive pedagogical approaches.

In practical terms, pertaining to disability, inclusive education at compulsory age level in Morocco has followed a trajectory that will be familiar to many in the Global North. It started with special needs schools as totally isolated educational settings, then special needs classrooms were established within mainstream schools, with the aim of providing learners with special educational needs a basic education that would enable them to enter the regular school path. More recently, initiatives have concentrated at ending an isolatory approach to special education, with efforts concentrated on enabling development of whole-school strategies for inclusive learning of all students.

To a large extent, this situation is also mirrored at the HE and FE level. In practice, while laudable and ambitious policies are in place, they are far from reaching their intended goals due to a lack of exemplified operational processes and an absence of clear guidelines for implementation. Educators need insights as to how policy can be transformed into effective whole organizational approaches and how these, in turn, will be actualised in the shared learning spaces. The situation is also compounded by a lack of research in the field, where there are a very limited number of published papers outlining how inclusion might be realised in the post-secondary domain. One exception is the small-scale study by Clouder et al. (2019) that looked at the role of accessible technologies in facilitating access to the curriculum in university. However, this study is an exception.

In strategising how best to overcome the current barriers to learning, four major attributes for change come to mind. Firstly, there is a pressing need for a reconsideration of how curriculum and assessment can meet the learning requirements of a more diverse student cohort. Secondly, educators and support staff who are responsible for facilitating learning through more accessible modes of teaching and through the use of effective technological and other pedagogical resources, require additional and ongoing support and professional enhancement. Drawing on insights from Hanesworth et al. (2019), who argued for a UDL strategy that would be cognisant of local socio-cultural factors, the third facet of developing the whole organisational approach is to consider the ambient learning environment, both in terms of its affordances and its potential for social, psychological, and geographic barriers. As with other studies that highlight how inclusion can be realised systematically in education, Hanesworth et al. (2019) also accentuate the need for key stakeholder involvement. Indeed, this critical fourth factor in successful holistic inclusive planning and implementation was identified by UNESCO (2020b) as being of particular relevance in countries such as Côte d'Ivoire, where some close parallels can be drawn between practices in different jurisdictions.

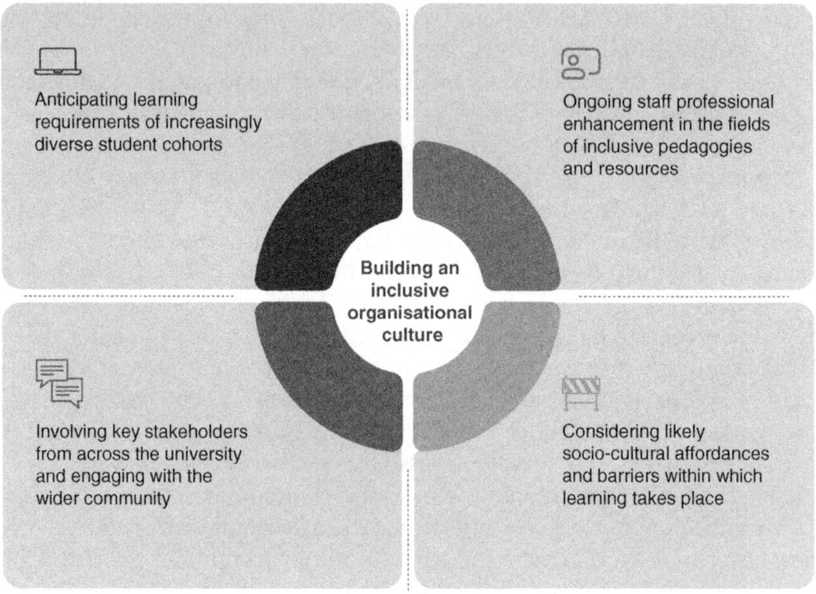

Figure 5.3 Building an inclusive organisational culture; attributes for consideration

There is a need then for the voices of the wider community, especially the learners in Higher Education, to actively inform change processes for inclusion (Seale, 2009). Nonetheless, in many instances, current approaches are a lot more akin to integration models that require learners to adapt to a 'one size fits all' strategy rather than offering anticipatory and adaptive designs that will better meet learning requirements for a diverse student cohort. As lucidly expressed below in one of INCLUDE's student blogs, written by Oussama, a 19-year-old Law student at UIZ, students with additional learning requirements tend to face a new and unfamiliar learning terrain once they join university:

> I am a first-year university student studying law in French. I needed to multiply my efforts to be able to succeed and get to this point because since childhood I've had dyslexia. Studying was never an easy undertaking for me. This year, everything has changed. Studying at the university is different from school. Before, I was able to have a supporting tutor, generally one of my teachers. I could find a variety of digital resources that helped me understand my lessons. This year, I feel lost … I cannot focus or understand the lectures which are exclusively presented verbally without providing a choice of alternative formats and resources. If only my university adopted the UDL principles, I would certainly have had the opportunity to study with fewer barriers since the courses would have been presented and adapted in a way that meets my needs too.
>
> (El Jamyly, 2021)

With educator awareness of what learners require to access their sessions, comes a greater responsibility to consider these learning requirements during course design and as classes are scheduled. Here, Oussama shares how the UDL framework has the capacity to provide a pathway to multiple means of engagement and thereby facilitate access to the curriculum. Such an approach should move beyond an isolated case and become threaded through the cultural fabric of the university. The section below explores how that may be possible when the culture within a large HE organisation incrementally begins to reorient itself towards inclusive practices.

If only my university adopted UDL: The role of INCLUDE

UIZ is the largest university in Morocco providing for the student population of 53 per cent of the national territory. In normal circumstances, the notion of normality being relative, three to four undergraduate groups are taught every semester, each group consisting of about 200 students or so. A large number of these students come from lower socio-economic backgrounds; others are the first in their family to attend university. Sometimes these students come from distant areas, so they cannot access wider community social support networks upon which they relied to ensure their wellbeing while they lived with extended families. In reality, disabled students rarely show up for their lectures because many classrooms and the course instructional materials are not accessible. Given their size and diversity and the limited class time (an average of two hours a week), it is practically impossible to retrofit the curriculum. Given this context, UDL is particularly appealing for Moroccan universities as it facilitates a proactive anticipation of learners' requirements by designing flexibility into the course materials, the assessment of, and for, learning (O'Neill and Maguire, 2019), and by seeking ways in which the classroom space can also become a more socially aware and socially supportive inclusive space. That is how local interest in UDL through INCLUDE started. Senior HE leaders recognised that the framework had the potential to respond intentionally to a complex web of seemingly intractable problems which could be addressed in a cohesive way through ongoing capacity building.

Increasing awareness and understanding of UDL through the student lens

In Morocco, as elsewhere, given the significant role that disability rights have played in striving for equity, the conceptual scope of inclusive education as a whole is associated with disability rather than applying to all learners who have variability in how they approach learning. For the past two decades, throughout the United States the association with UDL as an indispensable, research-informed framework enabling access to the curriculum has been enshrined in the Individuals with Disabilities Act, so there has been an established traction with UDL implementation and research (Hitchcock et al., 2002). In other parts of the world, the conceptual underpinnings of UDL have gained traction more slowly. In Morocco, as with many countries in the Global South, until relatively recently little was known of UDL and its potential to inform pedagogy not only for disabled learners but also for other minoritised groups such as migrants or those whose first language was not the same as that spoken in the host country, or for whom the curriculum or the learning spaces may have been designed inaccessibly (Chita-Tegmark et al., 2012). Research in the field is negligible, and the very concept of anticipatory inclusive design was somewhat alien. Instead, educators sought to 'differentiate' the curriculum, that is to make sub-groups of learners 'different', rather than to fashion space and learning content according to learners' diverse requirements early in the planning stages. Nevertheless, as a country with a proud heritage of enabling access to HE (Arbaoui, 2012), educators in Morocco are keen to engage proactively with notions of how best to widen participation and to plan effectively for diversity.

Thus, when the opportunity arose in 2020 for learners and staff from UIZ to become partners with the International Collaboratory for Leadership in Universally Designed Education (INCLUDE), the fit between the Collaboratory's action-oriented values and those of agents for positive change within UIZ was noticeable. The wider Collaboratory sought to help change the university's educational world for the better through provision of "professional expertise for those interested in gaining knowledge or implementing change based on UDL" (INCLUDE, 2019). This led to a sea-change in awareness and agency, especially when students from UIZ were invited to write blogs for the learner voice section of INCLUDE's website. In a reciprocal way, students learned about UDL and were empowered to evaluate their university learning experiences using the UDL framework as a means to reflect on the extent to which their learning was accessibly designed. Blogs by students like Oussama quoted above or Samara, a dyslexic student's story presented in the blog titled, "I am not disabled, I am different" (El Amiri, 2021), were transformative in a cultural context where people with cognitive, or other impairments, tend to avoid revealing their differences because of the disabling environments within which they learn.

In time, educators and students from UIZ were recognised as contributing knowledge to the wider inclusion agenda beyond Morocco. A critically reflective engagement with the blogs identified they were not only facilitative in strengthening learner self-efficacy and executive functioning but they also played a pivotal role in altering academics' mindsets towards disabled learners (Rossi and Aabi, 2020). Further, the momentum for learner agency led to the organization of the first international Student Voice Conference held in the Maghreb. The event was opened by the Moroccan Minister for Higher Education, with the aim of promoting student engagement and strengthening learner agency. The attendance of the Minister for Education and some senior policy advisors at the Student Voice Conference was reported by *Morocco World News* (2021). It was seen as the type of initiative that could provide an impetus to realising the relatively recent Framework Law 51.17 (Kingdom of Morocco, 2019), a legislative initiative stipulating that:

> The principles of equity and equal opportunity are manifested in the free provision of public education by the state in all fields and specialties and in the efforts of the state to mobilize and guarantee all available capacities to make it accessible to all citizens and to provide disadvantaged learners with the benefits of social services related to housing food and scholarship.
>
> (Ayad, Bennani, and Elhachloufi, 2020, p. 99).

Learner voice and agency are seen as pivotal in strengthening an educational system that is striving to posit inclusion at the heart of a quality educational experience for all learners. The Student Voice Conference provided an empowering and creatively dynamic workspace for students to interact and to collaborate with others, including faculty and senior University leaders, and to take ownership of event organisation.

Orienting a way forward: Capacity building and research

As identified above, in a relatively short period of time, UDL, as facilitated through INCLUDE, has played an important role in developing policy and practice at UIZ, and its impact was especially important as learning shifted online during COVID-19. As attested to by the President of the University during his keynote to the Student Voice Conference (Bendou, 2021):

> We have seen learning shifting largely to online, with a considerable social media component encouraging peer-to-peer and student-to-teacher communications in new inclusive contexts. This shift has provided our teachers with a conducive environment to universally designed education, which INCLUDE helped introduce among colleagues and students in their teaching and learning practices and their research.

However, despite these earnest observations, there is still somewhat of a lacuna in the research space for the role of UDL in HE within Morocco. However, there is hope that the situation may change as students and faculty at UIZ continue to forge knowledge exchange and research links with colleagues and partner universities within Morocco and, more broadly, throughout Africa. It is promising that several colleagues from UIZ have joined INCLUDE research and professional development task teams and they have cultivated UDL practices along with extended networks of other colleagues. Further, several doctoral students have begun researching the application of UDL in disciplines beyond education; it has also become a core component of two Masters programmes, both introduced by local colleagues who have been involved with INCLUDE.

Ultimately, however, in our experience the UDL framework cannot be transposed directly from its initial application within schools in North America onto educational contexts that are significantly different in relation to their socio-cultural, historical, and legislative pathways. However, there are significant affordances associated with UDL, and, as shown by the University of Ibn Zohr, these can provide very helpful tools, strategies and orientations, as well as enabling empowering collegiate links from beyond the local, for those seeking to forge new inclusive cultures and practices. Powerful creative synergies between global influences and ways of thinking and doing can emerge that facilitate local aspirations when ownership and action is determined by those who have most to gain; namely, the local educators and their learners.

References

Arbaoui, L. (2012). Al Karueein of Fez: The oldest university in the world. *Morocco World News.* Available at: www.moroccoworldnews.com (accessed 8 February 2022).

Ayad, K., Bennani, K.D., and Elhachloufi, M. (2020). Evolution of university governance in Morocco: What is the impact?International Journal of Higher Education, 9(5), 94–104.

Bendou, A. (2021). Student Voice in Moroccan Higher Education. The First International Student Voice Conference, organised virtually by the International Conference on Education Quality (ICEQ) and The International Collaboratory for Leadership in Universally Designed Education (INCLUDE), 8 April 2021.

Chita-Tegmark, M., Gravel, J.W., Maria De Lourdes, B.S., Domings, Y., and Rose, D. H. (2012). Using the Universal Design for Learning framework to support culturally diverse learners. *Journal of Education*, 192(1), 17–22.

Clouder, L., Cawston, J., Wimpenny, K., Mehanna, A.K.A., Hdouch, Y., Raissouni, I., and Selmaoui, K. (2019). The role of assistive technology in renegotiating the inclusion of students with disabilities in higher education in North Africa. *Studies in Higher Education* (Dorchester-on-Thames), 44(8), 1344–1357. Available at: https://doi.org/10.1080/03075079.2018.1437721

El Amiri, Y. (2021). I'm not disabled, I'm DIFFERENT. INCLUDE website blog. Available at: https://include.wp.worc.ac.uk/im-not-disabled-im-different/ (accessed 7 February 2022).

El Jamyly, S. (2021) Pourquoi je souhaite que mon Université ait la CUA? INCLUDE website blog. Available at: https://include.wp.worc.ac.uk/pourquoi-je-souhaite-que-mon-universite-ait-la-cua/ (accessed 7 February 2022).

Hanesworth, P., Bracken, S., and Elkington, S. (2019). A typology for a social justice approach to assessment: Learning from universal design and culturally sustaining pedagogy. *Teaching in Higher Education*, 24(1), 98–114. Available at: https://doi.org/10.1080/13562517.2018.1465405

Hitchcock, C., Meyer, A., Rose, D., and Jackson, R. (2002). Providing new access to the general curriculum: Universal Design for Learning. *Teaching Exceptional Children*, 35(2), 8–17.

INCLUDE (2019). *Action Oriented Values.* Available at: https://include.wp.worc.ac.uk/action-oriented-values/ (accessed 8 February 2022).

Kingdom of Morocco (2019). *New Framework Law n° 51.17*. Available at: http://www.sgg.gov.ma/Portals/0/BO/2020/BO_6944_Fr.pdf?ver=2020-12-24-133647-943 (accessed 1 February 2022).

Morocco World News (2021). First International Student Voice Conference to take place April 8. Available at: https://www.moroccoworldnews.com/2021/04/339094/first-international-student-voice-conference-to-take-place-april-8 (accessed 8 February 2022).

O'Neill, G. and Maguire, T. (2019). Developing assessment and feedback approaches to empower and engage students. In S. Bracken and K. Novak (eds), *Transforming Higher Education Through Universal Design for Learning: An International Perspective*. Abingdon, UK: Routledge, pp. 259–277.

Rossi, V. and Aabi, M. (2020). *360° inclusive feedback: A case study of a classroom blog*. Keynote presentation at the Assessment and Feedback Symposium: Inclusive Assessment, University of the Highlands and Islands, UK.

Seale, J. (2009). Doing student voice work in higher education: An exploration of the value of participatory methods. *British Educational Research Journal*, 36(6), 995–1015.

UNESCO (2020a). *Global Education Monitoring Report*. Available at: https://unesdoc.unesco.org/ark:/48223/pf0000373721 (accessed 7 February 2022).

UNESCO (2020b). *Towards Inclusion in Education: Status, Trends and Challenges: The UNESCO Salamanca Statement 25 Years On*. Available at: https://unesdoc.unesco.org/ark:/48223/pf0000374246

5.3 Achieving culturally inclusive teaching utilising the Universal Design for Learning framework

Linda Hui Yang

The higher education landscape has changed significantly in the past 20 years. The student populations of universities throughout the world are increasingly multicultural (Bhandari and Blumenthal, 2010). Understanding how to support learning needs among diverse groups of students has become increasingly important to universities worldwide, as what once worked in the typical university classroom may no longer be sufficient (Rich, 2020). In this case study, the author shares a Universal Design for Learning (UDL) for Culturally Inclusive Teaching (CIT) approach she developed to help instructors achieve culturally inclusive teaching in the higher education context.

Teaching diverse students in times of change

It has been well documented that, while studying abroad, international students experience various challenges. Academic adjustment appears to be the most challenging (Wu et al., 2015; Wang, 2018). Other documented challenges include social cultural adjustment and psychological distress due to cultural differences (O'Reilly et al., 2010). Faculty who seek to accommodate diverse learning needs have expressed a desire for targeted support and training to equip them with knowledge and skills to achieve culturally inclusive teaching (Clarke et al., 2018; Beelen, 2017).

Hofstede's cultural values framework

Many researchers have attempted to define culture, including Samovar and Porter (1988), Lustig and Koester (2003), and Collier (1989). One of the most widely accepted definitions of culture was proposed by Hofstede (1984, p. 6):

> Culture consists of the unwritten rules of the social game. It is the collective programming of the mind that distinguishes the members of one group or category of people from others.

DOI: 10.4324/9781003253631-18

Hofstede (1986, p. 303) observed four fundamental problems in cross-cultural learning institutions, where the educator and the student are from different cultural backgrounds, including:

1 Differences in the social positions of educators and students in the two societies
2 Differences in the relevance of the curriculum in the two societies
3 Differences in profiles of cognitive abilities between the populations from which educator and student are drawn
4 Differences in expected patterns of educator/student and student/student interaction.

Hofstede developed a 4-D model of cultural differences among societies (Hofstede, 1986) and later extended the model to 6-D (Hofstede and Hofstede, 2005; Hofstede et al., 2010). This model has been described as "probably the dominant explanation of behavioural differences between nations" (Williamson, 2001, p. 1392).

Despite the popularity of Hofstede's model, his approach has been challenged, notably by Harrison and McKinnon (1999), McSweeney (2002), and Signorini et al. (2009). However, the model has proven to be a useful framework for analysing cultural differences (Clark, 1990) in teaching and learning (Wang, 2018). Empirical studies in the higher education context have found two particular cultural dimensions – **individualism** and **power distance** – useful in explaining cultural differences in learning behaviours and preferences, in particular, educator/student and student/student interaction, including Gu (2009), Cronjé (2011), and Arnold and Versluis (2019).

Individualism (IDV) as a characteristic of a culture opposes collectivism, and measures the degree of independence in the way people work. In countries that score high on IDV, people look primarily after their own interest and the interest of their own family. In contrast, countries scoring low on IDV are collectivistic, where any person belongs to one or more right 'in-groups' (e.g. extended family, clan or organisation) from which they cannot detach themselves.

Power distance (PDI) as a characteristic of a culture defines the extent to which the less powerful persons in a society accept inequality in power and consider it as normal. Inequality exists in any culture, but the degree of it that is tolerated varies from one to another.

Cultural differences in teaching and learning

The impact of these two cultural dimensions on teaching and learning are illustrated in Tables 5.1 and 5.2. Hofstede's observations (1986) have been validated by other empirical findings, including Gu (2009), Wang (2018), Zhu (2012), and Cronjé (2011).

Table 5.1 Individualist /collective societies and teaching and learning

Individualist Societies	*Collective Societies*
Students expect to learn how to learn	Students expect to learn how to do
Individual students will speak up in class in response to a general invitation by the teacher	Individual students will only speak up in class when called upon personally by the teacher
Individuals speak up in large groups	Individuals will only speak up in small groups
Confrontation in learning situations can be salutary; conflicts can be brought into the open	Formal harmony in learning situations should be maintained at all times
Face-consciousness is weak	Neither the teacher nor a student should ever be made to lose face

Table 5.2 Power distance and teaching and learning

Small Power Distance Societies	*Large Power Distance Societies*
A teacher merits the respect of their students	A teacher should respect the independence of their students
Student-centred education	Teacher-centred education
Teacher expects students to initiate communication	Students expect teacher to initiate communication
Students may speak up spontaneously in class	Students speak up in class only when invited by the teacher
Students are allowed to contradict or criticise teacher	Teacher is never contradicted nor publicly criticised
Effectiveness of learning related to amount of two-way communication in class	Effectiveness of learning related to excellence of teacher

UDL for culturally inclusive teaching

According to Ginsberg and Wlodkowski (2009), based on an extensive analysis of empirical literature on culture, diversity, inclusion, teaching, and motivation, culturally responsive (or inclusive) teaching has five salient characteristics:

1 Establishes inclusion by making students feel welcome, safe to express their point of view, and respected and connected to one another.
2 Relies upon teaching methodologies and assessments that address multiple learning styles and allows students to learn from and about each other (cooperative learning).
3 Includes content in multiple formats that are linked to best practices for access.

4 Incorporates content that is representative of real-world events and perspectives and voices of those who have been traditionally under-represented.
5 Makes a case for appreciating diversity and different perspectives as an essential outcome of the class.

Drawing on Ginsberg and Wlodkowski's work, the author has developed a UDL approach for CIT to help educators to plan and deliver their teaching in an inclusive manner. This approach is detailed in Table 5.3.

One important element of this approach is the development of intercultural competence. The author developed an Intercultural Development Programme

Table 5.3 UDL for CIT

Engagement	*Representation*	*Action & Expression*
The why of learning	The what of learning	The how of learning
Engaging students in multiple ways helps them to become **purposeful and motivated**. Engagement captures **interest** while helping students to sustain the required **effort** at the same time as developing necessary strategies and skills.	Providing content in a **variety** of ways means that your students have opportunities to comprehend your material and become **knowledgeable learners**. Using audio, video, text, activities, and other means of presenting information gives students a chance to learn in a way that works for them.	Providing students with various options for **physical action, expression and communication**, fosters active learning, encouraging them to be strategic and goal oriented.
Academic orientation Help students to understand the academic practice, teaching activities, assessment etc. **Intercultural competence** Equip students with an important set of knowledge and skills to be able to function effectively in a multicultural setting. **Safe space** Create a safe space where students feel welcome and safe to express views by setting ground rules, codes for productive discussion, and classroom behaviour. **Learning community** Help students feel sense of belonging to the learning community.	**Flipped class** Deliver information transmission outside of the classroom. **Multimedia** Offer content in multiple formats that are linked to best practices for access. **Glossaries** Clarifying key vocabulary while highlighting main ideas and relationships. **Core readings** Highlight core readings to help students prioritise their learning.	**Structuring learning** Provide pre-learning material, making underpinning structure explicit. **Communication** Clear and explicit communication. Use simple language. Avoid making jokes. Check understanding. **Note-taking** Encourage note-taking to reinforce students' understanding and memory of the key learnings. **Participation in class** Use techniques such as pre-warning and online platforms to encourage participation in class.

(ICD) (Yang, 2022) at UCD Michael Smurfit Graduate Business School in 2018. While developing students' intercultural competence, other sets of essential transferable skills are also enhanced, including communication, adaptability, teamwork, critical thinking, creativity, conflict management, problem-solving, decision-making, listening and observing, emotional intelligence, and global mindset. The programme has been in high demand since its introduction. ICD has seen an explosion in popularity, with participation numbers increasing from 128 in the first year to 1,573 in 2021 – 98.6 per cent of the school's total student population, representing over 50 nationalities. In 2022, the ICD won the Silver Award for the AMBA & BGA Excellences Award, Best Culture Diversity and Inclusion Initiative.

Feedback from students has shown that participating in the ICD had a significant impact on their overall student experience. Three annual ICD Students' Experience Surveys indicated that 87 per cent of students believed that ICD helped them with working in diverse groups, 96 per cent of students indicated that ICD has met their expectations, and 100 per cent of students would definitely recommend ICD to future students.

Below are some key reflections on utilising the UDL approach for CIT in the delivery of the ICD programme to postgraduate business students.

Establish the why of learning pre-arrival

It is essential to establish the reason why students need to commit to learning in increasingly globalised workplaces. For postgraduate business students, the positive impact of the learning outcome on their career development and overall personal development directly links to their intrinsic motivation. This should be established as early as possible, preferably before students arrive on campus by, for example, delivering an information webinar and making the video recording available afterwards.

Provide learning content in a variety of means

To make the content as easily accessible as possible, I used the flipped classroom approach, which was highly valued by all the students. This means students can learn essential theories before coming to the class. International students for whom English is not their first language, as well as students who have an independent learning style, particularly value the online learning material because they can spend more time on the knowledge transmission outside of the class which can help them achieve deep learning and be better prepared for class participation (Yang, 2021).

In terms of the online learning materials, students particularly valued the short videos (no longer than 10 minutes) rather than slides with voice over. Instead of giving students a long reading list, I give them no more than three core recommended readings to help them prioritise their learning (see Yang (2021) for more information on making online materials more engaging).

Interact with diverse students in the class

Due to cultural differences and different levels of English proficiency, in order to enhance students' engagement with their learning, as well as class participation, I put a lot of effort into making my communication with the students as explicit as possible, to ensure they were clear about my expectations. This was achieved by using simple words, providing visual aids (e.g. slides, pictures), allocating Q&A time, as well as making online office-hours available so that students from collective cultures, who are not comfortable asking questions in front of others, could approach me individually.

To help students from diverse cultures to participate when in class, I provided various options. For example, for students from relatively lower power distance societies, I tended to ask open questions to the whole class and let them speak up voluntarily. For students from relatively higher power distance societies, I tended to organise small group discussions and invite a group representative to summarise what they had discussed. I gave the students opportunities to ask questions in the class verbally, as well as anonymously online.

Conclusion

As the world, and the higher education classroom, is increasingly globalised, university educators must build an understanding of the impact of cultural dimensions on the approaches and expectations of students from cultural backgrounds which are different from their own. They must adapt their own teaching approach to ensure that their teaching is culturally inclusive. This case study offers an approach to CIT based on UDL, an important component of which is the development of intercultural competence.

References

Arnold, I.J. and Versluis, I. (2019). The influence of cultural values and nationality on student evaluation of teaching. *International Journal of Educational Research*, 98, 13–24.

Beelen, J. (2017). The missing link in internationalisation: Developing the skills of lecturers. *Zeitschrift für Hochschulentwicklung*, 12(4), 133–150.

Bhandari, R. and Blumenthal, P. (2010). *International Students and Global Mobility in Higher Education: National Trends and New Directions*. New York: Springer.

Clark, T. (1990). International marketing and national character: A review and proposal for an integrative theory. *Journal of Marketing*, 54(4), 66–79.

Clarke, M., Yang, L.H., and Herman, D. (2018). *The Internationalisation of Irish Higher Education*. Dublin: Higher Education Authority.

Collier, M.J. (1989). Cultural and intercultural communication competence: Current approaches and directions for future research. *International Journal of Intercultural Relations*, 13(3), 287–302.

Cronjé, J.C. (2011). Using Hofstede's cultural dimensions to interpret cross-cultural blended teaching and learning. *Computers & Education*, 56(3), 596–603.

Ginsberg, M.B. and Wlodkowski, R.J. (2009). *Diversity and Motivation: Culturally Responsive Teaching in College*. New York: John Wiley & Sons.

Gu, Q. (2009). Maturity and interculturality: Chinese students' experiences in UK higher education. *European Journal of Education*, 44(1), 37–52.

Harrison, G.L. and McKinnon, J.L. (1999). Cross-cultural research in management control systems design: A review of the current state. *Accounting, Organizations and Society*, 24(5–6), 483–506.

Hofstede, G. (1984). *Culture's Consequences: International Differences in Work-related Values*. Newbury Park, CA: Sage.

Hofstede, G. (1986). Cultural differences in teaching and learning. *International Journal of Intercultural Relations*, 10(3), 301–320.

Hofstede, G. and Hofstede, G.J. (2005). *Cultures and Organizations: Software of the Mind*, 2nd edn. New York: McGraw-Hill.

Hofstede, G., Hofstede, G.J., and Minkov, M. (2010). *Cultures and Organizations: Software of the Mind*, 3rd edn. New York: McGraw-Hill.

Lustig, M.W. and Koester, J. (2003). *Intercultural Competence: Interpersonal Communication Across Cultures*. Boston, MA: Allyn & Bacon.

McSweeney, B. (2002). Hofstede's model of national cultural differences and their consequences: A triumph of faith – a failure of analysis. *Human Relations*, 55(1), 89–118.

O'Reilly, A., Ryan, D., and Hickey, T. (2010). The psychological well-being and sociocultural adaptation of short-term international students in Ireland. *Journal of College Student Development*, 51(5), 584–598.

Rich, B.L. (2020). How are culturally inclusive teaching practices integrated into business school's curriculum? An analysis of syllabi from the United States. *International Journal of Inclusive Education* [online], pp.1–24.

Samovar, L. and Porter, R. (1988). *Intercultural Communication: A Reader*. Belmont, CA: Wadsworth Publishing Company.

Signorini, P., Rolf, W., and Roger, M. (2009). Developing alternative frameworks for exploring intercultural learning: A critique of Hofstede's cultural difference model. *Teaching in Higher Education*, 14(3), 253–264.

Wang, I.K.H. (2018). Long-term Chinese students' transitional experiences in UK higher education: A particular focus on their academic adjustment. *International Journal of Teaching and Learning in Higher Education*, 30(1), 12–25.

Williamson, D. (2002). Forward from a critique of Hofstede's model of national culture. *Human Relations*, 55(11), 1373–1395.

Wu, H.P., Garza, E., and Guzman, N. (2015). International student's challenge and adjustment to college. *Education Research International*, issue 20, 1–9.

Yang, L.H. (2022). *Intercultural Development Programme (ICD)*. UCD Michael Smurfit Graduate Business School. (Dr Linda Hui Yang was the programme developer and leader from 2018 to 2022.) Available at: https://www.smurfitschool.ie/icd/

Yang, L.H. (2021). Online learning experiences of Irish university students during the COVID-19 pandemic. *All Ireland Journal of Higher Education*, 13(1).

Zhu, J. (2012). *Academic Adjustment of Chinese Students at German Universities*, Dissertation, Philosophischen Fakultät IV Humboldt-Universität zuBerlin.

Chapter 6

Student Supports & Services

6.1 The structures and status of student support

Bairbre Fleming

The concept of a scaffold is regularly used to describe supports for students, and Seamus Heaney's description of scaffolding in the poem Scaffolding (Heaney, 1991) evokes the spirit and value of a scaffold and the promise of the completed "walls of sure and solid stone". However, both the status of the supports and the perception of them can be somewhat ambiguous, and the foundations somewhat unclear. This chapter will explore two critical aspects of student support in higher education. The first is the nature of student supports and how we sequence and build that scaffold. The second, and related theme, is the status of the staff who offer support, or the uprights in the scaffold.

The changing face of higher education

Access to higher education is fundamental to securing opportunities and options. Globally, higher education has moved from the preserve of the élite to mass participation. The last one hundred years has seen the transformation of higher education from a collection of small elite institutions to a mass system. Trow outlines how growth in Europe was initially "beyond the tiny numbers enrolled in a few European universities before the war to the 30 to 40 percent of the age grade currently enrolled in all forms of postsecondary education" (2000, 1). The more recently coined concept of High Participation Systems (HPS) of higher education captures this growth (Marginson, 2016a). Worldwide participation is increasing very rapidly by historical standards, at 1 per cent a year, and now constitutes one-third of the nominal school leaver age group (Marginson, 2016b). However, this expansion is not evenly distributed globally, as all high-income countries and most middle-income countries are tending towards or have exceeded the 50 per cent mark (Marginson, 2016b). This growth has generated new challenges in respect to the logistics of selection, funding, resources, organisation, and governance. In addition, there are more complex challenges to creating different conditions for teaching new types of students with diverse aspirations and academic talents. Higher education expansion also raises a series of challenges about the nature of higher education and management and is well explored

DOI: 10.4324/9781003253631-20

elsewhere. The aspect of higher education that is most relevant to this chapter is the diversification of the sector and the changing nature of the student support roles within higher education.

Pillar 2 – Student Supports & Services

The importance of the first year experience as the foundation stone to successful student engagement, student retention, and student learning is well established in the literature (Tinto, 2006, 2017; Kuh, 2009; Brinkworth, 2009). Student engagement, which is defined as a key part of student success, encompasses both social and academic aspects of the student experience and is influenced by activities inside and outside of the classroom (Krause and Coates, 2008).

The provision of student support, therefore, is clearly critical in the foundation and construction of the higher education experience. We could extend the metaphor to consider student supports as a scaffold, which can fortify and enhance the construction of, in this case, an engaged and successful student.

The student supports on offer in higher education institutions can be extensive and varied. Sometimes, they are clearly accessible and navigable, and occasionally they are not. The size of the institution can determine what is available and how readily a student can find their way to it. The university in this case study developed a Student Experience Map in 2019 to establish a student perspective into how students see and navigate the university ecosystem (UCD Agile, 2019).[1]

In developing the map in Figure 6.1, the project team met with students to establish their perspective on how they see and navigate what they describe as

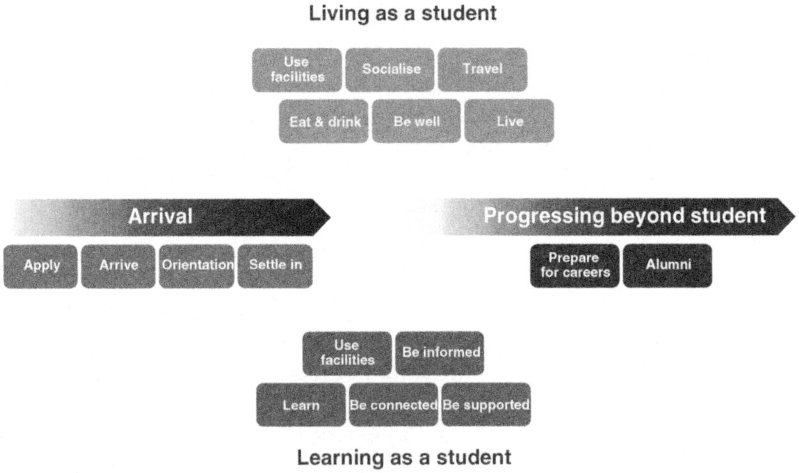

Figure 6.1 UCD Student Experience Map, 2019

the university ecosystem. One of the take-aways from this process is noted in Figure 6.2:

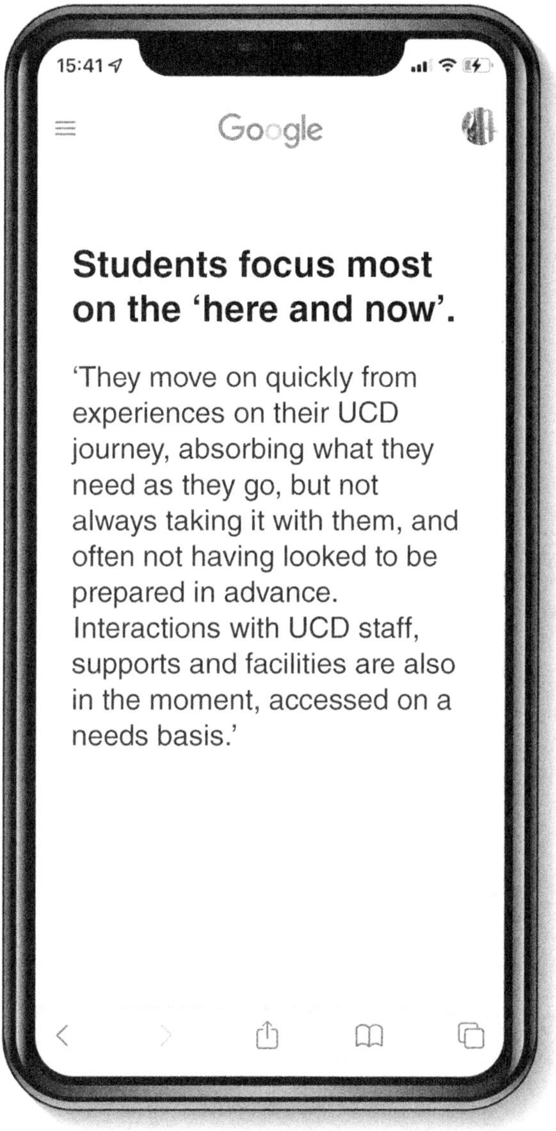

Figure 6.2 A statement from the summary of students' perspective of their UCD experience documented as part of the UCD Student Experience mapping project

The navigation of this, or any, ecosystem is challenging for students. The manner in which we offer supports is discussed in more detail later in the section 'You can start from anywhere'. The status and location of the staff who offer these supports is discussed in more detail in the section 'The status of Student Support Staff'.

Education and capital – its role in student support

Education can, and does, play a significant role in both perpetuating and reinforcing class differences (Reay et al., 2005). Using social reproduction as a mechanism for exploring equality of access is useful as it provides us with a framework for understanding inequality and relatively low participation rates of some groups in our higher education institutions. It highlights the manner in which institutions confer advantage on some groups while reinforcing disadvantage on others.

Michael Apple offers the analogy of a swimming pool to illustrate the potency and potential of social reproduction to advantage one group over another:

> In all too many cases, the situation that has been created is the equivalent of an Olympic-length swimming pool in which a large number of children already drown. The response is to lengthen the pool from 100 meters to 200 meters and give everyone an "equal opportunity" to stand at the far end of the pool, jump in, and then swim the doubled length. However, some children come from families who are affluent enough to have given their children swimming lessons or have sent them to expensive summer camps, whereas others could not even swim the earlier length because of not having such economic advantages. Yes, we guaranteed equality of opportunity, but basically all we really did was put in place another stratifying device that ratified prior advantages in cultural and economic capital.
>
> (Apple, 2001, pp. 725–6).

Apple's swimming pool acts as a metaphor in this chapter for student support in higher education. The various initiatives and structures have to consider how to design equitable support that will allow a more diverse group of students to access the pool. Critically, the students will also need to have the stamina and resources to thrive in that pool.

Social Reproduction Theory highlights the role that formal education can play in reinforcing the dominant culture. The French sociologist, Bourdieu, became interested in the dynamics of social class and how members of higher social groups adopted various methods to protect and reproduce their social positions. Bourdieu's (1986) conceptual toolkit of capitals, field, and habitus offer a critical perspective on the dynamics that can either reproduce or frustrate advantage. He uses the evocative image of those who enter a landscape or habitus with which they are familiar, such as a university, as being like "a fish in water". He developed the concept of 'capital' to include areas such as cultural capital, social capital, and symbolic capital.

Using Bourdieu's framework, American sociologist, Annette Lareau (2003), explores how social inequality is perpetuated from generation to generation. She explores the role of class in childrearing practices in families, studying the differences between middle-class and working-class groups. While Lareau's work is based on social class and parents' involvement in their children's lives, it has applicability to any educational context. Her most recent work looks at classism in higher education among college students. She introduces the term 'hostile ignorance' to capture challenges working-class students, from a variety of racial and ethnic groups, face from students from higher social class backgrounds (Ferguson and Lareau, 2021). They define hostile ignorance as what happens when more affluent students ask questions or make comments to working-class students in a critical or hostile manner (rather than a neutral or positive one) on a matter connected to the class position of the students or their families. As an illustration, they include examples of when students of privilege pass comments of judgements on the daily lives of lower-income students. This theme is also identified by Reay who describes the students in a study as "working class survivors of meritocracy" (Reay, 2021, p. 60). She describes a disconnect caused by successful students being trapped by an academic success that disconnects them from their working-class roots which "generates discomfort, intimidation, withdrawal, lack of confidence, even terror, pain and isolation for some of the working-class students" (Reay, 2021, p. 61).

The work of social scientists such as Reay and Lareau is of relevance to this chapter on student support as there are clear parallels between the middle-class sense of 'entitlement' and the dominance of middle-class learners in higher education. In that context, 'non-traditional' students can be positioned as the 'other' to an assumed norm, and the capacities of these students can be considered the 'wrong' capacities, such that privilege prevails (Mulcahy and Martinussen, 2022).

Lareau uses a horticultural analogy to define parenting styles. Middle-class parents tend to adopt a cultural logic of child rearing that stresses the concerted cultivation of children. *Concerted cultivation* is characterised by parents encouraging negotiation and discussion involving extensive participation in organised extra-curricular activity. This style empowers students to challenge those in authority, to be articulate and comfortable in advocating their needs. Lareau suggests that the middle-class children in her study exhibited an emergent version of sense of entitlement, characteristic of the middle class. They acted "as though they had a right to pursue their own individual preferences and to actively manage interactions in institutional settings" (Lareau, 2003, p. 6).

Working-class parents, by contrast, tend to undertake the accomplishment of natural growth. This parenting style is characterised by parents being more directive with their children and not encouraging negotiation or discussion. Conversely, parents from lower income households were more likely to encourage their children to accept and follow direction from those in authority. This style of parenting also facilitated greater autonomy among children by facilitating more free time and fewer structured activities. Lareau concluded that the 'natural growth' mindset was more likely to encourage children to respect and take the advice of people in authority.

The children in the study were subsequently followed up as college-age students and the middle-class children maintained their entitled status – they were 'fish in water'. By contrast, the working-class children showed an emerging sense of constraint in their interactions in institutional settings. They were less likely to try to influence actions to suit their own preferences. Like their parents, the working-class children accepted the actions of figures in positions of authority.

By extending Lareau's concept to student support in higher education, we can consider how those students who have been immersed in a culture of 'concerted cultivation' may be better served in the current context of maximising their access to all available supports and opportunities. By inference, those students who have absorbed the pattern of 'natural growth' may not recognise their entitlement to support, or the merits in them cultivating an approach to maximising their opportunities in higher education. It would, therefore, seem reasonable to conclude that the work of those of us in student support is to cultivate a sense of entitlement to the campus and all relevant supports.

Reshaping student supports would have the impact of disrupting deficit framings (Mulcahy and Martinussen, 2022). To do this, we must reconsider how we offer student supports and ensure that we provide a range of supports that are easy to access and navigate.

So what has this to do with student support?

The concept of capital and how it relates to student support can therefore be further explored. Bourdieu's theories of capital can be used as a framework to explore how to structure student supports to make that swimming pool more navigable for all. The significance of the various forms of capital are further illustrated in Liz Thomas' contribution later. Her work and observations reflect similar experiences in our university.

We hosted an inclusive University for All Welcome at the start of the 2019–20 Academic Year. During the Welcome, which is designed to give access students a sense of entitlement and to cultivate their opportunities as students, we asked them to indicate what their main goal was for the year ahead. Their responses illustrated a disconnect between the capital we thought they would want and the aspirations they had for themselves.

The question asked was an open one, and the students wrote anonymously on a green luggage tag. Over 45 per cent of the handwritten Goal Tags referred to some aspect of social capital. 120 (19 per cent) of the respondents wrote specifically about 'making friends' or a version of wishing to connect and make new friends. The short and unambiguous ambition to 'make friends' was powerful. In that context, offering advice on other aspects of student life or information capital is ill-advised and poorly timed. In that 2019 Welcome, students were offered specific sessions on financial support, on academic writing, and a range of information sessions on various aspects of student life. In that exercise, only seven (1 per cent) of the students noted that their main goal was to figure out a financial strategy. All these information sessions were offered by university staff and were detailed and expert in their delivery and content.

> Make as much friends as possible. Be confident where I'm at and what I'm doing.
>
> [Student Goal, ALL Welcome 2019–20]

Following our analysis of the Goal Tags and feedback from the Welcome event, we adapted our Welcome Programme for the following year. The amended Welcome Programme recognises that students want to meet other students. They want time to learn from each other and connect with each other. We, therefore, co-created the welcome sessions with Access Leaders, who are student leaders, and have amended the programme to reduce the informational content and maximise student interactions. This change has been significant and requires a change in mindset, as staff are predisposed towards sharing information and detail at point of entry, rather than disseminating it through other media or outlets, such as our student leaders.

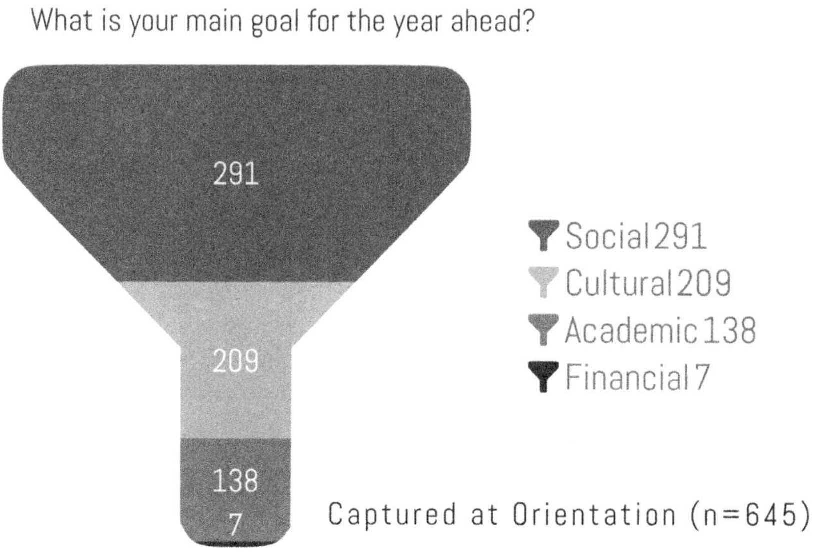

Figure 6.3 Coding of Student Goals from incoming students who described their key goal for the semester ahead

You can start from anywhere

> A GENIAL Irishman … was once asked by a pedestrian Englishman to direct him on his way to Letterfrack… The Irishman flung himself into the problem and, taking the wayfarer to the top of a hill commanding a wide prospect of bogs, lakes, and mountains, proceeded to give him, with more eloquence than precision, a copious account of the route to be taken. He then concluded as follows: **'… I wouldn't start from here'**.

The original version of this well quoted joke 'I wouldn't start from here' is attributed to the *Hibbert Journal*, written in 1924 (Hibbert Journal, 1924). The sentiment almost a century later remains familiar. Those of us working in student support globally tend to approach our work with the same enthusiasm as the genial man in the joke. We want to impart as much as we can to those we meet, offering them a series of directions, details, and observations. However, we should consider what message we share with students, and when we should offer these directions.

This exercise described in Figure 6.3, and a related one Liz Thomas offers later, illustrates the need to reconsider what students are looking for, and in what sequence. The traditional Orientation exercises, laden with lessons and information content, may not be transecting at the right points for students as they transition to university, with an overwhelming number of students (45 per cent) in our study prioritising the need to make friends and social networks.

Navigating student supports

As was noted in the student feedback on their goals at Orientation, outlined in Figure 6.3, new entrants to the university are preoccupied and distracted. Our instinct for offering guidance and direction is comparable to attempting to absorb detailed directions when all you need to know is what needs to be done in the 'here and now'.

Picturing student supports as different forms of capital may help structure and shape supports. Using the different forms of capital described earlier, student supports could be considered as a series of routes that students will need or will travel. The myriad supports could be grouped as Information (Cultural Capital), Financial Capital, Academic Capital, and Social Capital. The key messages shared with students in our university are used below as an illustration. The complexity, detail, and number of supports outlined in Figure 6.4 illustrate the density and inaccessibility of what we try to share with students at the start of their journey. Knowing that students want the information when they need it, we should reconsider student supports as a range of journeys and offer directions accordingly. We can, therefore, offer direction in varied sequences, remembering that some of the routes, in particular the one for social supports, will be of more immediate relevance than some of the others.

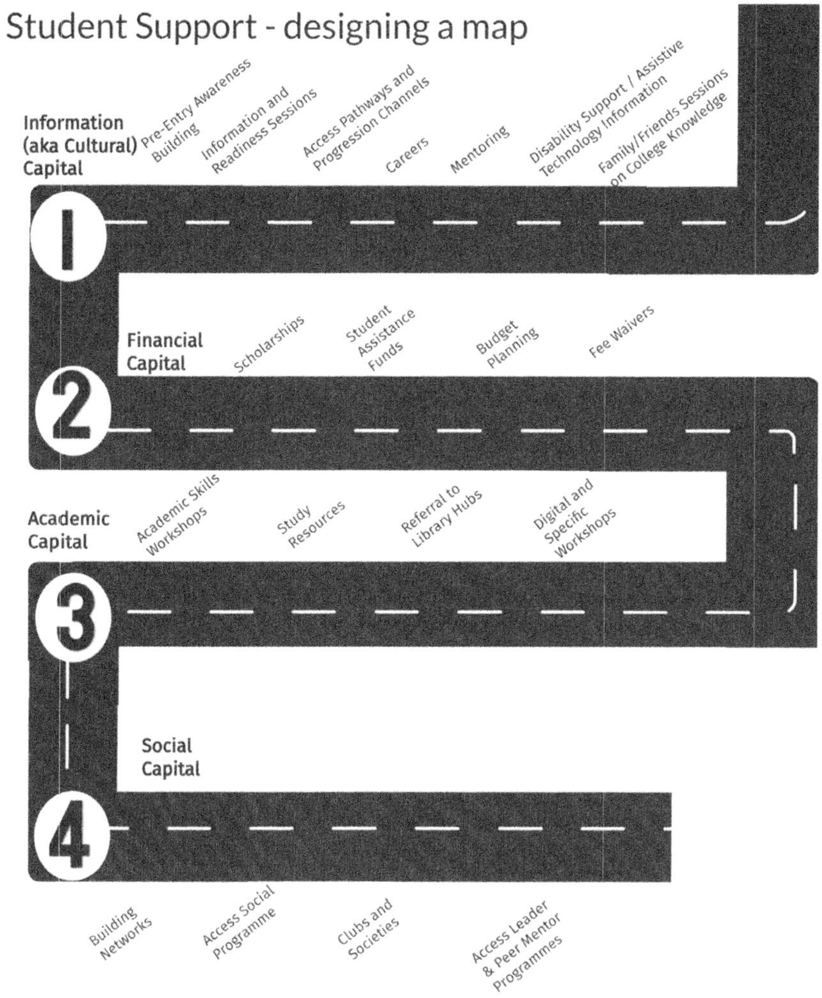

Figure 6.4 Student Support as a detailed map offered to students at Orientation

But, however we offer the supports, we can reassure the students that they can start from anywhere on that map and absorb the directions as and when they are ready and relevant.

We also must consider the extent to which our supports are universally designed so that our students from a non-dominant background are not required to assimilate to succeed in education. This e*mbourgeoisement* has been described as being "strangers in a strange land" (Benn, 1995) or, as "Strangers in Paradise" (Reay et al., 2009). Reay and her colleagues describe the arrival on campus for working-class students as being an 'out of field' experience, as the new students had no familiarity with the field. They are fish out of water.

Those of us working in student supports must, therefore, consider the impact of this transition for some students to a strange land, with its potential for 'othering'. The inferred assimilation into an alternative habitus risks prompting students to create an alternative narrative, or what Reay and her colleagues refer to as 'reinvention':

> Unlike their middle-class counterparts, they are engaged in acts of invention or more accurately reinvention – making dreams come true rather than doing what everyone like us does.
>
> (Reay et al., 2009b, p.8).

Inevitably, this clash of cultures must be anticipated and considered in the context of student support.

The language and approach being used in the context of widening participation is being challenged. The concept of 'raising aspirations' is vexed, as it implies that potential students could access higher education if they had aspirations (Rainford, 2021). An alternative view, of 'raising expectations' or 'realising aspirations', is a more inclusive and positive approach in our messaging to students in student support. Rainford also offers the possibility of formulating a 'possible selves' approach to outreach and engagement (Rainford, 2021).

The alternative approaches to language around inclusion and widening participation will also impact on how we offer student support. The challenge around assumptions that we make, and the impact of our 'hostile ignorance' on student experience, is a sobering one. The aspiration to be a University for All embraces that challenge and can use that 'possible selves' approach in a range of mentoring, peer-support, and access leader engagement to see students' possible self within our higher education institutions.

Universal Design and student support

In the context of a university as an eco-system, student supports, typically, have been differentiated with many so-called non-traditional or under-represented student cohorts supported by specialised services; e.g. mature students meet a dedicated mature student officer for all needs (Kelly and Padden, 2018). In an inclusive higher education institution, our approach is to treat all students equitably – and to frame it that 'a student is a student' regardless of background, age, disability, and pace of study. This equitable approach, therefore, determines that all supports will be offered to all students. For example, students requiring writing support or academic advice will be able to receive this support in the same way, regardless of entry route. Similarly, part-time students will have the same access and entitlement as those who are full time.

Where supplementary supports such as assistive technology or learning support are required, these are usually provided by specialists. In this context, these supports augment, rather than replace, mainstream services. This approach strengthens inclusion and mitigates the tendency to consider under-represented student cohorts as 'other'.

Ron Mace (1998) offers us the following: "'universal design' means the design of products, environments, programmes and services to be usable by all people, to the greatest extent possible, without the need for adaptation or specialized design" (Dolmage, 2017, p. 115). In that context, student support is an obvious canvas for universal design. The construction of student supports as 'other' has been replaced with an emerging ambition to mainstream supports for all students. This aspiration will be further enhanced by the delivery of a national digital badge for student support and engagement that is currently in development, and a collaboration between the higher and further education sectors.

In that context, reviewing the Student Experience Map in Figure 6.5 offers a new structure to consider Student Supports in a higher education institution. This new construction borrows the theoretical frameworks and tools referred to in this chapter.

However, this approach can be challenging to resource and mainstream. The typical higher education institution works across the student lifecycle where the work is characterised by Liz Thomas as follows: "Too often, fundamental and important changes to improve student learning experiences and outcomes are

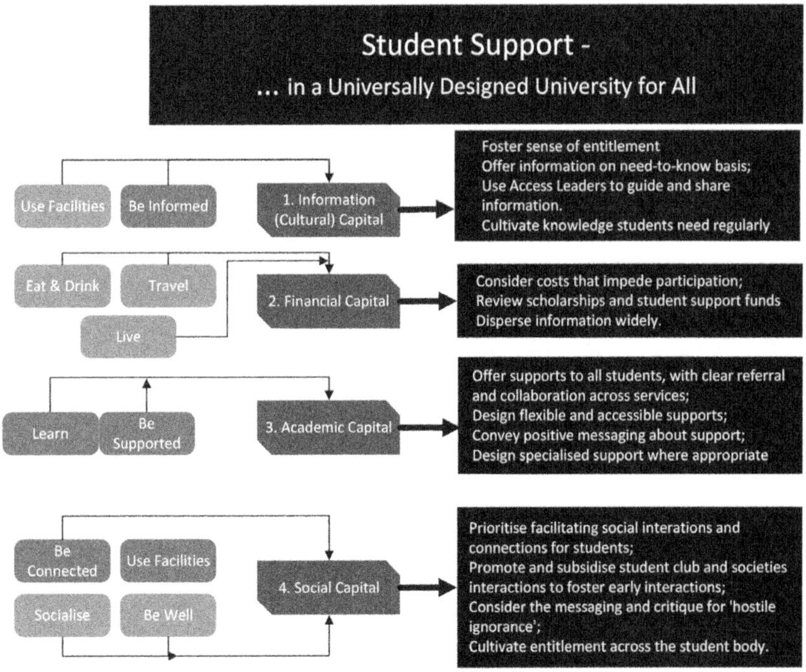

Figure 6.5 Revisiting a Student Experience Map to consider Universally Designed student supports

reliant on the good will of staff champions, who often undertake additional work in their own time" (Thomas et al., 2017, p. 93). This gap between the systemic ambition for moving from the margins to mainstreaming will require a significant change in both ambition and mindset, which

> necessitates a shift away from supporting specific student groups through a discrete set of policies or timebound interventions, towards equity considerations being embedded within all functions of the institution and treated as an ongoing process of quality enhancement. Making a shift of such magnitude requires cultural and systemic change at both the policy and practice levels.
>
> (May and Bridger, 2010, p. 2)

If the nature of the student experience and supports are varied and contested, so too are the status and roles of those working in the academy. The following section considers the status and role of those scaffolders – the professional staff who engage in supporting students in higher education through a range of initiatives, projects, and specialised and generalised supports.

The status of student support staff

Roles in the Academy

Max Weber referred to academic life as "an utter gamble" (Ruser, 2020, p. 162). While the context of his description has changed over time, so too has the nature of the academic role. In her case study in Chapter 4, Mary Farrelly notes that accessibility and inclusion problems for staff and students do not only exist in parallel but also feed into and perpetuate one another: "Too often the day-to-day work of making inclusive higher education a reality for students reproduces structures of exclusion and marginalisation for staff, undermining from the start the impact of those very initiatives in the classroom".

Rosewell and Ashwin (2019) distil the perceptions of the academic role to being either a researcher, a teacher, a researcher and teacher, an academic, a professional, or a manager. Similarly, the role of 'professional staff' has also changed. The earlier description of roles being either 'academic' or 'non-academic' has been challenged as the "binary perceptions tend to polarise academic and non-academic activity, with the result that the two are often seen as being in tension with each other" (Whitchurch, 2013, p. 5). In his study of academics' perception of professional staff, Gray (2015) refers to a perception of a divide between academic and professional staff, with the latter being comparatively impotent or largely invisible, in spite of the contributions they make to their institutions. In his observations in 'Culture clash or ties that bind?', Gray explores the themes of the professional other, managerialism, bureaucracy, and the Third Space.

Emergence of the Third Space

The application of the concept of Third Space captures an alternative to the binary perception. Whitchurch proposes the use of Third Space to explore the emergence of broadly based, extended projects across the university, which are no longer contained within fixed boundaries and have generated new roles and activities. She has captured these in diagrammatic form, which has been adapted in Figure 6.6 below (Whitchurch, 2008).

The Third Space captures the complex, altering, and dynamic nature of the current higher education landscape, as even the term 'professional' is contestable. However, in general, professional now refers to staff who are not employed on academic contracts (Gordon and Whitchurch, 2007). While professional staff may not have academic contracts, many have academic credentials and experience and may be research active and teachers. Similarly, academic staff may also work in this Third Space, bringing a range of additional skills and competencies around project management, leadership, and innovation.

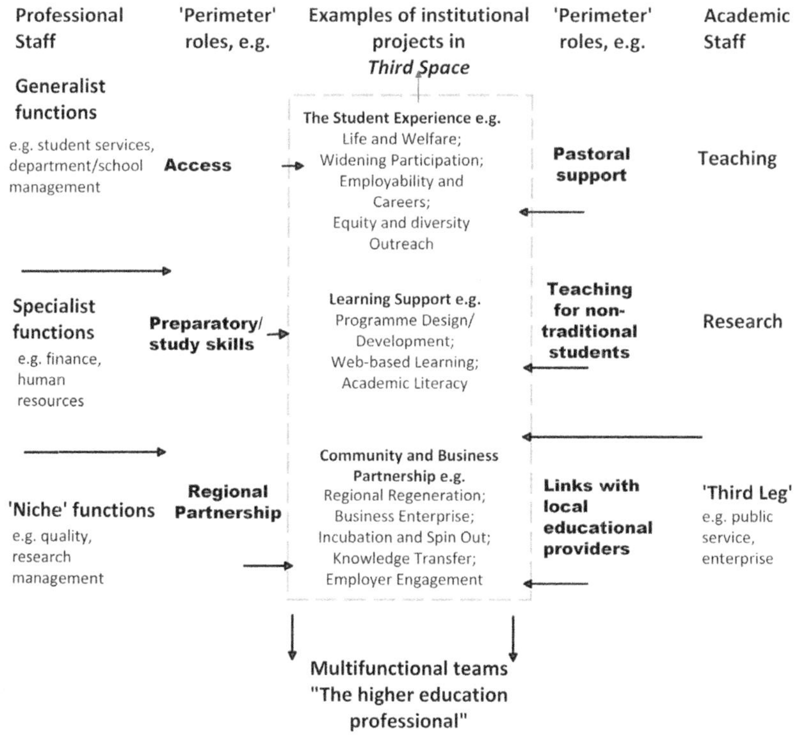

Figure 6.6 The identification of a Third Space
Adapted from (Whitchurch, 2008) and further developed in (Whitchurch, 2013).

Higher education structures are organisationally complex and contested. In the current system, student supports tend to be located outside the academic sphere. Consequently, they are typically located in administrative or professional units, serving and supporting but unlikely to be shaping. In our diagrammatic representation, staff working in student support may be in fixed roles in the 'Professional Staff' dimension. However, increasingly some of the roles are new and support staff may not have "ready-made scripts for their roles" (Ryttberg, 2019).[2] Their roles are more likely to be in that Third Space. The location and governance of student supports, therefore, runs the risk of undermining or devaluing the function, efficacy, and impact of student supports and services in supporting an inclusive university.

The earlier Weber description of academic life as 'an utter gamble' could be more appropriately assigned now to those working in professional or 'Third Space' roles. The experts working in student supports tend not to have equal status with their academic colleagues. In many cases, student support staff will have the credentials and competencies of their academic colleagues, but do not have the autonomy or benefits of the academic life. The valorisation of the 'academic' at the expense of all other staff working in the university could have a detrimental impact on this critical pillar of Student Supports & Services. The added paradox of this inequity is that the staff who are most likely to be leading the university in challenging issues of inclusion and diversity are the same colleagues who are undermined by the governance and culture of their institutions.

The potential for valorising a Third Activity

Thinking in fractions, one could see the potential for focusing on two different 'thirds'. If student support was recognised as having a comparable status to teaching and research, the status of those student specialists would be considerably enhanced. As an illustration, Conway's analysis of the relationship between academics and administrators in universities captures a perspective:

> Academics often assume that because support staff are there to support teaching and learning, they are therefore there to support academics, rather than both working to deliver teaching and learning in different ways.
>
> (Conway, 2012, p. 46)

The reimagining of the nature of student support, and the engagement of more colleagues, both academic and professional, would embed the activity and incorporate it as an integral aspect of the university mission. Student Support would then become the third leg of the university mission and help balance the student experience, enhance their engagement, and maximise student success.

Similarly, the recognition of the Third Space in a higher education context offers a framework for moving the debate from what was described as the 'academic–administrator divide' and the generally negative characteristics associated with the relationship between these two core groups of university staff (Conway, 2012). That 'Third Space' alters the binary and recognises the new space as one that has the potential to forge links between staff and to create new synergies and outcomes.

Conclusion

In the generations since Newman first imagined the idea of a university, our higher education sector has changed. One of those key changes is in how we design and deliver student support in an integrated and student-centric way. When we meet students for the first time now, we talk to them about student autonomy and everything that is implied in that. In our planning for student transition to higher education, we can consider the analogy of a car. For many incoming first years, their experience of second-level education involves sitting in the back seat of that car, travelling on a predetermined route at a predetermined speed. The student has minimal choice or input on the decisions being made on that journey.

Then, the students transition to higher education and, over the course of a few short weeks in some cases, our first-year students are moved directly into the driver's seat. The student now directs where they are going with their study, how often they will attend, how they will participate, and what their workload input will be for each module they study. Typically, students are given some version of a road map when they attend their orientation. As with any set of directions, the instinct is to offer as much detail as possible to the recipient. What is clear from the Goal Tags mentioned earlier, and reinforced by other student inputs, is that we need to consider how we offer those directions, or how we shape that scaffold. The various capitals, or directions or supports that students need, are required at different times.

This analogy of the student as autonomous driver, and its implications, also relates to the professional staff involved in student support in higher education. The staff have also been involved in change and reflecting on how to support student autonomy. In that context, staff have shifted their focus from the role of chauffeur or oracle and now guide or empower students.

As outlined earlier, these student support professionals are engaged in a complex 'third' space, not just engaged in operational tasks or 'fixes', but facilitating a learner strategy towards empowerment as a strategy to embed student success. In this context, the newly launched Student Success Strategy from the Teaching and Learning Forum highlights the need for staff to be supported, motivated, and recognised for their commitment to the enhancement of teaching and learning and student success (National Forum, 2021). Professional staff who support our students have developed new and complex skills to allow them to adapt and design supports that have universal application for our twenty-first century institutions. They can be reflective practitioners who can observe changes in student needs, who can co-create with students, and who can support students in an inclusive and sustainable way.

> If you want to build a ship, don't drum up the men to gather wood, divide the work, and give orders. Instead, teach them to yearn for the vast and endless sea.
>
> – Antoine de Saint-Exupéry[3]

The over-quoted analogy of '*Give a man a fish…*' has direct relevance to our work in student support. Our inclusive universities teach our students to fish, or drive, or direct their own work. They do this through researching their areas of expertise and harnessing the best practice in our field. To do this, our colleagues in student support are earning the same respect that we offer teaching and research in our institutions. Yet, in higher education we tend to be slow to recognise, celebrate, and reward that work. To be truly inclusive in our ambition, we need to be inclusive in how we recognise all activities in our institutions and to recognise the contribution of student support and engagement in our mission.

In an inclusive university, we could reflect on how inclusive we are in the parity of esteem and treatment offered to all who play key roles in the students' educational experience through the opportunities, rewards, and recognition offered and the status conferred on the activity of student support.

An inclusive culture demands that we grapple with such issues as we structure our scaffolding. This act of inclusion would promote our idea of a university – a university for all…

Notes

1 The UCD Student Experience mapping project involved the contribution of over 200 staff/faculty and students. Experience mapping was used as the approach for uncovering the student perspective. The project was co-ordinated by UCD Agile and chaired by the Dean of Students.

2 The specific role and identities of librarians as professional staff is not addressed here but has generated significant debate elsewhere. See Wasserman, V. and Berkovich, I. (2022). Higher education professionals in the age of NPM and digital knowledge: Distinction strategies for forming new occupational capital. *Studies in Higher Education (Dorchester-on-Thames)*, 47, 146–158.

3 Cited in Karakhanyan, S., van Veen, K., and Bergen, Th.C.M. (2011). Teachers' voices in the context of higher education reforms in Armenia. *European Journal of Education*, 46, 508–523.

References

Anon (1924). *Hibbert Journal: A Quarterly Review of Religion, Theology, and Philosophy.*

Apple, M.W. (2001). *Will Standards Save Public Education?*Thousand Oaks, CA: Sage Publications.

Benn, R. (1995). Strangers in a strange land: Participation and withdrawals on university certificates. *Studies in the Education of Adults*, 27, 187–199.

Bourdieu, P. (1986). The forms of capital. In J.G. Robinson (ed.), *Handbook of Theory and Research for the Sociology of Education*. New York: Greenwood Press.

Brinkworth, R. (2009). First year expectations and experiences: Student and teacher perspectives. *Higher Education*, 58, 157–173.

Conway, M. (2012). Using causal layered analysis to explore the relationship between academics and administrators in universities. *Journal of Futures Studies*, 17, 37–58.

Dolmage, J.T. (2017). Universal Design. In *Academic Ableism*. Ann Arbor, MI: University of Michigan Press.

Ferguson, S. and Lareau, A. (2021). Hostile ignorance, class, and same-race friendships: Perspectives of working-class college students. *Socius: Sociological Research for a Dynamic World*, 7. doi:10.1177/23780231211048305

Gordon, G. and Whitchurch, C. (2007). Managing human resources in higher education: The implications of a diversifying workforce. *Higher Education Management and Policy*, 19, 131–153.

Gray, S. (2015). Culture clash or ties that bind? What Australian academics think of professional staff. *Journal of Higher Education Policy and Management*, 37, 545–557.

Heaney, S. (1991). Scaffolding (1966). *Death Of a Naturalist*. London: Faber & Faber.

Karakhanyan, S., van Veen, K. and Bergen, Th.C.M. (2011). Teachers' voices in the context of higher education reforms in Armenia. *European Journal of Education*, 46, 508–523.

Kelly, A.M. and Padden, L. (2018). *Toolkit for Inclusive Higher Education Institutions: From Vision to Practice*. Dublin: UCD Access & Lifelong Learning.

Krause, K.L. and Coates, H. (2008). Students' engagement in first-year university. *Assessment & Evaluation in Higher Education*, 33, 493–505.

Kuh, G.D. (2009). What student affairs professionals need to know about student engagement. *Journal of College Student Development*, 50, 683–706.

Lareau, A. (2003). *Unequal Childhoods: Class, Race, and Family Life*. London and Berkeley, CA: University of California Press.

Lareau, A. (2011). *Unequal Childhoods: Class, Race, and Family Life*, 2nd edn. Berkeley, CA and London: University of California Press.

Mace, R. (June, 1998). *Designing for the 21st Century: An International Conference on Universal Design*. Paper Presented at the International Conference on Universal Design, Hofstra University, Hempstead, New York.

Marginson, S. (2016a). High Participation Systems of higher education. *The Journal of Higher Education*, 87, 243–271.

Marginson, S. (2016b). The worldwide trend to high participation higher education: Dynamics of social stratification in inclusive systems. *Higher Education*, 72, 413–434.

May, H. and Bridger, K. (2010). *Developing and Embedding Inclusive Policy and Practice in Higher Education*. York: Higher Education Academy.

Mulcahy, D. and Martinussen, M. (2022). Affecting advantage: Class relations in contemporary higher education. *Critical Studies in Education*, 1–16.

Rainford, J. (2021). Are we still "raising aspirations"? The complex relationship between aspiration and widening participation practices in English higher education institutions. *Educational Review*, 1–18.

Reay, D. (2021). The working classes and higher education: Meritocratic fallacies of upward mobility in the United Kingdom. *European Journal of Education*, 56, 53–64.

Reay, D., Crozier, G., and Clayton, J. (2009). 'Strangers in Paradise'? Working-class students in elite universities. *Sociology (Oxford)*, 43, 1103–1121.

Reay, D., David, M., and Ball, S. (2005). *Degrees of Choice: Social Class, Race and Gender in Higher Education*. Stoke on Trent: Trentham Books.

Rosewell, K. and Ashwin, P. (2019). Academics' perceptions of what it means to be an academic. *Studies in higher education (Dorchester-on-Thames)*, 44, 2374–2384.

Ruser, A. (2020). From gamble to conformity? Academic careers, ethical neutrality and the role of 'professional' social sciences. *Social Epistemology*, 34, 162–173.

Ryttberg, M. and Geschwind, L. (2019). Professional support staff in higher education: Networks and associations as sense givers. *Higher Education*, 78, 1059–1074.

Thomas, L., Hill, M., Mahony, J.O., and Yorke, M. (2017). *Supporting Student Success: Strategies for Institutional Change What Works?* Student Retention & Success programme. York: Higher Education Academy.

Tinto, V. (2006). Research and practice of student retention: What next? *Journal of College Student Retention: Research, Theory & Practice*, 8, 1–19.

Tinto, V. (2017). Reflections on student persistence. *Student Success*, 8, 1–8.

Trow, M. (2000). From mass higher education to universal access: The American advantage. *Minerva*, 37, 1–26.

UCD AGILE (2019). *Mapping Our Students' Experience – The Student Perspective* [online]. Available at: https://www.ucd.ie/agile/whatagiledoes/mappingourstudentsexperience/thestudentperspective/ (accessed 1 April 2022).

Wasserman, V. and Berkovich, I. (2022). Higher education professionals in the age of NPM and digital knowledge: Distinction strategies for forming new occupational capital. *Studies in Higher Education (Dorchester-on-Thames)*, 47, 146–158.

Whitchurch, C. (2008). Shifting identities and blurring boundaries: The emergence of Third Space professionals in UK higher education. *Higher Education Quarterly*, 62, 377–396.

Whitchurch, C. (2013). *Reconstructing Identities in Higher Education: The Rise of Third Space Professionals*. Abingdon, UK and New York: Routledge.

6.2 Putting student support centre-stage to improve diversity, belonging, and success – the #Ibelong project

Liz Thomas

Introduction

For too long, student support has been sidelined, positioned as a remedial intervention for students who are struggling and may be at risk of withdrawing, rather than a mainstream activity for all students, and to be undertaken by all staff. The term student services, professional services, and student support are not tightly defined, or used consistently. Previous research has taken a broad approach, encompassing academic and pastoral support and other student services, such as finance and careers and employment services (Thomas et al., 2002, p. 80), and specifically listed the following services: careers and employability services including volunteering; student advisers, counselling, and wellbeing services; disability services; financial support and advice; IT skills and support; library services; support for religion or belief; study skills in the widest sense; and students' union services (Woodfield and Thomas, 2012, p. 4).

This piece considers the evidence about why student support needs to be mainstreamed and presents a case study based on the #Ibelong project, funded by the European Erasmus+ programme. #Ibelong aimed to improve the belonging of diverse students in an inclusive learning environment through a series of interconnected course-level interventions, which were implemented in universities in the Netherlands, Germany, Portugal, and the UK between 2019 and 2021. The COVID-19 pandemic interrupted and fundamentally changed the delivery of the activities and made the evaluation (based in part on historical baselines) problematic. The piece, therefore, concludes with recommendations which draw on both the experiences and the aspirations of the #Ibelong project, and the wider literature.

Moving student support into the mainstream

In 2002, a team of researchers at Staffordshire University were commissioned by the UK Department for Education and Skills to undertake a research project to examine the role of student services in retaining students in the context of greater student diversity (Thomas et al., 2002). The overriding

DOI: 10.4324/9781003253631-21

concern was to consider how student services could play a more strategic and influential role in the emerging widening participation agenda by contributing to the retention and completion of students from 'non-traditional' student groups. This was amid concerns that students may fear being stigmatised if they needed support (NAO, 2002), especially those most likely to need support (Dodgson and Bolam, 2002; Harris, 2001). A survey respondent optimistically wrote:

> I believe that the role of student services is in a process of transition from a reactive, welfare orientated service for institutions to a pro-active developmental service that is fundamental to the work of the HEI as a whole, in particular with regard to recruitment, retention and completion, the employability of students and to the overall quality of the student experience. For many years the role of student services has been just outside the core business of the institution. I believe that has now changed and that with the increasing professionalisation of all constituent areas of student services, such a department has a great deal more to offer an HEI than supporting students with problems (Head of Student Support Services).
>
> (Thomas et al., 2002, p. 17)

Around the same time, Owen (2002) described the 'curriculum model', which provides support through academic courses. This overcomes many of the problems associated with a one-to-one, centralised student support, which, in a mass university, she argues "works only at a huge cost in terms of people-hours and stress" (p. 20).

A decade later, Woodfield and Thomas (2012) examined gendered engagement with academic and pastoral support services; the model of service delivery had remained largely unchanged, although there was growing recognition of the role of personal tutors and academic advisers (Thomas and Hixenbaugh, 2006). Woodfield and Thomas found "students' knowledge about specific services was often vague and their awareness of a particular service was sometimes arrived at by chance" and "male students who participated in the research were generally less aware than female students of all services" (p. 11). The study also found that "many services had low levels of use by students" and "male survey respondents used most services less than female respondents" (p. 12).

Of those who had considered withdrawing from their studies, men were less likely than women to report accessing university services to help them resolve their issues. When male respondents were asked what helped them to stay at university, only 24 per cent cited support from their HEI's services and from their tutors, compared with 32 per cent of women – 10 per cent of men and 18 per cent of women reported that support from tutors, in particular, had helped them to stay on the course (Woodfield and Thomas, 2012, p. 13).

The *What Works?* student retention and success programme (Thomas, 2012) found that the majority of students who think about leaving do not make use of institutional support and professional services; rather, they seek advice from friends and family (McCary et al., 2011). More recent research with commuter students (Thomas, 2020a) – who are more likely to be from a lower socio-economic group, be the first generation in their families to enter higher education, have a lower income, be mature, be from an ethnic minority background and have studied in a state school (Donnelly and Gamsu, 2018; Maguire and Morris, 2018) – tend to prioritise academic engagement at the expense of engagement in enhancement and social activities, including accessing support services. Students cited practical challenges, the lack of relevance to them, and the desire to focus on getting a good degree to enable them to progress into graduate employment, which inhibited their engagement with the wider university experience (p. 10).

#Ibelong

The #Ibelong project sought to work with the whole course team to enable diverse students to be successful, by embedding activities about diversity, belonging, and success into the learning experience (e.g. Owen, 2002; Thomas, 2012; Thomas et al., 2017). The focus is on students who are first generation entrants, from ethnic minorities or who have a 'migrant background'but the activities were delivered to all students in the cohort. #Ibelong developed three inter-connected interventions: Dialogue Days (DD), Team Teacher Reflection (TTR), and Student Community Mentoring (SCM). This case study focuses primarily on DDs.

DDs bring together students, staff, and student community mentors from a particular course or programme of study and create a safe space in which to discuss diversity, belonging, and success. DD1, at the time of transition into higher education, focuses on dialogue about diversity in relation to past experiences and expectations of the forthcoming HE programmes, promoting interaction between students and with staff to develop belonging and thinking about how the course can support students to be successful. DD2, towards the end of the academic year, reflects on the first-year experience of studying, belonging, and succeeding in HE, and empowers students to feel safe and supported in looking ahead to be successful in their second year of study, where there are increased academic demands and higher expectations of student autonomy. The DDs developed a series of activities to achieve these goals; they were initially delivered in-person but were subsequently adapted and delivered both online and in a blended format (Thomas, forthcoming).

The #Ibelong project has drawn upon the idea of being colour-brave, as opposed to colour-blind (Hobson, 2014); #Ibelong reframed it as 'diversity brave', as the project did not just address issues of race and ethnicity. This approach acknowledges and talks about difference and explicitly addresses the issues arising, rather than ignoring diversity and difference; Baboeram

(2020) describes this as "getting comfortable with the uncomfortable". This approach helps to develop an environment in which alternative perspectives and experiences can be raised, and which promotes awareness and understanding amongst students and staff. It also reflects our commitment to being inclusive, rather than devising specific interventions for individual students, and frequently improves the experience for all students.

To enact a diversity-brave approach, which hears, values, and validates experiences, staff and student mentors share their personal experiences of diversity and success. This helps break down power differentials, creating 'connection' between teaching staff and students (Butcher, 2006) and generating 'meaningful experiences' for students which contribute to "agency, belonging, and competence—three assets that are essential to youth development" (Mitra, 2004, p. 651). This story-telling approach enables students to feel more able to engage with staff and mentors, and to imagine their future selves (Markus and Nurius, 1986; Harrison, 2018), who belong in HE and overcome any challenges they experience. Again, this approach demonstrates institutional and course commitment to recognising, valuing, and discussing diversity rather than ignoring or denigrating difference. The candid conversations empower students to belong and succeed, while also providing staff with insights to help them ensure learning and support is inclusive of the students enrolled in the course. Other group activities, such as taking, selecting, and captioning photos about belonging and not belonging, promote peer interaction and contribute to the early development of networks of support and relationships with peers that contribute to belonging (Thomas, 2012).

Towards the end of the first DD, when there has been significant time spent on acknowledging and discussing diversity, belonging and success, and relationships and trust have started to be nurtured, the 'snowballs and aeroplanes' activity (Thomas, forthcoming) has been effective. This final activity is designed to provide students with an opportunity to anonymously share information with the staff team. Students are asked to write on a separate piece of paper and complete the sentences: "I want you to know this about me… " and "You can support me to be successful by…". They then make the paper into a 'snowball' or an 'aeroplane' and throw it to the front of the room. (This has been adapted for online delivery, to use an anonymous message board for people to post their answers and providing students with a personal email to encourage them to get in touch.)

In 2019, DD1 was undertaken, with around 300 Primary Education students in a tiered lecture theatre on the second day of term. The snowballs and aeroplanes activity received 226 responses. 23 students identified serious issues and included their name and a request for support (this is just over 10 per cent). Nine students provided their name but wrote positive comments, including looking forward to the course and offering to support other students. 160 students (over 70 per cent) identified issues and ways in which they would like to be supported to be successful. These included quite serious concerns relating to anxiety, caring responsibilities, and about their ability to be a good teacher. Others noted nervousness, shyness, the need to be organised, along with challenges with commuting and car parking, in particular. Frequent ways to be supported included: to be friendly, to ask if I'm OK even if I look OK, to be patient, to explain things simply, to be available to offer support and to provide academic guidance with assignments, presentations and developing confidence/public speaking.

- I would like you to know that I can be shy and unorganised but you can help me by involving me in discussions and being patient with me.
- I'm very anxious and quiet in new situations and around new people. You can help by knowing I'm not being rude or lazy it just takes me a bit of time to settle in.
- You should know that I like learning visually and I like to ask questions when learning to ensure I am doing the task correctly. You can help me by having regular check-ins and knowing that I struggle getting information to stay in my brain.
- I'd like you to know that I sometimes overthink and get anxious about assignments You can help me to be successful by explaining and giving an estimated time of how long it should take.
- I like you to know I get quiet on certain days. You can help me by knowing I'm not upset, angry or annoyed with anyone, it's just extra hard on those days.
- I am an introvert. You can help me by asking me questions directly to include me in a conversation.
- I'd like you to know… that I sometimes struggle to make friends You can help me be successful by… being friendly and approachable.
- You should no that I am not very confident in my English ability. You can help me to be successful by giving me advise on different ways I can go about improving my English skills.

This activity generated important information about the new cohort of students and indicates that the DD was successful in enabling students to trust and share some insecurities. In the first year, the information was grouped into themes and shared with personal tutors, many of whom had not attended the DD. In the coming weeks, the value of the DD was recognised, and this made it easier to engage the whole staff team in, not only attending, but leading and contributing to future DDs, and learning first hand with their students about diversity, belonging, and success. Thus, in the second year of implementation, the student responses to the snowballs and aeroplanes activity went directly to tutors who facilitated the activity; of those shared back to the #Ibelong team, very similar themes emerged.

Tutors having (early) access to this information, and engaging in the DD to develop connections, trust, and understanding, allows them to address many of the issues and concerns through the group tutorial process. This developmental approach was reinforced by the TTR activities, which worked through course team meetings to develop a frame of reference for a sense of belonging for the teaching team, and to address real challenges identified by DDs, SCMs or by staff. Learning from the snowballs and aeroplanes activity in 2019 informed a new initiative called 'Just ask me if I'm OK', which checked-in on students each week by email during the first semester, only requiring them to respond with a number, and allowing tutors to follow up students who indicated they were not OK (this was inspired by an intervention at St Marys University – Thomas et al., 2017, pp. 52–53).

The student mentors, who contributed to the design and delivery of the DDs, and who shared their stories, also played an on-going student support role through one-to-one and group peer mentoring sessions. Feedback from mentors suggested that reflecting on diversity, belonging, and success had enhanced their understanding of these issues. Sharing their personal stories enabled students to approach them for support, especially about specific issues they spoke about.

Conclusions, implications, and recommendations

The DDs were evaluated using a programme evaluation tool (Thomas, 2020b); students benefitted by making friends, getting to know staff, gaining understanding about diversity and the importance and challenges of belonging and success; and staff developed understanding about the diversity of their students and their support needs. Subsequently, staff were able to build changes and support into their teaching and tutoring to help all students prosper, and they were able to make early contact with those who identified specific challenges. The impact of the DDs were greater because they were delivered to the course in conjunction with TTR and SCM initiatives. The evaluation also identified the following lessons about DDs:

1 DD1 is most effective during the first week of the academic year
2 DDs need to be embedded into the teaching, both in terms of the timetable, and making links to the curriculum if possible
3 Teaching staff need to participate fully in the DDs
4 Smaller groups (e.g. led by tutors or mentors) are an effective way of promoting more active engagement by students – and staff
5 DDs need to be organised for a specific student cohort, rather than several courses
6 Online learning or a blended approach allows the activities to take place over a longer period of time, allowing the issues to be addressed in more detail, embedding the learning into the course, and intensifying the impact.

Student support needs to be made available to all students in an accessible way through the curriculum. Focusing on diversity, belonging, and success, using a diversity-brave approach has proven to be effective in building connections, breaking down barriers, and allowing students to share concerns and support needs. It is, therefore, suggested that other institutions and courses consider what they could learn from embedding student support through a model such as #Ibelong, which has created a safe space for students to discuss and share issues. A further strength is the complementary staff development (TTR) and the active role of mentors (SCMs) in DDs and in delivering support sessions.

References

Baboeram, P. (2020). Getting comfortable with the uncomfortable: 5 uncomfortable situations in the classroom (or other educational settings) and how to constructively deal with them. #Ibelong. Available at: https://ibelong.eu/2020/11/24/getting-comfortable-with-the-uncomfortable-5-uncomfortable-situations-in-the-classroom-or-other-educational-settings-and-how-to-constructively-deal-with-them/ (accessed 9 March 2022)

Butcher, S. (2006). Narrative as a teaching strategy. *Journal of Correctional Education*, 57(3), 195–208.

Dodgson, R and Bolam, H. (2002). *Student Retention, Support and Widening Participation in the North East of England*. Sunderland: Universities for the North East.

Donnelly, M. and Gamsu, S. (2018). *Home and Away—Social, Ethnic and Spatial Inequalities in Student Mobility*. London, UK: The Sutton Trust.

Harris, M. (2001). *Developing Modern HE Careers Services*. Available at: www.dfes.gov.uk/hecareersservice/pdfshecaereersservicereview.pdf

Harrison, N. (2018). Using the lens of "possible selves" to explore access to higher education: A new conceptual model for practice, policy, and research. *Social Sciences*, 7(10), 209.

Hobson, M. (2014). Color blind or color brave? TED Talk. Available at: https://www.ted.com/talks/mellody_hobson_color_blind_or_color_brave?language=en

Maguire, D. and Morris, D. (2018). *Homeward Bound: Defining, Understanding and Aiding 'Commuter Students'*. Oxford: Higher Education Policy Institute.

Markus, H. and Nurius, P. (1986). Possible selves. *American Psychologist*, 41(9), 954–969.

McCary, J., Pankhurst, S., Valentine, H., and Berry, A. (2011). *A Comparative Evaluation of the Roles of Student Adviser and Personal Tutor in Relation to Undergraduate Student Retention. What Works Final Report*. Cambridge: Anglia Ruskin University.

Mitra, D.L. (2004). The significance of students: Can increasing "student voice" in schools lead to gains in youth development? *Teachers College Record*, 106(4), 651–688.

National Audit Office (NAO) (2002). *Improving Student Achievement in English Higher Education*. London: The Stationery Office.

Owen, M. (2002). Sometimes you feel you're in niche time: The personal tutor system, a case study. *Active Learning in Higher Education*, 3(1), 7–23.

Thomas, L. (2012). *Building Student Engagement and Belonging in Higher Education at a Time of Change: Final Report from the What Works? Student Retention & Success Programme*. London: Paul Hamlyn Foundation.

Thomas, L. (2020a). "I am happy just doing the work…". Commuter student engagement and success and lessons for other equity groups. *Higher Education Quarterly*, 74(3), 290–303.

Thomas, L. (2020b). Using logic chain and theory of change tools to evaluate widening participation: Learning from the What Works? Student Retention and Success programme. *Widening Participation and Lifelong Learning*, 22(2), 67–82.

Thomas, L. (forthcoming) *Dialogue Days (IO1). #Ibelong: Towards a Sense of Belonging in an Inclusive Learning Environment*. Rotterdam: Erasmus University.

Thomas, L., Hill, M., O' Mahony, J., and Yorke, M. (2017). *Supporting Student Success: Strategies for Institutional Change. What Works? Student Retention and Success Programme. Final Report*. London: Paul Hamlyn Foundation.

Thomas, L. and Hixenbaugh, P. (2006). *Personal Tutoring in Higher Education*. Stoke-on-Trent: Trentham Books.

Thomas, L., Quinn, J., Slack, K., and Casey, L. (2002). *Student Services: Effective Approaches to Retaining Students in Higher Education*. Stoke-on-Trent: Institute for Access Studies, Staffordshire University.

Woodfield, R. and Thomas, L. (2012). *Male Students: Engagement with Academic and Pastoral Support Services*. London: Equality Challenge Unit.

Chapter 7

Physical Campus & Built Environment

7.1 The campus as a canvas

How the built environment embodies a university's journey towards inclusion for all

Kim Lombard

An inclusive university physical campus and built environment is one that caters for the diverse needs of the population so that as many users as possible can access, navigate, and use the campus facilities without the need for specific accommodations, modifications, or assistive technologies and, hence, can engage in all aspects of university life. Within occupational therapy, much of practice revolves around analysing the transactive relationship between the person (i.e. motor, cognitive, and affective aspects), their environment (i.e. physical, social, cultural, socio-economic, and institutional environments), and the occupations or activities with which they need or want to perform in their everyday lives (Law et al., 1996), which is demonstrated in the Person–Environment–Occupation Model (PEO) diagram in Figure 7.1. The aim of this model is to identify environmental or occupational adaptations that can be made to support participation, health, and well-being through occupational performance (i.e. how well one is able to engage in their everyday activities) by understanding how the person, their environments, and their occupations are interrelated (American Occupational Therapy Association, 2020). Occupational performance is a lifelong experience, constantly being influenced by the transactive relationship between these three factors (Law et al., 1996). In relation to the environment, we are concerned with 'environmental impact', which is how the opportunities, constraints, demands, and resources of one's physical, social, cultural, economic, and political environments influence occupational engagement (Kielhofner, 2008).

Within the context of a higher education institution, the physical campus and built environment greatly influence how well users can engage in everyday university activities, including teaching and learning, research, recreation, residential activities, retail, sport, and well-being activities. Moreover, it cannot be forgotten that a university is as much a workplace for faculty and professional staff as it is an educational environment for students. Considering the PEO Model (Law et al., 1996), the greater the overlap or congruence between the users of a university, the university environment, and the activities in which the users seek to engage in, the greater levels of occupational performance and inclusivity that can be achieved. Conversely, if the environment and set-up of activities within a university conflict with the diversity of needs experienced by its users across their lifespan, this threatens inclusivity and accessibility, and may

DOI: 10.4324/9781003253631-23

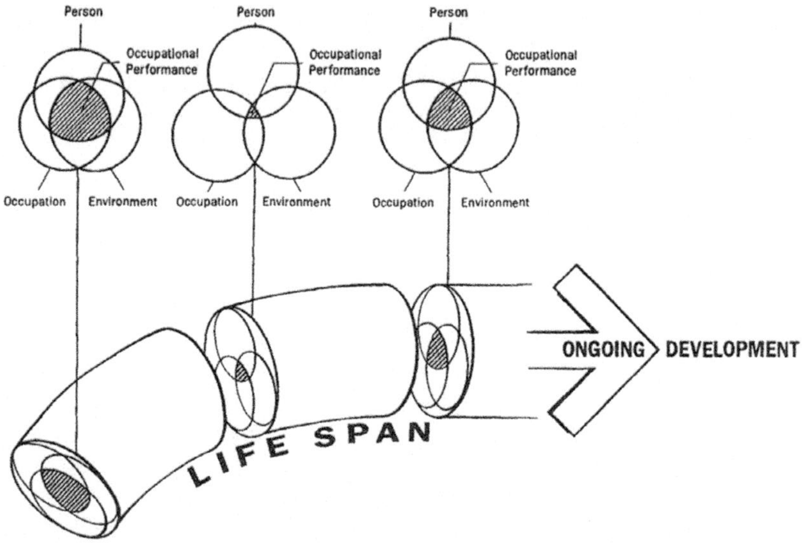

Figure 7.1 Person–Environment–Occupation Model of Occupational Performance
Source: Law, M. et al. (1996) 'The Person–Environment–Occupation Model: A transactive approach to occupational performance', Canadian Journal of Occupational Therapy, 63(1), 9–23.

discourage diversity within the university population. It is for this reason that higher education institutions should not only seek to understand the diversity of their users' needs across the range of university activities, but should also seek to understand and appreciate the role that the university environment plays within the process of creating a university for all.

The primary focus of this chapter will be on the physical campus and built environment of a university, but it is acknowledged that other elements of the university environment are equally important to consider together in creating a university for all, which is highlighted in other chapters of this book. For example, having an inclusive built environment for all students is ideal, but is made redundant if the institutional policies and procedures exclude students from diverse backgrounds from accessing the university system in the first instance. The physical campus environment is the most tangible aspect of an institution's environment and hence can arguably be viewed as the most tangible display of an institution's commitment to, and progress towards, inclusion. For many campuses, older campus infrastructure was built at a time in which accessibility and inclusion was not a high priority and in which diversifying the population of higher education was not desired. As a result, many institutions are faced with balancing addressing legacy accessibility issues with developing more inclusive buildings in the future.

In order for all students to be able to engage in all aspects of student life, it is imperative that the university built environment fosters inclusion and is responsive to the diverse needs of the student population. One group which might come to mind when thinking about inclusion in the built environment is people with disabilities. Imrie (2012) and Shuayb (2020) document the historical developments in paradigm and attitude shifts that have occurred regarding creating more accessible built environments for people with disabilities in order to have equitable opportunities for engaging in everyday life as anyone else in society. This has been the product of the disability rights movement beginning in the 1960s which has advocated for a shift in how we view disability from a medical model (i.e. one's impairment was the main reason they could not interact with the environment) towards a social model of disability (i.e. disability is a result of society providing disabling environments hence excluding certain groups from engagement) (Barnes, 1991; Shuayb, 2020). Around the world, this has resulted in the development of regulations and guidelines which provide tools for designers to design spaces that can be accessed and used by people with disabilities (Shuayb, 2020). However, this often results in designs for the built environment catering for the minimum standard of accessibility (Imrie, 2012; Ringaert, 2003) rather than the inclusion of as many people as possible. Developing a physical environment that is inclusive of people with disabilities is captured in the following response to a survey conducted with access students from University College Dublin (UCD) in November 2017 which asked, 'What does "University for All" mean to you?':

> "A university where I can get around without needing to wait for someone to open a door or go the long way around away from my friends and other students. A university where we all go to class together and no one is left separate".

There are several case studies investigating the implementation of inclusive design within the physical campus and built environment for people with disabilities. For example, students studying in the Faculty of Architecture, Slovak University of Technology in Bratislava, were involved in a project entitled 'Universal Design of the built environment focused on the inclusion of people with disabilities into the education and the work process' (Ceresnova, 2014). One aspect of this project involved students conducting simulation exercises in buildings with full adaptations, partial adaptations, and within new buildings which sought to have no physical barriers from the perspective of a person with either a physical disability or a sensory disability. Through these simulations, students identified some supports within the environment such as easy to find entrances, ramps, and tactile guiding lines on raised platforms but encountered several accessibility challenges in all three types of buildings, such as: lack of multisensory wayfinding; access to rooms but lack of appropriate usage for services such as a reception desk being too high; separated space for wheelchair users in lecture theatres; difficult navigation routes from transport to the main entrance; and challenges with self-closing door systems. Raheja and Suryawanshi's (2014) participatory research in Jawaharlal Nehru University (JNU), New Delhi, aimed to capture the lived experiences of 89 students with visual impairments, as well as students with physical disabilities who used mobility aids, regarding the identification, auditing, and planning of retrofitting solutions within the campus environment. One aspect of the study involved focus groups with the students to gather their qualitative experiences of barriers within the physical environment, such as the absence of path navigation blocks, difficulties with undulating sites, unpaved surfaces resulting in students having to use longer and more inconvenient routes between buildings and experiencing high levels of fatigue, challenges with inaccessible toilets, obstructions within corridors, and the absence of railings for safety. Nevertheless, the students highlighted supportive aspects of the environment, including access to screen reading software such as Jaws, access to a Braille printer, and engaging with staff who were sensitive to their needs. Another aspect of the study involved developing, piloting, and validating an audit tool and conducting accessibility audits on campus buildings. The audits identified issues and potential solutions for parking and entrances, horizontal and vertical circulation of buildings, access to services such as accessible toilets and drinking water fountains, aspects of building interiors such as ramps, handrails, and the height of door latches, as well as appropriate signage and wayfinding systems on campus. However, due to funding issues, implementation of the recommendations was prioritised according to the number of people with specific disabilities, the severity of the physical barriers, and the site in which the barriers existed.

As can be seen, the above studies focused primarily on the accessibility needs of people with sensory and physical disabilities. However, the studies did not consider the needs within the physical environment of people with other disabilities such as autism, mental health difficulties, dyspraxia, dyslexia, attention deficit hyperactivity disorder, or significant ongoing illnesses. Not only is it essential to consider the needs of all people with disabilities, but also the needs of users from other diverse backgrounds who may experience various challenges when attempting to engage with the physical campus and built environment. There are many kinds of users in a university (e.g. students, staff, visitors, research participants, service personnel) from various backgrounds who have particular needs at different points in time, including, but not limited to, users with a physical, cognitive, sensory, or mental health disability, low-income users, mature entrants, people from international backgrounds with different languages and cultures, part-time users, users who are pregnant, users who have a temporary illness or injury, or users of various ages and genders. For the physical campus environment to be truly inclusive, the needs of this wide range of users must be considered holistically. An inclusive physical campus not only considers accessible ramps and doors but also expands the scope to consider the inclusivity of campus facilities and amenities for the diversity of users. This is where Universal Design comes into the equation, as it aims to develop environments and products within the environment that are usable by as many people as possible (Mace, 1985;

Steinfeld and Maisel, 2012). Universal Design aims to go beyond mere compliance with accessibility standards for people with disabilities, seeking to design environments in which all users are enabled to engage, as captured by Salmen (2011):

> Accessibility is a function of compliance with regulations or criteria that establish a minimum level of design necessary to accommodate people with disabilities. Universal design, however, is the art and practice of design to accommodate the widest variety and number of people throughout their life spans.
>
> (p. 6.1)

This raises the question – What does a Universally Designed physical campus and built environment look like? How can it cater for the needs of various users? First and foremost, there must be an appreciation for the breadth and depth of potential human functioning (Ringaert, 2003) within the university built environment. This can be achieved by involving and consulting diverse user-experts in the design process who can assist in identifying the barriers that exist within the environment and in developing strategies to overcome these (Ostroff, 1997). Incorporating user voices into the design process can highlight elements of the physical environment that may not have been considered by designers who are not going to be using that environment directly themselves. When considering the built environment, each aspect should be examined, including external considerations (e.g. access to buildings, wayfinding, parking, service dog facilities, etc.), internal considerations (e.g. wayfinding, inclusive WC facilities, communication systems, accessible lecture theatres, use of light, use of materials, noise levels, quiet spaces, etc.), as well as appropriately designed student accommodation (Kelly and Padden, 2018). This applies to both upgrading existing buildings as well as developing plans for future campus infrastructure. Capturing user-oriented data can help inform priorities for improving inclusivity of the physical campus, as the accessibility issues that exist may be context specific.

An example of this is the University for All Student and Staff surveys that were conducted in University College Dublin (UCD) in 2020 (outlined in the introduction to this book). These surveys aimed to gather the experiences of both students and staff in each Pillar of the University for All Toolkit (Kelly and Padden, 2018) and were completed by students and staff from various backgrounds. In relation to 'Pillar 3: Physical Campus & Built Environment', respondents were given the opportunity to comment on and make suggestions for improvement, some of which are illustrated in Table 7.1. This highlighted unique ways in which UCD's physical campus could be improved for the benefit of all users. For example, having access to a cross-campus shuttle service would benefit users with disabilities who may experience fatigue issues, while also benefiting the likes of a pregnant user, a user who is transporting heavy or bulky items across campus, or making a campus more easily

Table 7.1 Sample responses to Physical Campus & Built Environment question on the 2020 University for All Student and Staff surveys

External considerations	• Sufficient parking and appropriate costs especially for commuters who are dependent on a car or part-time students • Appropriate signage and wayfinding that caters for diverse abilities (e.g. Braille, ISL etc.) and languages • Accessibility of the campus (e.g., widening corridors/doors, functioning automated doors, considering the distance/routes between buildings) • Benefits of having green spaces for relaxation and exercise • Coverage of walkways and appropriate drainage of footpaths • Sufficient lighting on walkways, especially for accessing public transport at night • Sufficient bike parking and separate cycle lanes for cyclists • Access to a regular cross-campus trolley/shuttle to assist with getting across campus in a timely manner.
Internal considerations	• Need for increased seating and areas for students to either study and/or socialise in between classes • Appropriate signage and wayfinding within buildings and representing diversity in posters throughout the campus • Accessibility and materials used in lecture theatres (e.g. comfortable seating, non-fixed/standing desks, options for wheelchair users) • Sufficient library opening hours, seating, and quieter study spaces • Accessible changing rooms and hot water in the university gym • Catering to students' sensory needs by considering the acoustics, crowd-control, quiet spaces, temperature, and lighting • Greater access to inclusive toilets for users of any ability, height, gender • Access to other spaces such as prayer rooms, respite/napping space, breastfeeding facilities • Increased access to facilities such as water fountains, charging outlets, microwaves, and recycling bins across all buildings.
Student accommodation	• Providing more affordable on-campus accommodation for students from low-income backgrounds • Opportunities for commuter/part-time students to book accommodation to promote engagement in social events/ irregular classes or exams • More consideration for on-campus accommodation to cater for mature or international students who have families.

accessible for those whose discipline is located in more remote areas. Moreover, increasing the availability of versatile spaces for students to socialise or study together can improve overall student experience and well-being, while bookable accommodation by commuter or part-time students can enhance their engagement with certain campus activities such as evening social events.

Nonetheless, creating an inclusive physical campus and built environment relies on advancements within the other aspects of the social, cultural, socio-economic, and institutional environments of a university. As described in Chapter 2, university institutions are complex organisations, and the reality is that creating a university for all requires a journey of cultural and institutional change – a journey which takes considerable time and effort to implement. The case studies illustrated in this chapter tell a story of how a university can go about starting this journey in order to create an inclusive university built environment by using both systems-approaches and grassroots approaches while being informed by user-oriented data and collaboration/empowerment of campus services, all the while being underpinned by a whole institution approach to inclusion (Figure 7.2).

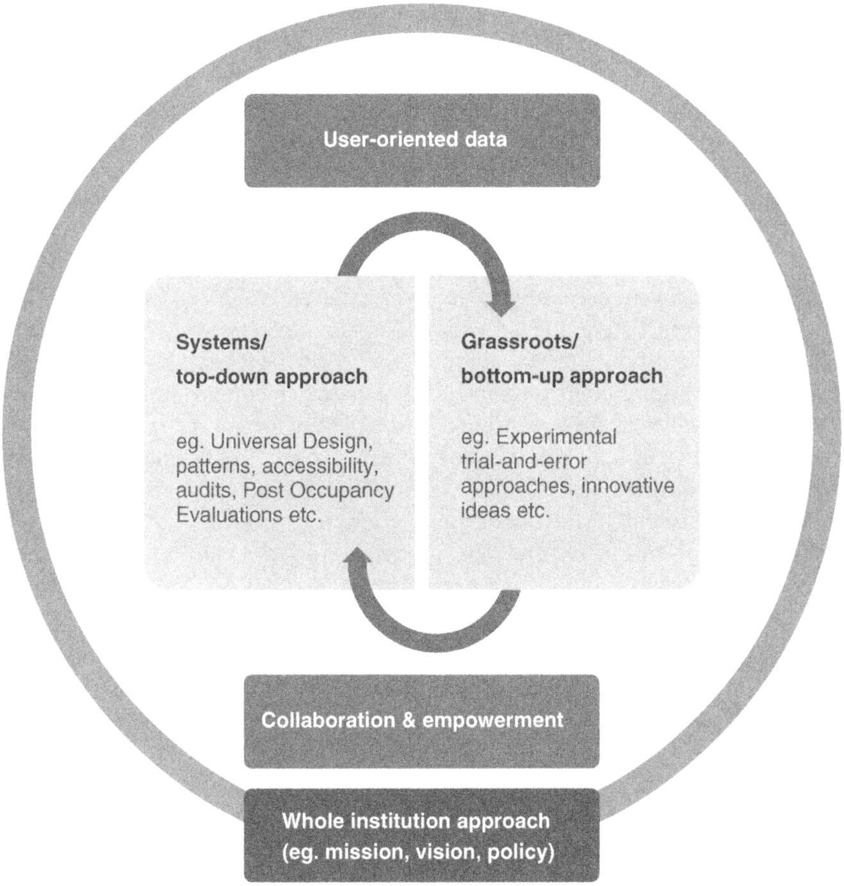

Figure 7.2 Approaches to creating an inclusive physical campus and built environment

The first case study (7.2) by international contributor Hubert Froyen provides an architecture-theoretical perspective on the importance of Universal Design for creating inclusive campus environments for all users. Froyen argues the need for architecture curricula to embed Universal Design, the importance of developing dynamic databases of Universal Design Patterns which captures both user-oriented design and advancements in technological solutions and which provides experimental plans for transforming conventional sanitary facilities into universally designed 'care rooms'. However, throughout Froyen's piece, the real-life challenges of creating an inclusive campus and physical environment are captured – namely, a lack of a whole-institutional approach and commitment towards creating an inclusive university, as well as subsequent budgetary roadblocks in implementing projects to improve the inclusivity of the built environment.

Following on from this, the second case study (7.3) by Fiona Sweeney and Tina Lowe and the final case study (7.4) by Tadgh Corcoran and Thomas Hamill, respectively, capture the journey towards developing an inclusive physical campus and built environment using a whole-institutional approach from the perspectives of a university access service and a university estate service working collaboratively towards a shared goal. Sweeney and Lowe provide practical guidance on how the university access service began this process, documenting the progress that has been made to date. This includes establishing dedicated roles for campus accessibility, providing consultation and awareness raising, and fostering collaborative relationships with Estate Services while ultimately mainstreaming the responsibility and financial commitment of campus accessibility to Estate Services. Corcoran and Hamill provide the perspective from a university Estate Service of this journey, including the evolution of the campus, how they deal with and consistently monitor legacy accessibility challenges of existing buildings, and how they are embedding Universal Design principles into plans for future campus projects as they acknowledge the benefits of an inclusive built environment of a university. Overall, these case studies acknowledge the need for time, effort, and commitment using a whole-institution approach to ensure that access and inclusion of all within the physical campus and built environment becomes everyone's business.

References

American Occupational Therapy Association (2020). *Occupational Therapy Practice Framework: Domain and Process*, 4th edn. *The American Journal of Occupational Therapy*, 74(Supplement 2).

Barnes, C. (1991). *Disabled People in Britain and Discrimination*. London: Hurst and Co.

Ceresnova, Z. (2014). Student engagement in assessment of universal access of university buildings. In P.M. Langdon, J. Lazar, A. Heylighen, and H. Dong (eds), *Inclusive Designing: Joining Usability, Accessibility, and Inclusion*. Switzerland: Springer International Publishing, pp. 143–151.

Imrie, R. (2012). Universalism, universal design and equitable access to the built environment. *Disability and Rehabilitation*, 34(10), 873–882.

Kelly, A.M. and Padden, L. (2018). *University for All Toolkit for Inclusive Higher Education Institutions – From Vision to Practice.* University College Dublin Access & Lifelong Learning. Available at: https://www.ucd.ie/all/t4media/0274_UCD_TOOLKIT_1118_ONLINE_LR.pdf (accessed 15 March 2022).

Kielhofner, G. (2008). The environment and human occupation. In G. Kielhofner G (ed.), *Model of Human Occupation: Theory and Application*, 4th edn. Baltimore, MD: Lippincott Williams & Wilkins, pp. 85–100.

Law, M., Cooper, B.A., Strong, S., Stewart, D., Rigby, P., and Letts, L. (1996). The Person–Environment–Occupation Model: A transactive approach to occupational performance. *Canadian Journal of Occupational Therapy*, 63(1), 9–23.

Mace, R. (1985). Universal design: Barrier-free environments for everyone. *Designer West*, 3, 147–152.

Ostroff, E. (1997). Mining our natural resources: The user as expert. *Innovation, the Quarterly Journal of the Industrial Designers Society of America*, 16, 33–35.

Raheja, G. and Suryawanshi, S. (2014). Inclusive strategies for universal access in educational campus environments. In P.M. Langdon, J. Lazar, A. Heylighen, and H. Dong (eds), *Inclusive Designing: Joining Usability, Accessibility, and Inclusion.* Switzerland: Springer International Publishing, pp. 165–174.

Ringaert, L. (2003). Universal design of the built environment to enable occupational performance. In L. Letts, P. Rigby, and D. Stewart (eds), *Using Environments to Enable Occupational Performance.* Thorofare, NJ: SLACK Incorporated, pp. 97–116.

Salmen, J.P.S. (2011). U.S. Accessibility Codes and Standards: Challenges for Universal Design. In W.F.E. Preiser and K.H. Smith (eds), *Universal Design Handbook*, 2nd edn. New York: McGraw-Hill, pp. 6. 1–6. 7.

Shauyb, T. (2020). Emergence of design standards and inclusive design. In T. Shauyb (ed.), *Inclusive University Built Environments: The Impact of Approved Document M for Architects, Designers, and Engineers.* Cham, Switzerland: Springer Nature Switzerland, pp. 35–62.

Steinfeld, E. and Maisel, J. (2012). *Universal Design: Creating Inclusive Environments.* Hoboken, NJ: Wiley & Sons.

7.2 Universal Design Patterns for enabling physical environments

Hubert Froyen

Introduction

This piece approaches the general theme of physical spaces for "integral & inclusive education for all" from an architecture-theoretical point of view. The piece outlines a conceptual framework that is nurtured and coloured by the symbiosis of personal experience of physical dis-ability (sic), plus in-depth academic Teaching & Research relative to a methodological approach to the new design paradigm of Universal Design (Froyen, 2012). Emphasis is placed on human-made physical environments and objects, and more specifically on the question of how these can be systematically made more enabling for the wide variety of abilities and disabilities of users.

Over recent decades, there has been a gradual paradigm shift surrounding the understanding of human functioning and factors leading to functional difficulties. On the threshold of the twenty-first century, in 2001, the World Health Organization published the ground-breaking "International Classification of Functioning, Disability and Health" (WHO, 2001). For the first time, in addition to human functioning and functional problems, external environmental and personal factors were also taken into account. This broadens the focus from a human-related disability to possible disabling misfits in the Human–Environment interface.

Decision makers and designers now adopt the Social model / Cultural model, with a special role they have to play in the creation of enabling objects and enabling physical environments. Integral and inclusive design processes go beyond the needs of the stigmatised group of people with permanent health related impairments, adopting an integral and inclusive "Design for All" approach. Designers first analyse misfits in the Human–Environment interface, in so-called Dis-abilty[1] Situations (sic) (Froyen, 2009a). If we design, for example, a portable device that requires two-handed operation, then we create potential Dis-ability Situations (sic) for a whole range of people, both without and with disabling health conditions. Examples include someone riding a bicycle, pushing a pram, injured, suffering from arthritis, a person with congenital limb deficiencies, arm in plaster cast, someone opening a door or using a stair railing, someone who carries a heavy box, a person

DOI: 10.4324/9781003253631-24

with temporary loss or restrictions in manual dexterity, someone pulling a shopping trolley. The English architect, Selwyn Goldsmith, describes, in that regard, the "architecturally disabled" as those who are "disabled because the architect who designed the building did not anticipate their needs, or did not care about them" (Goldsmith, 1997, p. vii).

It is imperative then that decision-makers and designers make thorough (non-medical) analyses of "dis-ability situations" and can then conceptually contribute to environments that are enabling and genuinely comfortable for many more people. To encourage this practice, in 2001 the Council of Europe adopted Resolution ResAP(2001)1, specifically the 'Tomar Resolution', which advocates for the "introduction of the principles of universal design into the curricula of all occupations working on the built environment". Supported by the recommendations of this European Resolution, in the same year, 2001, three Flemish architecture schools received grants from the Government of Flanders' Equal Opportunities Team for a five-year "Universal Design Education Project" (UDEP, 2001–2006). Teachers from the three schools integrated Universal Design (UD) into the educational curricula, and they shared their pedagogical-didactic experiences and insights in a published "Universal Design Toolkit" (Froyen et al., 2006). What lessons were learned from this systematic exploration of the new Universal Design paradigm in the field of architecture education in Flanders? The academic UD Education Project was an excellent incubator to explore the new UD paradigm and to develop adapted education and research. Yet, the broader objective of integrating the theme more permanently into the study programmes of each of the participating architecture schools, in terms of policy and structure, and to disseminate it bottom-up to other study programmes, initially failed.

There were temporary and isolated silos of inspirational good practice, but the new UD paradigm was not yet strong enough to be embedded in the social, the academic, or the professional field. However, the UDEP 2001–2006 did provide a fertile ground for successful thematic workshops, seminars, conferences, publications, design competitions, 24-hour challenges, science communication to the general public and to policymakers, UD doctoral research (Herssens, 2011; Ielegems, 2017; Kapedani, 2021), and even setting up a physical UD Living Lab for demonstration and education (Figure 7.3). Although individual academics carried out the project and coordinated their own UD teaching and research, an institution-wide approach to inclusion and a structure for continuity was not yet attained. Now, two decades later, a new generation seems to build on more solid social, academic, and professional foundations in a multi-disciplinary academic approach (e.g. gradual integration of some aspects of Architecture and Occupational Therapy in an experimental Universal-Design-to-Care [UD2Care] programme).

Where do we go from here? What further work needs to be done to continue the movement towards built & social environments that are more enabling? The step-by-step progress towards "integral & inclusive education for all" is a lengthy and complex process that requires generative techniques.

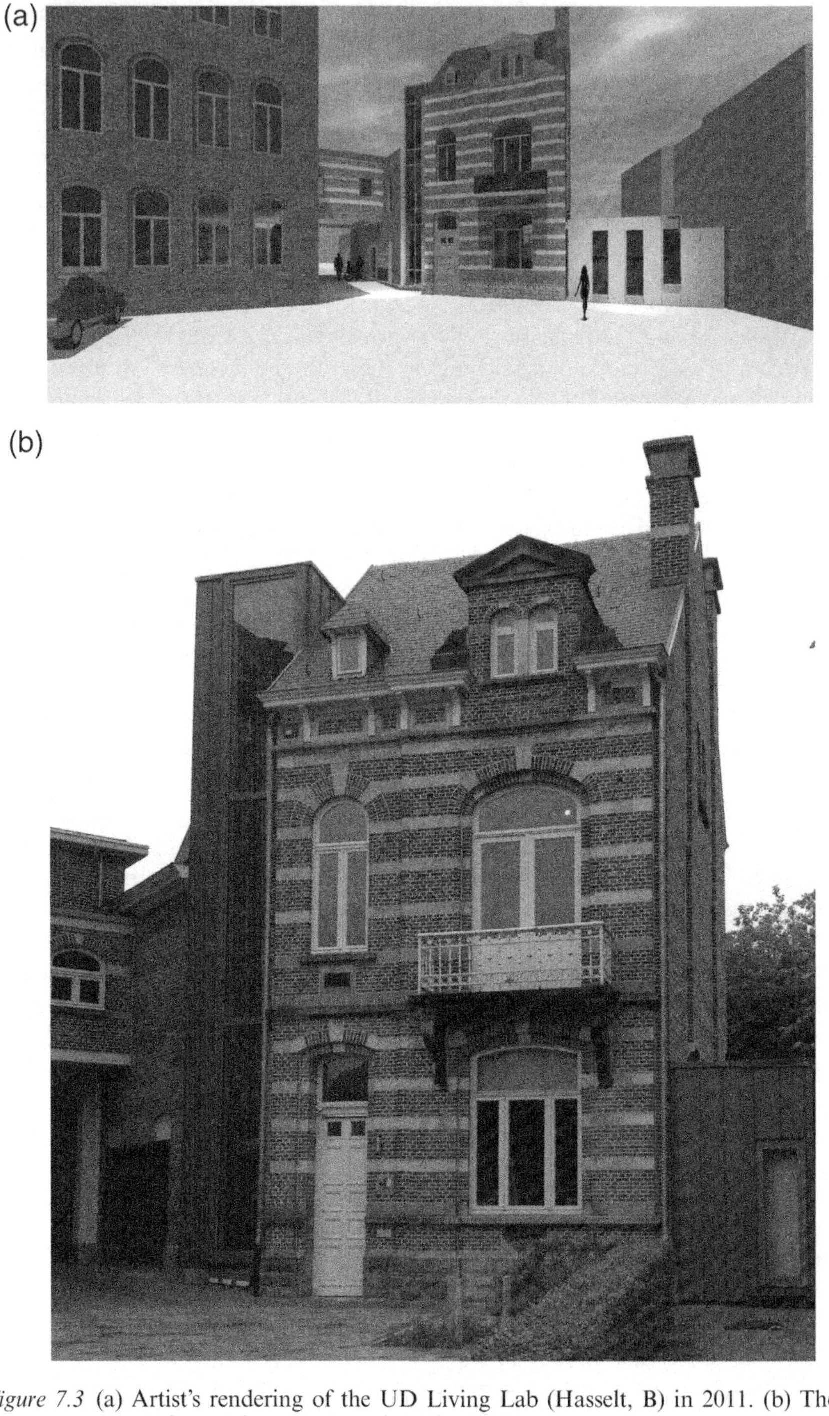

Figure 7.3 (a) Artist's rendering of the UD Living Lab (Hasselt, B) in 2011. (b) The renovation project was completed in 2013

First of all, there needs to be a mission statement, a clear vision of shared inclusion goals, plus an overall inclusion policy. Second, a system approach towards Design-for-All is essential. And last, but not least, a diversity of trial-and-error grassroots approaches that will gradually lead to a more consistent body of knowledge and experience. The next two sections will focus on two research projects carried out at UHasselt (Hasselt University, B). In the first section, I discuss a methodological approach to the Universal Design paradigm through the development of reusable UD Patterns (Systems approach). The second section describes an experimental design for "Rooms for Care & Well-being" in public spaces (Grassroots approach).

Universal Design Patterns for enabling physical environments (Systems approach)

> In the epistemological fault zone that designers are currently traversing, the renaissance ideal of designing for the universal person is gradually being transformed into a contemporary goal of universal designing for the relevant variety of real people in real situations.
>
> The notion of the normality of users of human-made environments is becoming less exclusive and is gradually also including people with permanent, temporary and / or situational functional limitations throughout all phases of the life cycle.
>
> (Froyen, 2008, p. 249)

In order to design a physical campus and a built environment that is inclusive for all, there needs to be a shift in the guides used to inform architectural design. Classic prescriptive design guides such as *Architects' Data* (German title: *Bauentwurfslehre*; Neufert et al., 2019) are outdated. They are based on model people without physical, sensory, mental, or functional limitations. We regard the original German *Bauentwurfslehre* (BEL) as an exponent of the modern pursuit of the "ideal architecture for the ideal human being". Hence, a large amount of additional empirical information in connection with human disabilities, related to disabling physical environments, is needed.

As a contemporary alternative to outdated and static design guides we propose, in our research and methodological approach, a dynamic database of descriptive Universal Design Patterns (UD Patterns) (Froyen, 2008). These reusable design patterns are in permanent dialogue with all involved parties because insights into functional limitations and disability situations are continuously evolving, and the possible morphological/technological solutions are improving.

> UD Patterns form the core elements of the proposed methodological approach. They provide relevant information in a structured way, both about Problems (CONFLICTS) that are experienced in handicap (sic) situations by users (with specific permanent limitations or non-permanent

> temporary or situational limitations) and empirically supported Architectural/Technological Solutions (RESOLUTIONS). Since the documented solutions are always tentative and a large amount of room remains open for innovative concepts, we prefer to describe the UD Pattern approach as an adapted problem definition method. By explicitly giving attention in the UD Patterns to the Problem Definitions (CONFLICTS), we differ fundamentally from the many prescriptive ("do this") legal ordinances and building regulations that are presently used in design and building processes.
>
> UD Patterns accurately capture descriptions of the "why" for each design parameter. By their descriptive nature, they also contribute to a broad user-oriented design and building culture that complements the prescriptive national and European laws and norms. For the development and the continual updating and improvement of UD Patterns, we propose that conventional empirical research be combined with peer review (user-experts) and with a broad exchange of (Open Content, OC) information and communication via the Internet.
>
> (Froyen, 2008, pp. 253–254)

For further Research & Development, a possible online Wiki-like database of UD Patterns for human-made environments could be fed by user-experts representing a broad spectrum of disabilities. They would serve as "miner's canaries" to reveal and expose problems and difficulties as "they can most precisely analyse the characteristics of the misfit and help in finding better universal design solutions" (Froyen, 2003, p. 20). Not only do user-experts detect and formulate impeding situations, but often they have also sought and found directly applicable innovative solutions. People with permanent or long-term functional disabilities can make unique and valuable contributions to the ongoing advancement of society, as envisioned in the "cultural model" (Devlieger et al., 2003) of disability perception.

The initial concept, the structure, and the academic use of UD Patterns have been extensively researched, tested in experimental academic settings, and published (Froyen, 2008, 2012). A major next step in the process of operationalisation is the development of multiple media strategies to recruit user-experts in the real world, to disseminate knowledge about UD, to collect and to edit the data generated, and to transfer UD-knowledge to decision makers and designers. A dedicated Wiki-site, which is designed for all user-experts, academics, and professionals, to easily formulate and share experienced misfits in physical environments, plus to suggest possible solutions for enabling environments, ought to be developed in reality and tested next. In addition to researching existing thematic design guidelines for accessibility and usability, and in addition to interviews and workshops, we also want to take full advantage of advanced technology and digitization, and of popular aspects of internet culture such as forums and social media. In light of this, the UD Patterns project could be web-based and multiple media strategies could be utilised to recruit citizen scientists, to educate the participants on the concept of Universal Design, on collecting data, and to discuss and co-create the optimal design solutions for all.

To achieve this, a university could start with regular annual "Occupancy Evaluations" in the field which could primarily focus on accessibility and usability for all, and have the overall physical environment of the campus checked by a mixed group of users, user-experts, and other stakeholders, who map and document misfits and barriers. Secondly, a basic set of online accessibility standards could be documented and updated. This could include a limited number of specific UD Patterns for campus facilities, such as small seminar rooms, lecture halls, administrative facilities, cafeterias, gyms, laboratories, sanitary facilities, etc. Finally, interactive online training could be developed. An example of this is the accessibility e-learning training developed by Scandic (n.d.) – the largest Nordic hotel operator. This interactive online training focuses on advice, tips, tests, and instructional videos showing how to provide good service and create Universal Design facilities, home-away-from-home, in an inclusive setting. Hotel rooms constitute an interesting hybrid form of permanent private versus temporary public accommodation.

Rooms for Care & Well-being (Grassroots approach)

In their private living spaces, in every situation and in every phase of life, people make suitable provisions for their personal needs for eating and drinking, intimacy and privacy, body care and healing, being together or being alone, work and relaxation. It is important that similar facilities also be available and accessible for everyone in public spaces and buildings, in all universities and higher education institutions. We can have a general goal of providing an adapted experience of "*Home away-from-home*" in all human-made environments.

From that point of view, conventional "sanitary facilities" could become true "care rooms", with facilities for more extensive body and mind care for young and old, for rest and recovery, intimacy, and privacy. As an example in that regard, in 2016–2017 several researchers at the Faculty of Architecture of Hasselt University developed a project "Universal Design Rooms for Care & Well-being in public spaces" (Froyen and Bosserez, 2019; Froyen, 2021, pp. 57–58). In Building E, the Faculty of Architecture building on the Diepenbeek Campus of Hasselt University, two existing wheelchair-accessible toilets, a small one (Figure 7.4) and a larger one (Figure 7.5), were redesigned for provision of more integral & inclusive care facilities. The two toilets are on different floors that are connected by stairs and a steel-glass wheelchair accessible elevator. In the experimental design, both rooms are gender-neutral, with adapted facilities for a diversity of standard users, plus for people with motor, sensory, stature, and organ-related functional limitations and those with mental, psychological, and neural diversity. Specific design attention is paid to stoma care (Froyen et al., 2009b), obesity, MCS (multiple

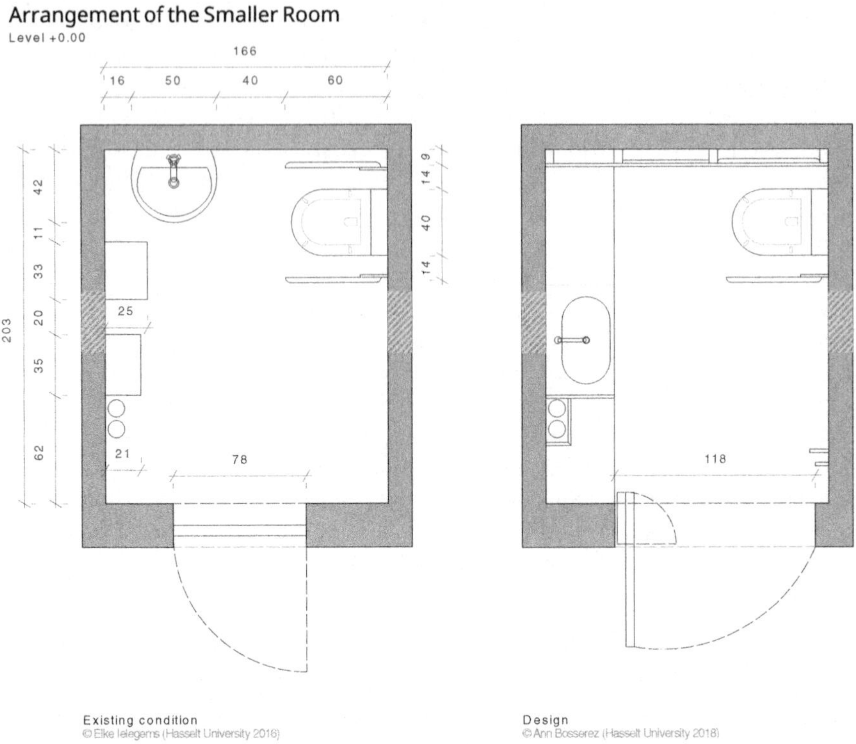

Figure 7.4 Smaller room (166 cm × 203 cm). Existing situation (left) and UD concept for more "Care & Well-being" (right)

chemical hypersensitivity), limited power and reduced stamina, shower facilities, supine care (infant and adult), breastfeeding, daylight entry, artificial light with adjusted colour temperature for mood / body inspection, acoustics, heating / cooling and balanced ventilation. Elements and space are provided for wider doors, shower toilet (WhirlSpray shower technology), support elements, for personal assistance, for a (folding) rest and care bed, guide dog, walker, wheelchair, pram, personal care products, handbag / book bag, clothes hooks, and sanitary waste bins (for women and for men).

However, the experimental project has not been installed. The University's Material Services Department has not provided any means for implementation, highlighting the need to secure appropriate institutional-level annual budgets for adaptation and renovation to implement both at the small-scale renovation level towards major building projects. A fundamental problem was that the experimental process started as a truly bottom-up project without integration in the top-down decision process of the University. Secondly, the pragmatic and restricted plan for renovation was in conflict with the ambitious "Design for All" concept (e.g. dimensions of the rooms remained unchanged, and for budgetary reasons, position and direction of the toilet

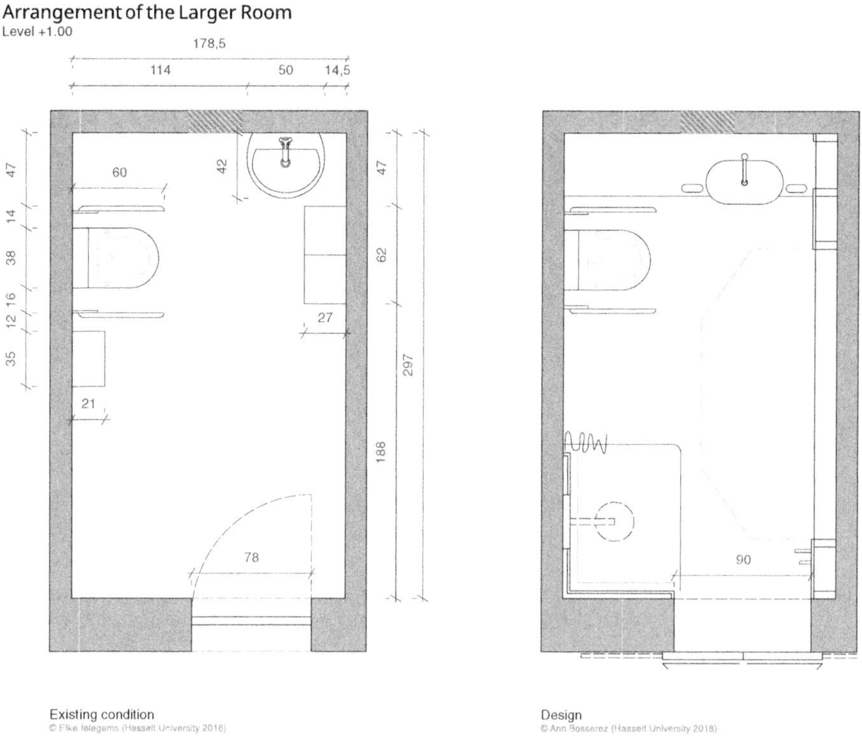

Figure 7.5 Larger room (178 cm × 297 cm). Existing situation (left) and UD for more "Care & Well-being" (right); Graphics: dr. arch. Elke Ielegems, dr. arch. Anne Bosserez, interior arch. Kaat Berben.

bowl was left unaltered, etc.). This is not convincing enough, and is even in conflict with some of the actual building regulations for wheelchair access.

Conclusion

How can universities start with the aim of developing more inclusive physical campus environments? The answer lies through Universal Design. However, this requires an institutional commitment as well as time and effort to engage in both systems and grassroots approaches to develop solutions for inclusivity. The commitment of a university is fundamental for all further inclusivity initiatives.

Finally, the World Health Organization recommends thematic education to address the spatial needs of (older) people in urban settings: "The common recommendation for addressing these concerns is education, particularly for urban planners and architects, about the needs of older people" (WHO, 2007, pp. 15). We can easily widen this pragmatic goal beyond specific needs and can argue that education, from Kindergarten up to university level and lifelong learning, is the cornerstone of social, academic, and professional innovation and progress. Inclusion is an important lever to strengthen our society, to bring comfort and elegance for all, to make it more diverse and more sustainable, and to ultimately promote social justice and equality.

Note

1 The word "disability" invokes (socio-cultural) negative and stigmatising connotations, in addition to its literal or primary meaning. Human beings are almost never 100 per cent abled bodied, nor 100 per cent disabled. Hence dis-ability. Precise wording matters. Dis-ability refers to fluid capacities.

References

Council of Europe (2001). *Resolution ResAP(2001)1 on the Introduction of the Principles of Universal Design into the Curricula of all Occupations Working on the Built Environment*. Available at: https://www.coe.int/en/web/disability/adopted-texts (accessed 4 December 2021).

Devlieger, P., Rusch, F., and Pfeiffer, D. (2003). Rethinking disability as same and different! Towards a cultural model of disability. In P. Devlieger, F. Rusch, and D. Pfeiffer (eds), *Rethinking Disability. The Emergence of New Definitions, Concepts and Communities.* Antwerpen – Apeldoorn: Garant, pp. 9–16.

Froyen, H. (2003). Universal design education. In M. Dujardin and I. Dua (eds), *Universal Design Education. Proceedings of the Scientific Contact Forum, Brussels, Belgium, May 17, 2002*. Brussels: Royal Flemish Academy of Belgium for Science and the Arts, pp.17–21.

Froyen, H., Asaert, C., Dujardin, M., and Herssens, J. (2006). *Ontwerpen voor Iedereen, integraal en inclusief. Universal Design Toolkit*. Brussels: Ministerie van de Vlaamse Gemeenschap, Gelijke Kansen in Vlaanderen.

Froyen, H. (2008). Universal Design Patterns and their use in designing inclusive environments. In P. Langdon, J. Clarkson, and P. Robinson (eds), *Designing Inclusive Futures.* London: Springer-Verlag, pp. 249–260.

Froyen, H., Verdonck, E., De Meester, D., and Heylighen, A. (2009a). Documenting handicap situations and eliminations through Universal Design Patterns. *Australasian Medical Journal, AMJ,* 1(12), 199–203.

Froyen, H., Verdonck, E., De Meester, D., and Heylighen, A. (2009b). Universal Design Patterns for stoma care away-from-home. *Australasian Medical Journal, AMJ,* 1(13), 213–216.

Froyen, H. (2012). *Universal Design. A Methodological Approach. A Pathway to Human-Friendly and Elegant Architecture.* Boston, MA: Institute for Human Centered Design.

Froyen, H. and Bosserez, A. (2019). 'Universal Design Rooms for Care & Well-being in public spaces', unpublished article. Hasselt University, Faculty of Architecture.

Froyen, H. (2021). *Universal Design als basis, Leersteun voor iedereen.* Architectuur maakt school. Brussels: Politeia, pp. 45–67.

Goldsmith, S. (1997). *Designing for the Disabled, The New Paradigm.* Oxford: Architectural Press / Butterworth-Heinemann.

Herssens, J. (2011). *Designing Architecture for More. A Framework of Haptic Design Parameters with the Experience of People Born Blind*, unpublished PhD thesis, PHL University College / Hasselt University.

Ielegems, E. (2017). *Designers' Knowledge Building in (Universal) Design Processes*, unpublished PhD thesis, Faculty of Architecture and Arts, Hasselt University,

Kapedani, E. (2021). *Indoor Environmental Comfort – Integrating Universal Design & Energy Efficiency in Home Renovations*, unpublished PhD thesis, Faculty of Architecture and Arts, Hasselt University.

Neufert, E., Neufert, P., and Kister, J. (2019). *Architect's Data*, 5th edn. Hoboken, NJ: Wiley Blackwell.

Scandic (n.d.). Accessibility at Scandic. Available at: https://www.scandichotels.com/explore-scandic/accessibility/accessibility-training (accessed 12 March 2022).

World Health Organization (2001). *International Classification of Functioning, Disability and Health (ICF), Resolution WHA 54.21*. Available at: https://www.who.int/standards/classifications/international-classification-of-functioning-disability-and-health (accessed 5 December 2021).

World Health Organization (2007). *Global Age-friendly Cities: A Guide*. Geneva: WHO Press.

7.3 Mainstreaming inclusion and accessibility of the University built environment through collaboration with and empowerment of Campus Services

Fiona Sweeney and Tina Lowe

Introduction

An accessible built environment is one that fosters inclusion and can be accessed and used by all, without the need for adaptations or modifications (Government of Ireland, 2005, pp. 46). Kelly and Padden (2018, pp. 67) highlight how an inclusive physical campus and built environment is one in which "campus infrastructure meets the needs of the entire student cohort". Over the last decade, the subject 'University' has embarked on a journey, from compliance towards its vision of inclusion, and, although it is not quite there yet, significant progress has been made over time in reshaping the accessibility of the University built environment. This piece will focus on how inclusion and accessibility of the physical campus and built environment have been mainstreamed from a university access service to Estates Services through collaboration and empowerment. The piece provides an opportunity to consider this journey, articulate the strategies used, elucidate models of good practice, and reflect on lessons learned with the intention of providing practical guidance for other institutions embarking on a journey of creating a university for all. Dedicated roles, fostering effective collaborative working relationships and mainstreaming the responsibility, ownership, and financial commitment of campus accessibility with senior leadership and key Estate Services staff, along with consulting with all users, are just some of the examples of good practice that have contributed to the evolving journey of this University.

The campus was originally built in the late 1960s and spread out over 360 acres, with a combination of period houses, listed and modern buildings, all interspersed with woodlands, walkways, trails, and lakes. The main spine of the campus was built in a geometric design and included steps as part of the architectural design. As accessibility and inclusion was not a priority when the campus was originally built, this resulted in legacy accessibility challenges, especially for users of the campus who have a disability. Not only was there a need to improve the accessibility for people with disabilities on campus, but also a need to consider how the physical campus environment can promote the inclusion of the wide diversity of campus users using Universal Design.

DOI: 10.4324/9781003253631-25

As a result, the University's current approach to accessibility and inclusion of the built environment is grounded in national policy such as national guidelines for universal design (Centre for Excellence in Universal Design, 2012), institutional policy such as the Toolkit for Inclusive Higher Education Institutions (Kelly and Padden, 2018), the Disability Act (Government of Ireland, 2005), National Disability Inclusion Strategy (Department of Justice and Equality, 2017), and research and data (AHEAD, 2017; CSO, 2017; Hamraie, 2017; Irish Wheelchair Association, 2014).

Designated responsibility and resources for accessibility audits

Initially, the starting point to developing an inclusive campus was a practical demonstration of the University's commitment to their responsibilities under the 2005 Disability Act with the creation of a dedicated Access Officer role, now known as Campus Accessibility Officer. The focus of the role was to create awareness of accessibility, provide training, signpost, and advise staff, students, and members of the public on accessibility issues, and to build collaborative working relationships within the University community. The post is based in the University's Access & Lifelong Learning centre (ALL) and collaborates closely with the University's Estate Services and the wider University community.

Initially, a series of ten accessibility audits of key buildings along the main spine of the campus were commissioned. Utilising professional expertise and following accessibility audit templates, the buildings were examined for accessibility pertaining to external access, internal access, circulation, entrances, and navigation to identify priority actions. The audits provided the foundations for the annual accessibility Minor Works programme. Since then, continual reviews and annual setting of priorities form the mainstay of the day-to-day operations of the university Campus Accessibility Officer and Estate Services in making the campus more inclusive.

It is a valid concern, when undertaking accessibility audits, that the cost of implementing the recommendations could be prohibitive. The University has found adopting a long-term approach and incorporating the recommendations as part of on-going maintenance and refurbishments has successfully contributed to reducing an onerous task and ensuring retrofitting is financially achievable. With each refurbishment, accessibility is incrementally improved, supporting the plus one approach of Universal Design which involves breaking down a project or task into manageable chunks to practically apply Universal Design in day-to-day operations (Tobin, 2014) A dedicated central budget is essential to ensuring that these works are completed in a timely manner. Initially, this dedicated budget was housed in ALL. Through the mainstreaming of responsibility of inclusion, it was relocated to Estate Services. This mainstreaming has contributed towards more efficient and effective implementation of the priorities identified in the accessible Minor Works projects.

Collaboration and innovation

Developing effective collaborative relationships with Estate Services staff has been integral in mainstreaming inclusion. Adopting a coordinated approach with work-around solutions, ongoing awareness raising of accessibility issues, coupled with the development of accessibility expertise, particularly regarding building regulations (e.g. Part M [Bright, 2017]) across the wider Estate Services' staff, resulted in accessibility being embedded into management and maintenance systems.

Capitalising on innovative ideas is key to mainstreaming inclusion and accessibility of the built environment, as evidenced by the recent Sensory Garden Project. This project emerged from the need for quiet spaces to support neurodiverse students on campus. Utilizing a series of linked open spaces across the campus, which have been adapted for accessible use and planted with sensory plants (e.g. *Jasminum nudiflorum*) and tactile trees (e.g. *Luma apiculate*) to encourage the natural environment, bird life and insects, along with water features and bamboo planting, has created spaces that soothe the senses and are of benefit to all campus users.

Continued consultation, awareness raising, and opportunities for feedback across the wider University community can never be underestimated. When undertaking the Accessible Signage Strategy in 2014/2015, regular consultations and feedback opportunities were held as part of the strategy development stage. However, it was not until the implementation of the accessible signs that the project became relevant to all users, especially as students' perspectives and voices were central here. Student focus groups during the concept and pilot stages and students walking the route at implementation, were approaches used to include their voices throughout the process.

Lessons learned

To date, there has been significant progress in mainstreaming accessibility and inclusion of the campus built environment from the University's access service to the university's Estate Services. Accessibility and inclusion are priorities for the Estate Services team, and this is reflected in both the ongoing refurbishment works of existing buildings and in plans for future campus infrastructure. However, it must be acknowledged that this process takes time, effort, and commitment. On reflection, there have been some lessons learned that other higher education institutions can consider. Firstly, establishing an institutional commitment towards a vision of an accessible and inclusive campus with buy-in from senior leadership is imperative. Embedding accessibility into the roles and responsibilities in Estates Services or situating the role of a dedicated accessibility officer within Estate Services may assist with bringing inclusion to the forefront of discussions regarding the development of the physical campus and built environment. Utilising expertise early in projects with adequate funding ring fenced in Estate Services' overall budget can enable greater completion of retrofit projects. Nevertheless, establishing effective collaborative relationships, developing, and enhancing expertise and using incremental change has been some of the mechanisms that have advanced our vision and have contributed towards access and inclusion becoming everyone's business.

References

AHEAD (2017). *Universal Design for Learning*. Available at: https://www.ahead.ie/udl (accessed 15 March 2022).

Bright, K.T. (2017). Access to and use of buildings (Part M). In M.J. Billington, S.P. Barnshaw, K.T. Bright, and A. Crooks (eds), *The Building Regulations: Explained and Illustrated*, 14th edn. Chichester: John Wiley & Sons Ltd, pp. 17. 1–17. 51.

Centre for Excellence in Universal Design (2012). *Building for Everyone: A Universal Design Approach – Building Types*. Dublin: National Disability Authority. Available at: http://universaldesign.ie (accessed on 15 March 2022).

Department of Justice and Equality (July, 2017). *National Disability Inclusion Strategy 2017–2021*. Available at: https://www.gov.ie/en/publication/8072c0-national-disability-inclusion-strategy-2017-2021/ (accessed 15 March 2022).

Government of Ireland (2005). *Disability Act 2005*. Dublin: Stationery Office. Available at: http://www.irishstatutebook.ie/eli/2005/act/14/enacted/en/html (accessed 15 March 2022).

Hamraie, A. (2017). *Building Access: Universal Design and the Politics of Disability*. Minnesota, MN: University of Minnesota Press.

Irish Wheelchair Association (2014). *Irish Wheelchair Association Best Practice Access Guidelines 3*. Available at: https://www.iwa.ie/access/ (accessed 15 March 2022).

Kelly, A. and Padden L. (2018). *Toolkit for Inclusive Higher Education Institutions: From Vision to Practice*. Dublin: University College Dublin Access & Lifelong Learning.

Tobin T.J. (2014). Increase online student retention with Universal Design for Learning. *Quarterly Review of Distance Education*, 15(3), 13–24. Available at: http://www.engl.duq.edu/servus/cv/QRDE.UDL.Article.pdf (accessed 8 June 2022).

7.4 Beyond compliance

Embedding accessibility and creating community through inclusive design of the university built environment

Tadgh Corcoran and Thomas Hamill

Introduction

The Estate Services within any higher education institution holds the important responsibility for managing existing university property while planning accommodation for future generations of students, researchers, faculty, and staff. The subject University has over 33,000 students and 3,900 academic and support staff and has the largest campus portfolio in Ireland. The University's Estate Service aims to embed accessibility and inclusive design within the campus environment to promote the creation of a university for all but acknowledges the challenges that may arise while attempting to make this vision a reality. Hence, the Estate Services team consider Universal Design to hold solutions to these challenges, as this enables us to appraise how our campus facilities can be used to the greatest extent possible by all people, regardless of age, ability, gender, or background.

University Estate Services

The role of an Estates Services team is one of custodian of the campus and the campus experience. Our aim is to pass the campus onto future generations in better condition, and, as such, it is a journey of continuous improvement, not only of the campus but also in how we manage the estate and building portfolio of the University. In 2022, the key objectives of the "Estate Strategy" in the subject University are:

1. **Support university growth:** Like most higher education institutions, UCD is growing rapidly with the University growing by 25 per cent or 6,600 full-time equivalents between 2018–2023. The University is diversifying this enrolment by engaging with access students, international students, and students with diverse abilities. Growth is manifested not only in the academic buildings but also in the residential and student amenities on campus that support student life and community promoting work, rest, and play
2. **Enhance the campus experience:** Fostering an inclusive and fulfilling experience of the physical campus and built environments for all users is

DOI: 10.4324/9781003253631-26

Figure 7.6 UCD Belfield campus

fundamental to the role of Estate Services in higher education institutions. In UCD's context, the early campus design in the 1960s reflected the ambitions of a modern egalitarian university, and the University recently celebrated 50 years of UCD at the Belfield campus (University College Dublin, 2020). The University seeks to improve the campus experience holistically, from the full-scale capital refurbishment projects, to targeted interventions through minor works projects and maintenance interventions of existing buildings, all which offer opportunities to embed accessibility and inclusive design to improve the campus experience

3 **Improve sustainability and transition to a low carbon campus:** It is no surprise that a university's buildings are the most significant contributor to energy consumption and carbon footprint. Our challenge as a University community is to learn to adapt how we use our buildings for a low carbon future.

As a higher education institution with a large campus portfolio (Figure 7.6) of buildings ranging from period to current day, it is our firm belief that these key objectives can only be met and the campus can only benefit by embedding accessibility and creating community through inclusive design, truly creating a university campus for all.

The evolution of university campuses

Often, higher education institutions have existing campus buildings and infrastructure which require refurbishment, as well as plans for future campus buildings to promote university activities. University Estate Services have the job of balancing priorities for refurbishment and developing future campus infrastructure. To understand the inclusivity journey that the Estates Services' team are on in UCD, one must firstly understand the campus' origin and the subsequent challenges posed.

As Ireland's largest University, the estate facilities are predominantly based at the Belfield campus with additional accommodation provided at Blackrock, Lyons Research Farm, Newman House, and various hospital locations. With over 33,000 students, faculty, staff, and visitors using the Belfield campus on a daily basis, the campus hosts a multitude of stakeholder groups and manages significant transport infrastructure. The Belfield campus facilitates various functions and incorporates apartments, offices, laboratory and teaching facilities, restaurants, sports and parkland facilities, retail, and entertainment services.

Historically, the Belfield campus was the realisation of a utopian vision for a modern Irish university. It was Ireland's first purpose built modern campus and it changed the idea of what a university should look like. The campus design came out of an international competition in the 1960s, with the original masterplan by Polish architect, Andrzej Wejchert (Figure 7.7). The campus was organised around a central spine of circulation based on the idea of movement and flexibility. The campus plan needed to be flexible, to allow for on-going development over future decades.

However, if you consider the campus in the context of the design principles at that time, accessibility, as we understand it now, was not a priority. This has left Estate Services with numerous challenges. As an example, although a number of the university buildings received Royal Institute of Architects of Ireland (RIAI) gold medals for their design, the Restaurant in 1970 (RIAI, 1970) and the Administration (Tierney) Building (Figure 7.8) in 1972 (RIAI, 1973) were developed with a series of steps at the front/main entrances. There are also the magnificent period estate houses whose lands make up the Belfield campus. Estate Services have established a Programme for the Preservation of Period Houses and although accessibility is always a priority in the sympathetic restoration of these historic properties, this is not as straightforward a process as developing a green field site. However, to give these properties a modern purpose, which is essential to their preservation, it is equally important that they are open and accessible to the entire university

Figure 7.7 Andrzsj Wejchert's sketch of his proposed campus layout

Figure 7.8 UCD Tierney Building 1972

community. Such legacy accessibility challenges are evident throughout the campus and highlight the impact of not embedding Universal Design and accessibility principles during the design stages of campus projects.

Promoting inclusion through building care and management

Although conscious of our obligations under the relevant legislation, statutory requirements are not the main driver in our inclusivity journey. Instead, the Estate Services' objective is to go beyond mere compliance and to understand that inclusivity and diversity are to be embraced and encouraged in the University community, and that the built environment of the University should be equally inclusive by design. We have realised that the accessibility and usability of a campus relies heavily on the good management and excellent care of our existing buildings. Building care and management encompasses the many practical tasks involved in the day-to-day operation of a building, including building maintenance, planning for emergency evacuation, customer service, and staff training.

The introduction of an Accessibility Systems Management Plan for all buildings across the campus is an example of how we have attempted to embed inclusivity in our day-to-day operations. Too often in the past, such systems were installed without any focus on ongoing maintenance and monitoring. Estates Services developed this systematic plan to regularly check and monitor accessibility systems in buildings, including accessible toilet and bedroom alarms, refuge point intercom systems, and power assisted doors. Ensuring the systems are working when required is a basic element of good building management.

Furthermore, through our accessibility minor works projects (small scale focused improvement works), we aim to make impactful alterations in a legacy campus environment, or put another way, we aim to make a big difference with small changes. These accessibility projects are a collaborative effort with colleagues in the University's access service, based on consultation and the identification of priorities. Projects completed have consisted of both external (e.g. access to buildings, wayfinding, parking, service dog facilities, etc.) and internal (e.g. wayfinding, inclusive Changing and WC facilities, communication systems, etc.) considerations.

Incorporating inclusion into future campus project and University capital programme

In a university's Capital Programme to support University Growth, ensuring Universal Design and University for All principles are considered right from the project inception is fundamental to moving from a focus on compliance to inclusive design. Examples within campus plans for UCD include the Centre for Creativity and the Centre for Learning (Figure 7.9). In conjunction with accessibility consultants O'Herily Access Consultancy, a 43-point checklist of Universal Design criteria (Appendix A) was developed for both projects which were based on the University for All Toolkit (Kelly and Padden, 2018) and review of national and international best practice. Through regular accessibility workshops, Universal Design reviews of the building's designs, Universal Design feasibility reports, and on-going accessibility advice from

Figure 7.9 Architect's impression of the UCD Centre for Creativity

the University accessibility consultants, inclusivity and accessibility were key principles throughout the design of both buildings.

With inclusivity being considered at all stages, and with the collaborative approach adopted by the University and our design team, it was possible to ensure Universal Design was incorporated fully into our future campus plans. Having successfully incorporated the process, we are very pleased to embed this into the design process for other major capital projects such as the Science Centre and the Sports and Student Amenities project, as the Estate Services' team acknowledge how embedding inclusivity from the design stage benefits all users of the campus.

Conclusion

As an Estate Service for a large university, we recognise that we are on a journey, a journey of continuous improvement. While we believe that we can take pride in the campus that the team has developed to date, there is still plenty of room for improvement and work to be done, all of which will take time. As we undertake that work, we are attempting to ensure inclusive practice across the spectrum of the services that Estates Services provide. From effective day to day building operation and campus management, to smaller scale accessibility focused renovation works, and all the way to our major future building projects, we are working to enhance the campus for future generations of students to come and provide a legacy of good design practice in which accessibility and inclusion for all are our driving principles.

We have made progress. The student funded Student Centre SLLS Building won the 2013 RIAI Universal Design Award (Centre for Excellence in Universal Design, 2013), and our integration of the inclusivity principle into our future campus design process is an innovation which enhances the design process and are examples of good universal design in operation. Most importantly, they are an example of the University's and Estate Services' commitment to move beyond compliance. We aim to continue to go beyond the statutory and building regulations requirements, and we realise that developing a campus experience which exemplifies a culture of inclusion is a challenge requiring a commitment towards a process of continuous improvement and not a one-off initiative.

References

Centre for Excellence in Universal Design (2013). UCD Student Centre wins Universal Design Award. Available at: https://universaldesign.ie/news-events/news/ucd-student-centre-wins-universal-design-award.html#:~:text=The%20winners%20of%20the%20RIAI,Disability%20Authority%20supported%20the%20award (accessed 22 June 2022).

Kelly, A.M. and Padden, L. (2018). *University for All Toolkit for Inclusive Higher Education Institutions – From Vision to Practice.* Dublin: University College Dublin

Access & Lifelong Learning. Available at: https://www.ucd.ie/all/t4media/0274_UCD_TOOLKIT_1118_ONLINE_LR.pdf (accessed 15 March 2022).

Royal Institute of Architects of Ireland (1970). Restaurant Building, UCD. Available at: https://www.riai.ie/discover-architecture/awards-archive/restaurant-building-ucd (accessed 22 June 2022).

Royal Institute of Architects of Ireland (1973). The Administration Building, UCD (1971–1973). Available at: https://www.riai.ie/discover-architecture/awards-archive/the-administration-building-ucd (accessed 22 June 2022).

University College Dublin (2020). Official launch of Belfield 50. Available at: https://www.ucdbelfield50.com/official-launch-of-belfield-50/ (accessed 22 June 2022).

Chapter 8

IT Services & Infrastructure

8.1 Facilitating inclusion in an evolving digital world

Daniel Elliott

Digital technology has long had the power to make higher education more accessible and inclusive. However, the adoption and use of systems and software that are not universally designed means that many students cannot access their learning and are not all treated equitably. Many university websites continue to be inaccessible and hard to navigate, while learning materials are provided in formats that cannot be accessed using assistive technology tools, with teaching staff often not equipped with the technical knowledge and training to provide technology enhanced or hybrid learning (Lazar, 2021; National Disability Authority, 2021). The onset of the COVID-19 pandemic has rapidly advanced the accessibility agenda for higher education IT services and infrastructure. The need to move learning completely online in a short space of time has shown how quickly HEIs can mobilise to meet the needs of their students (Camilleri, 2021). The pandemic has also laid bare the inequalities faced by students in higher education, particularly the difficulties faced by many in accessing technology, adequate Wi-Fi connection, and online materials: "the digital divide" (AHEAD, 2020; USI, 2020). University IT departments must be committed to making IT services accessible to all students. This chapter offers the work of one university's Information Technology services department (University College Dublin) as a case study in how an IT department can meet the needs of diverse learners and how investment in new technologies and software is levelling the playing field for all students.

The problem with adopting accessible tech

Much like how the construction of a new building on campus is built with Universal Design principles, the acquisition of new technologies for students should consider these same principles and accessibility should be of paramount importance (Burgstahler and Vinten-Johansen, 2017). The O'Rourke, Teevan, and Collins case studies demonstrate cross-unit collaboration as an enabler for change and show a whole-institution approach to inclusion in action. IT Services worked in collaboration with other student support departments to procure and implement new software addressing web accessibility and accessible digital

DOI: 10.4324/9781003253631-28

learning content. Evidence has shown that early adopter communities are effective in technology change (Armstrong, 2019; Bennett, 2014), and this is again evidenced in the case study, where early adopters were engaged through multiple means, and have been pivotal in ensuring a wide uptake of this software. The implementation shows that, once teaching staff and students are provided with the right technology, accessibility can be improved rapidly and on an institution-wide scale. Adopting tech tools that are easy and straightforward to use is crucial – we cannot expect to persuade academic staff, who are constantly stretched, to make their materials accessible if the process is difficult for them. The adoption of specific technologies designed to improve the quality of learning for one group of marginalised students can often lead to an improved experience for all students (Chambers, 2020).

Furthermore, this case study, along with Alistair McNaught's contribution addressing digital accessibility in the UK context, highlight not only the importance of institutional willpower but also the importance of government policy and legislation to effect change. Both examples illustrate how accessibility leadership should come from different levels within an institution. Adopting a top-down approach only can be prohibitive and hamper the adoption of new technologies by teaching staff, as was the case in the University of Botswana (Dintoe, 2018). This example supports the recurring theme within this chapter: that universities can invest in the latest technologies, but if staff, faculty, and students are not trained in how to use these effectively, its benefits are not widely reaped (Singh et al., 2021b). Donegal Further Education and Training Board's (ETB) Technology Enhanced Learning (TEL) Mentors offer an excellent peer-to-peer solution to combatting this problem that could easily be replicated in a HEI setting (Donegal ETB, 2020). Studies carried out in Egypt and India point to the need for such solutions, with teaching staff grappling with the difficulties of executing technology enhanced and blended learning experiences that cater to the needs of all students (Megahed and Hassan, 2021; Bordoloi et al., 2021; Sharma and Alvi, 2021).

Online and blended learning

Having been provided with recorded lectures and the opportunity to engage with their studies off campus, it is no small surprise that students continue to demand lectures being recorded and that blended or hybrid learning should remain an option (AHEAD, 2021; IUA, 2021; Singh et al., 2021a; USI, 2020). Students with disabilities, parental and caring responsibilities, financial barriers, long commutes, and high rents will continue to look for flexible learning environments. Research carried out by the Irish Universities Association (IUA) shows that students are craving a blended learning model that "allows for flexibility and personal responsibility for students in their learning, while also providing opportunities for students to engage and interact in person with classmates and staff" (IUA, 2021). Students also reported an appreciation of the flexibilities that online learning offered: they reported feeling more independent as learners and 'they could fit their learning into their lives more easily' (Clarke, 2020, sec. 2). However, Clarke does caution against relying exclusively on tools for learning, advocating adherence to pedagogical principles of design and recommending that "all online/blended or hybrid activity adheres to the principles of Universal Design" (Clarke, 2020, sec. 5). Universities should and need to be more informed about which aspects of this blended experience that can be adopted as standard practice and reflect on the practices that warrant more attention and resources (StudentSurvey.ie, 2021). This must be done through a whole-institution approach with the student body fully involved in this process. One such illustration of this is the University of Calgary's Flanagan Foundation Initiative, which provides students and staff with the resources they need as it implements its vision for blended and online learning (Taylor Institute for Teaching and Learning, 2021).

As we have seen throughout this book, a student-centred approach is crucial, and this should be the case when developing IT services and infrastructure. The move to online learning during the pandemic highlighted that many students did not own or have access to a laptop, which led to much needed funding from the Department for Further and Higher Education, Research, Innovation and Science to create a laptop loan scheme in Ireland (Government of Ireland, 2020). However, it is not enough to simply provide funding for devices; students require support and training to be proficient learners (AHEAD, 2021). UCD established the Digital Ambassador programme in 2016: a form of peer-to-peer digital support which allowed struggling students to access IT help from fellow students in a quick and informal manner. This service evolved quickly and was a valuable resource for students during the pandemic, providing an alternative for students who may not be comfortable approaching professional supports.

If we are to truly empower students through UDL to take ownership of their learning, university IT services and infrastructure must move beyond students' surveys, focus groups, and testing and develop a true partnership with them. Students should be involved both in the procurement process as the end users of new technologies; equally, there should be greater opportunities for students to act as digital mentors for other students. The IUA's Enhancing Digital Teaching and Learning Project aims to enhance the digital attributes and educational experiences of university students through enabling the mainstreamed and integrated use of digital technologies across the teaching and learning process. Importantly, it has hired student interns, with the aim of engaging students as co-creators in developing digital teaching and learning resources. This project offers a model of how to create such a partnership (IUA, 2022). Although this is at the policy level, it can be easily replicated at an institutional level.

As HEIs grapple with how to engage/re-engage learners, they must consider standardised guidelines for digital accessibility, they must ensure faculty and staff have the training required to provide accessible hybrid learning, and they must listen to students (Singh et al., 2021a). Accessibility must be built into the procurement of new software and digital technologies. Annual IT planning must align with inclusion. This chapter provides examples of how these processes can happen.

References

AHEAD (2020). *Learning from Home During COVID-19: A Survey of Irish FET and HE Students with Disabilities.* Dublin: AHEAD Educational Press.

AHEAD (2021). *Learning from Home 2021: A Survey of Irish FET and HE Students with Disabilities Learning through COVID-19.* Dublin: AHEAD Educational Press.

Armstrong, E.J. (2019). Maximising motivators for technology-enhanced learning for further education teachers: Moving beyond the early adopters in a time of austerity. *Research in Learning Technology*, 27, 1–23.

Bennett, L. (2014). Learning from the early adopters: Developing the Digital Practitioner. *Research in Learning Technology*, 22, 1–13.

Bordoloi, R., Das, P., and Das, K. (2021). Perception towards online/blended learning at the time of COVID-19 pandemic: An academic analytics in the Indian context. *Asian Association of Open Universities Journal*, 16(1), 41–60.

Burgstahler, S. and Vinten-Johansen, C. (2017). Seven steps toward IT accessibility compliance. *EDUCAUSE Review*. Available at: https://er.educause.edu/articles/2017/9/seven-steps-toward-it-accessibility-compliance

Camilleri, M.A. (2021). Evaluating service quality and performance of higher education institutions: A systematic review and a post COVID-19 outlook [online]. Available at: www.um.edu.mt

Chambers, D. (2020). Assistive technology supporting inclusive education: Existing and emerging trends. In D. Chambers and C. Forlin (eds), *Assistive Technology to Support Inclusive Education*. Bingley, UK: Emerald Publishing Limited, pp. 1–17.

Clarke, M. (2020). *Report of the Working Group on Prioritised Resourcing to Support Teaching, Learning and Assessment in the Autumn Trimester 2020/21*. Dublin: University College Dublin.

Dintoe, S.S. (2018). Educational technology adopters: A case study in University of Botswana. *International Journal of Education and Development using Information and Communication Technology*, 14(1), 52–90.

Donegal ETB (2020). FET Service hosts first Technology Enhanced Learning (TEL) webinar series. Available at: https://www.donegaletb.ie/2020/05/25/fet-service-hosts-first-technology-enhanced-learning-tel-webinar-series/ (accessed 2 June 2022).

Government of Ireland (2020). Minister Harris announces 17,000 laptops ordered to assist students with online and blended learning. Available at: https://www.gov.ie/en/press-release/7143d-minister-harris-announces-17000-laptops-ordered-to-assist-students-with-online-and-blended-learning/# (accessed 13 June 2022).

Fitzpatrick, L. and McStravock, K. (2020). *National Report on Students and COVID-19*, Union of Students in Ireland (USI). Available at: https://usi.ie/wp-content/uploads/2020/07/COVID_RESEARCH_FINAL.pdf

Irish Universities Association (IUA) (2022). Students as partners: The EDTL Project as case study – webinar. Available at: https://edtl.blog/webinar-series/students-as-partners-the-edtl-project-as-case-study/ (accessed 6 May 2022).

IUA EDTL (2021). *Your Education, Your Voice, Your Vision – Results of the Student Campaign Run by the Enhancing Digital Teaching and Learning (EDTL) Project, April – May 2021*. Dublin: Irish Universities Association.

Lazar, J. (2021). Managing digital accessibility at universities during the COVID-19 pandemic. *Universal Access in the Information Society* [online]. Available at: https://doi.org/10.1007/s10209-021-00792-5

Megahed, N. and Hassan, A. (2021). A blended learning strategy: Reimagining the post-COVID-19 architectural education. *Archnet-IJAR: International Journal of Architectural Research*, 16(1), 184–202.

National Disability Authority, Centre for Excellence in Universal Design (2021). *Ireland's Monitoring Report for the EU Web Accessibility Directive*. Dublin: Centre for Excellence in Universal Design.

Sharma, A. and Alvi, I. (2021). Evaluating pre and post COVID 19 learning: An empirical study of learners' perception in higher education. *Education and Information Technologies* [online]. doi:10.1007/s10639-021-10521-3.

Singh, J., Evans, E., Wiersma, H., Reed, A., Karch, L., Qualey, K., and Singh, L. (2021a). Online, hybrid, and face-to-face learning through the eyes of faculty, students, administrators, and instructional designers: Lessons learned and directions for the post vaccine and post-pandemic/COVID-19 world. *Journal of Educational Technology Systems*, 50(3), 301–326.

Singh, J., Singh, L., and Steele, K. (2021b). Combining the best of online and face-to-face learning: Hybrid and blended learning approach for COVID-19, post-vaccine, & post-pandemic world. *Journal of Educational Technology Systems*, 50(2), 140–171.

StudentSurvey.ie (2021). *Irish Survey of Student Engagement, Interim Results Bulletin*. Available at: https://studentsurvey.ie/sites/default/files/users/user27/StudentSurvey.ie%20Interim%20Results%20Bulletin%202021_0.pdf

Taylor Institute for Teaching and Learning (2021). *Community Report 2021*. Calgary: University of Calgary. Available at: https://taylorinstitute.ucalgary.ca/about/reports-plans

8.2 Embedding inclusion and accessibility in higher education IT

Sinéad O'Rourke, Ryan Teevan and Janet Collins

Information Technology is critical to the success of any university, as it underpins all essential services required to enable students to complete their educational journey. It is a central part of a student's daily learning experience, and it is essential that it is diverse, inclusive, and accessible to all. The dependency of universities on reliable and functional IT services was reinforced during the COVID-19 pandemic. IT infrastructure encompasses all systems and processes, teaching environments including the virtual learning environment (VLE), and student information systems used for registration and reporting. As the diversity in our classrooms evolves, so too does the higher education landscape, and its technology infrastructure must respond and adapt. It is no longer acceptable to offer secondary support to students who may not be able to use mainstream technologies – these technologies need to be developed with the entire student body in mind. A university needs to adopt a whole-institution approach when developing its IT systems and infrastructure, tailoring its teaching environments, systems, and processes to ensure it permeates all areas. When procuring a new system, vendors must show that they comply with or exceed accessibility requirements during the evaluation process. Digital technology makes transformation possible and there is a need to focus on creating an integrated digital campus to provide an inclusive, modern, and intellectually stimulating learning, teaching, and research environment. Whilst UCD offers, in most parts, best in class systems and services for students, these services evolve and are streamlined to ensure the best possible service experience available by providing consistent, responsive services accessible to all.

IT support in UCD

IT support services are centrally advertised through a student guide issued to all new students and published online (Figure 8.1). New and existing services are advertised on the IT Services website and published at intervals throughout the academic year in a bi-weekly Student e-zine. UCD Connect provides access to all central applications available to students such as Google Mail, Brightspace Virtual Learning Environment, Calendar/Timetable, and Google

DOI: 10.4324/9781003253631-29

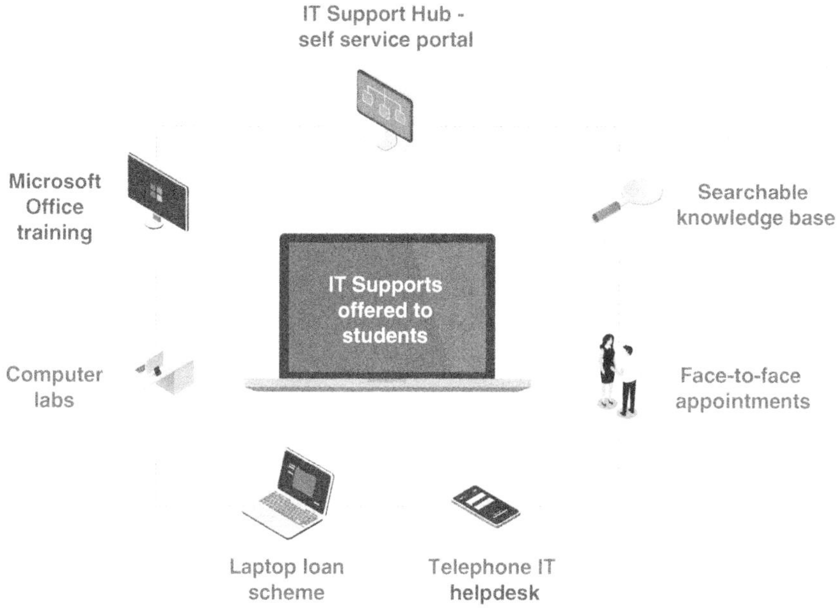

Figure 8.1 IT Supports and Services for students

Drive, together with software applications and other services such as Microsoft Office 365, library account, online file storage, UCD noticeboard, and news. Once a student has Wi-Fi, UCD Connect is available 24/7, whether the student is on or off campus.

UCD has a centralised integrated student information system called SISWeb. The system creates a comprehensive student information record capturing contact and programme information, allowing ease of use and easy access to course and timetable information via a secure portal. The record remains active throughout a student's studies and holds a record of support and services that a particular student has accessed. This record is also available to those who require it, such as module co-ordinators, and provides a full picture of a student's engagement with a support or a service.

However, while relationships exist between support services within the institution, there is currently no system that allows for a student query to be passed between one support unit to another. This may soon be addressed by an ongoing University-wide project to streamline services and processes. IT staff involved in supporting students have an opportunity to network with other support colleagues throughout the University via a number of working groups including Supports for Students, Orientation Oversight Group, and Remote Working Group meetings. These support groups offer the attendees an opportunity to share information and experiences and to learn from each other's practices. The two examples below outline the implementation process for new software in the University (see Figure 8.2).

Figure 8.2 IT implementation process

Case study: Implementation of accessibility tools for the Virtual Learning Environment

Every student at UCD has access to Brightspace – UCD's Virtual Learning Environment (VLE). This is an online platform that allows lecturers to share learning materials, announcements, assessments such as quizzes, and collect assignments. It also has additional features such as a plagiarism prevention tool, online virtual classroom facility, a range of learner activities, and other collaborative tools. All teaching materials are required to adhere to accessibility guidelines so that all students can partake fully in any online learning aspect of their university education. However, many of these materials still do not meet these requirements. To combat this, Ally, a tool provided by Blackboard, was introduced to support faculty and staff in understanding how accessible their learning content is, and to provide clear and easy information on how to create more accessible learning content for their students (Blackboard, 2021). It assists in improving the usability and accessibility of learning content within the VLE. Providing students with more accessible content ensures they can choose formats that work best for them, not only in terms of accessibility but also in terms of providing formats that assist students in understanding and digesting their module material in a manner that best suits their own learning preferences.

For faculty, this tool automatically scans the learning content, providing them with feedback and an accessibility score on each item and a series of steps to assist them in making content more accessible, in real time. Some students with disabilities need their module materials in alternative formats e.g. students with visual impairments who access their materials using a screen reader or students with specific learning difficulties who benefit from listening to their learning materials. This software facilitates these students by allowing them to access their module materials in a format that suits them at source, without the need to make special requests or use specialist software. It not only benefits students with disabilities but all students, who can now choose formats that best suit their learning needs, preferences, and environment.

Implementation

This software, for making digital course content more accessible (Ally), was licensed in February 2021, with a view to launching the service for the academic year 2021/22 (September 2021). IT Services engaged with other HEIs already using it, both within Ireland and the United Kingdom, to gain insights into their approach with launching the software. Feedback was very positive from these conversations, with indications that it was user friendly, and that students greatly benefited from its introduction across the board, particularly as these institutions had purchased it in the context of the global pandemic while supporting students studying remotely. It was decided after an initial testing period overseen by IT Services and Access & Lifelong Learning that it would be launched in April 2021 to support students ahead of the Summer Examination period. It was acknowledged that some work would be required in ensuring faculty understood why it was being introduced and the impact this would have on them. Positive feedback from students was received immediately after launch:

> "Just a quick line of thanks to all involved in getting the Ally software on Brightspace. After somewhat struggling with Zoomtext, this is a game-changer. It is simple to use and works every time. The time saved, compared to the previous laborious, and somewhat unreliable, methods is remarkable".

To build awareness of the software, the project team agreed to run an early adopter group for faculty who wanted to gain an understanding of the tool, and to assist the project team with developing appropriate support materials for faculty on its use in the VLE. Sign up to this group was very positive, with approximately 45 faculty joining over the summer. The group was involved in three group sessions hosted by the project team:

- The first session involved an overview of the software and provided the group with some scenarios that they could work through within their own modules in the VLE, including use of the Ally Module report.
- The second session provided an overview of the different alternative formats available in the VLE and when these might be used. It also allowed for some peer-to-peer discussion and support in breakout sessions with the project team to discuss how individuals were getting on.
- The final session involved a short recap of the first two sessions and allowed the group to provide some insights into the learnings or experience they have had using the tool and how they might bring this back to their local areas. Some pain points and possible resolutions were also discussed.

Weekly drop-in clinics were organised, where members of the group could meet and discuss any issues they were experiencing with a member of the project team, or share tips with other colleagues. A Google community was set up where members were encouraged to share their experience. The early adopter group ran from June to mid-August and allowed the project team to plan for the start of the next academic year where a full launch of the tool and support resources were made available for all staff and students.

Launch

In September 2021, the project team supported a full launch of Ally in Brightspace. It is now available to all staff and students across all modules. Communications were sent to the community informing them of the launch and detailing what this technology is and how it can be used. Training was incorporated within the IT Services VLE workshop schedule and was available for staff to sign up to ahead of the academic year. Online and on demand resources were created and published on the IT Services Knowledge Base and remain there for staff and students to use, should they wish to find out more information around using the tool. Blackboard also provides extensive information for staff and students on its use, which can be found on their website.

Student usage of the software has remained consistent during the first full trimester since it went live with over 38,000 downloads of alternative formats across approximately 1,750 individual modules. Instructor usage in the Autumn trimester saw over 370 fixes to module content across 86 modules. As of the end of March 2022, there have been over 830 content fixes across approximately 130 modules for this academic year. The overall data is rather consistent on a week-on-week basis and shows that the alternative format usage remains relatively high within the student population. In relation to the alternative formats being downloaded, the use of Tagged PDF is the most popular format, which follows a similar trend to other institutions in the EMEA region as reported by Blackboard. After Tagged PDFs, there is a preference towards the HTML and ePub formats followed by Audio. The project team recently ran a student survey to gain further insight into the student usage, and how it might be improved. The response numbers for this, however, were small and no tangible outputs could be made. Further student feedback will be sought and the means with which this is collected is being reconsidered.

Next steps

A full product review and evaluation will take place over the next 18 months. The review will focus on areas for improvement, increasing adoption, assessing the benefits it offers, and listening to the student voice. IT Services continue to participate in the Ally User Groups and roadmap sessions and have embedded learnings within our internal Brightspace workshops. IT Services continue to work with colleagues in Access and Lifelong Learning to promote this solution.

Understanding web accessibility

When we think of web accessibility, we might think of providing access to those with a permanent disability such as deafness or blindness. There are also temporary or even situational circumstances, whereby someone may require the use of an assistive technology. For example, in a noisy environment you might need subtitles on a video or when on the move you might require speech assistance. As a result, web accessibility should be seen as a requirement for all. Web accessibility is key to creating a more inclusive environment by eliminating barriers that restrict a person's access.

All universities in Ireland ensure they follow directives mandated by the European Union. The EU Web Accessibility Directive came into force in Ireland in September 2020 (European Union, 2020). This directive builds on existing obligations for public bodies to make websites and services offered to the public accessible by meeting its 'Essential Requirements' which can be achieved by complying with the Web Content Accessibility Guidelines (WAI). UCD is improving its web accessibility score in line with this directive. There are approximately 420 websites under the UCD domain, and the web accessibility score will be evaluated and published on the web accessibility statement at regular intervals to measure progress. In addition, the National Disability Authority (NDA) monitors and reviews the website domain since October 2021.

Part of this directive is the development of a web accessibility statement for each website or mobile application. Organisations publish an accessibility statement on their website to describe their policy, goals, and accomplishments related to web accessibility. The first version of the University's web accessibility statement outlines its commitment to improving its accessibility score. It outlines its compliance status and areas which can be improved, with a commitment to update the accessibility statement regularly and provide updates on its scoring (UCD.ie, 2021).

The content management system (CMS), Terminal 4, used for website development should allow for full accessibility in content development and use for all faculty and staff. This CMS is currently being used for approximately 150 sites within the University which allows for fully accessible content development. However, there are a large number of sites (>250) that do not use the CMS, and this presents a challenge to meeting the requirements of the directive. A new Design Library is being developed to make the standard approach to content development more user friendly and attractive to users and it is hoped that more website owners currently using alternative platforms will move to the CMS following its launch.

Case study: Implementation of an integrated web accessibility tool

To support the web accessibility improvement initiative, a web accessibility testing platform was procured to facilitate scheduled monitoring and fixing of accessibility issues. IT Services evaluated several web accessibility tools in 2021. The tool selected had to adhere to the following criteria:

- Audit to WCAG 2.1 AA Standard
- Cloud based with the capability to schedule regular audits

- Decentralised access
- Progressive scoring.

EU based, with support for Single Sign on and advanced mobile testing, was also a requirement. An integration with the CMS was also desirable.

Implementation

The software selected was Silktide 4.0 and was rolled out to the University's Websmart community (owners and managers of websites) in October 2021. The tool chosen is a web-based application that allows site owners to measure and improve the accessibility of their websites. It provides automated testing of sites, with comprehensive metrics that can be monitored, and useful tools that make improving websites as easy as possible. Those tasked with improving the accessibility of their websites can self-register and see the scoring of their website in the categories of content, accessibility, marketing, and user experience. The tool outlines where the issues are and allows the user to pinpoint where they need to implement fixes. The key metrics are: all webpages have a title, heading, offer alternative text for images, language that is easy to understand, as well as correct spelling and grammar. It also suggests the addition of captions for videos.

Launch

The platform was promoted in the University's Websmart community – 133 people – but not all of these are website editors. At the time of writing (April 2022), there are 53 users registered on the software's platform. Uptake of this technology is estimated to be about 50 per cent so far. When the first accessibility test was run in August, the overall score for the domain was 56. This is out of a possible score of 100, which is very difficult to achieve. The latest score, which was run in early December, had improved, to 59. IT Services have run several webinars, providing updates on implementation, along with the opportunity to share resources and information for the Google community. Efforts are being made to make this tool more visible and accessible to the wider University community.

Next steps

The use of this software will continue to be encouraged and advertised; it is hoped that more website owners will choose it as a standard accessibility tool when building and maintaining their site. It is intended that the University's accessibility score will continue to improve over time. The launch of the website design library in April 2022 will provide website owners with a suite of fully accessible templates that can be used to build internal sites for Colleges, Schools and Units. The library will contain up to 15 pre-built page layouts which have all been tested for accessibility on both mobile and desktop devices. Site owners can choose from a catalogue of components to build their website. It will offer clickable navigation layouts which offer a higher level of accessibility than standard navigation. This will further improve the University's accessibility score and it is hoped that the library will be an attractive option for some of those who currently use systems outside of the CMS to build and maintain their sites.

Using standard templates will also provide a much more streamlined experience for users offering a typical navigation and layout system that is more user friendly and familiar to all. The aim is to have slightly over one third of websites migrated to the new design library by June 2022 which will help to improve the overall accessibility score. More time can then be spent working with the remaining website owners to help improve their accessibility rating. IT Services engage with the National Disability Authority (NDA) and the National Council for the Blind of Ireland (NCBI) to help provide expertise and education needed to address accessibility issues.

Conclusion

Whilst UCD has made good progress in information technology working towards a University for All, there is a need to ensure that work continues to support inclusion, access and widening participation within the institution so that it is always at the forefront of thinking when implementing any new system or service. Annual IT project planning needs to consistently be aligned with the organisational strategy and work towards central goals of embedding accessibility and inclusion so that all students can fulfil their potential by using the vast array of IT resources available to them. IT involvement in the University level committees such as Equality, Diversity and Inclusion (EDI) and Widening Participation Committee, helps to integrate these specific priorities and aids the planning and implementation of mainstreaming inclusive projects within IT.

Our University, like any large organisation, uses an array of digital platforms and tools each of which require ongoing investment of money and resources. Bringing systems in line with accessibility standards can only take place over time and sometimes only small changes are evident. Institution wide change requires central policy to be aligned with academic and management support.

References

Ally for Blackboard. Available at: https://www.blackboard.com/en-eu/teaching-learning/accessibility-universal-design/blackboard-ally-lms#:~:text=Blackboard%20Ally%20is%20a%20revolutionary,digital%20course%20content%20more%20accessible

European Union (2020). *European Union (Accessibility of Websites and Mobile Applications of Public Sector Bodies) Regulations 2020*. Available at: https://www.irishstatutebook.ie/eli/2020/si/358/made/en/print.

Silktide. Available at: https://silktide.com/
UCD Connect Portal. Available at: https://www.ucd.ie/connect/
UCD Knowledge Base. Available at: https://fujitsuireland.service-now.com/itucd?id=kb_home_ucd
UCD SISWeb; Student Information System. Available at: https://hub.ucd.ie/usis/W_WEB_WELCOME_PAGE
UCD Student IT Guide. Available at: https://www.ucd.ie/itservices/startoftermguide/
UCD Web Accessibility Statement. Available at: https://www.ucd.ie/accessibility/
Web Content Accessibility Guidelines. Available at: https://www.w3.org/WAI/standards-guidelines/wcag/

8.3 Digital accessibility in the UK context

Alistair McNaught

The art of the possible

The paradigm shift is simple. It's about asking the question: "is the problem a disabled person or a disabled product?" If it's the latter, the follow-on question is: "why design/create/purchase disabling systems, tools or resources?"

The digital world has great potential for "un-disabling". For example:

- People who struggle to take meaning from printed text can listen instead
- A page created with heading styles can be skimmed, summarised, or navigated in seconds by dyslexic readers, blind readers, those with poor concentration or those whose confidence is easily overwhelmed
- Structured documents can transform to mind maps and vice versa
- Digital text can be recoloured, magnified, and reflowed so it still fits the screen.
- Information in images, video or audio can be conveyed in alternative ways to meet different needs.

Digital accessibility enables everyone. Courses can be accessed, books read, arguments discussed, tasks collaborated on, quizzes completed, and assessments performed, irrespective of disability. Digital, done well, is one of the most enabling environments on earth. But, ironically, it is often done badly.

A legacy of inexperience and ignorance

Digital accessibility is a marriage between imagination and training. With little experience of disability or little training in accessible practice, many struggle to imagine how differently disabled users access technology. Personal inexperience is compounded by institutional ignorance. Organisations purchase inaccessible digital systems or content. They create inaccessible branding and templates. Teaching content is created by people with no training in accessible practice, therefore users can't exploit accessibility benefits. The disconnect between good intention and good practice is evident, even at the highest levels where irony is rife.

DOI: 10.4324/9781003253631-30

Key reports and guidance to support disabled students remain inaccessible to their target audiences. Examples include the UK Office for Students' report 'Beyond the bare minimum – Are universities and colleges doing enough for disabled students?' and the Disabled Student's Commission guidance 'Considerations for disabled applicants to postgraduate study' (Office for Students, 2019; Disabled Students Commission, 2021). Both fail critical accessibility requirements like heading structures and reliable reflow. Reports that start as accessible documents are rendered inaccessible by graphic designers and marketing teams.

With its 50 compliance checkpoints, digital accessibility appears to be about coding, assistive technology, and disability. However, this is wrong, because:

- It is not about technical standards but good practices. True, a developer's "good practice" will involve technical standards. But if you just create documents and presentations, your good practices involve no technical standards at all, just a professionally informed way of working.
- It is not about disabled users. Accessible content makes all users more productive, working flexibly, comfortably, and efficiently.
- It is not about specialist teams. For anyone creating digital content – from social media posts to handouts and presentations – there is an inclusive way of doing it. If you don't know it, you probably exclude users.

Digital accessibility is not about expertise in technology or disability. It's about expertise in communicating without barriers.

Lessons from the UK context

The UK is not yet a paragon of digital accessibility – research (Rhodes, 2020) showed 80 per cent of Further Education Colleges had "no accessibility statement" or a "poor attempt" two years after the legislation came into force (The Public Sector Bodies (Websites and Mobile Applications) (No. 2) Accessibility Regulations 2018). Higher education was better – only 27 per cent with a poor or absent accessibility statement. However, despite such late adopters, legislation has created significant cultural shifts in many organisations. There are positives from the UK experience that are worth replicating.

At government level

In the UK, Government Digital Services (GDS) was responsible for implementing and auditing the legislation. In January 2018, a group of sector representatives requested an informal meeting with GDS to explore ways of collaborating. GDS agreed to an informal Digital Accessibility Working Group to improve understanding in both directions. The digital estate of a college/university is more complex than that of other public sector bodies so there were many things to understand. A Digital Accessibility Regulations mailing list (Jisc, 2018) was set up. It currently has over 1000 subscribers. The mailing list allowed:

- the working group to inform the sector of any new guidance from GDS
- managers and practitioners to raise issues on the mailing list. These were summarised for meetings with GDS then reported back
- relevant training to be advertised
- resources to be swapped
- problems to be debated.

Regular, honest meetings between the auditing body and the sector proved vital. For a culture change to be credible, it must be possible. However, education is complex. No other public sector institution has multiple platforms with multitudinous resources created weekly by non-specialists. Government bodies auditing institutions need to understand their challenges. A legalistic insistence on 100 per cent digital accessibility risks the unintended consequence of "ditching digital". Ironically, returning to chalk, talk, and handouts would create more barriers than the worst digital content.

At community level

Communities of practice are key for support and guidance. Many organisations (including services and suppliers) put on free training or support. Examples included:

- the Education and Training Foundation's free, self-access training modules on accessibility and several relevant webinars/recordings (Education and Training Foundation, 2019–2021)
- JISC's Teams channel and regular themed Accessibility Clinics helped coordinate guidance and resources.

The scale of the challenge encouraged a groundswell of sharing – some institutions like the University of York (2019) and Worcestershire County Council (2020) shared quality training resources with the sector. Others like the City of Westminster College used existing communities of practice to disseminate training and resources. Regular webinars from bodies as diverse as AbilityNet and the Future Teacher Project nurtured the sector's evolving understanding (AbilityNet, 2018; Future Teacher, 2017–2022). Further education struggled to access available support but the Association of Colleges' report on Creating a post-COVID-19 EdTech strategy (AoC, 2020) had four chapters on aspects of digital inclusion.

Conclusion

Digital accessibility is multi-layered, affecting everything from the digital platform to the way it is set up, the content it holds, and the skill of those who use it. Accessible content and systems make everyone more productive and are therefore better value. However, reality is complex. Content that is inaccessible to one person may be perfectly accessible to a person with different needs. Banning "inaccessible" content may discriminate against a different group of disabled users for whom the content added significant value. Organisations need to steer a careful path. They need to encourage teachers and lecturers to maximise digital content while minimising barriers due to lack of training or awareness. From experience in the UK, organisations making most significant progress are those where:

- Digital accessibility is driven from the top with senior managers actively involved.
- The process is transparent – students are involved with the journey and understand how it will benefit them. They are part of the solution, empowered to identify and report accessibility problems.
- Accessibility is seen holistically woven into procurement, policies, practice, and training. The accessibility maturity model for education (McNaught, AbilityNet, 2019) has helped dozens of UK organisations plan and prioritise in a strategic way that focuses on learner experience rather than technical standards.
- Knowledge of accessible digital practice is a "desirable" skill on any job applications involving creating online content or communications.
- Staff training in accessibility is focused on the skills required for the specific roles they perform.
- Progress is audited and reported on.
- The 'accessibility journey' – with its inevitable challenges, compromises, and contradictions – is openly shared between organisations via sector wide bodies and support networks.

Finally, organisations need to be proactive in defending staff and students from unintended consequences. Bodies responsible for auditing compliance often have little experience of the day-to-day complexities of further and higher education. Some UK universities experienced pushback from staff and unions where the demands of compliance were deemed to be unrealistic. Plan a marathon, not a sprint. Use the "disproportionate burden" derogation wisely as a breathing space to identify priorities, plan improvements, and implement quality assurance processes.

New technologies will create new challenges. New staff will need training. New standards will emerge, but the basics remain. Professional practice is accessible practice. Nobody chooses to design barriers for users.

References

AbilityNet (2018 onwards). AbilityNet webinars. Available at: https://abilitynet.org.uk/free-resources/webinars (accessed 4 January 2022).

AoC (2020). Creating a post-COVID-19 EdTech strategy. Association of Colleges. Available at: https://www.aoc.co.uk/policy/technology/creating-a-post-covid-19-edtech-strategy (accessed 4 January 2022).

Disabled Students Commission (2021). Considerations for disabled applicants to postgraduate study. Advance HE guide. Available at: https://www.advance-he.ac.uk/knowledge-hub/considerations-disabled-applicants-applying-postgraduate-courses (accessed 3 January 2022).

Education and Training Foundation (2019–2021). Enhance digital teaching platform. Available at: https://enhance.etfoundation.co.uk/category/accessibility (accessed 3 January 2022).

Education and Training Foundation (2020). Webinars to support remote working. Resources to support remote working. Available at: https://enhance.etfoundation.co.uk/remoteworking (accessed 3 January 2022).

Future Teacher (2017–2022). Future Teacher Talks UK. Future Teacher project. Available at: https://xot.futureteacher.eu/play.php?template_id=4#home (accessed 4 January 2022).

Jisc (2018). Digital accessibility regulations Home Page. Jiscmail. Available at: https://www.jiscmail.ac.uk/cgi-bin/wa-jisc.exe?A0=DIGITALACCESSIBILITYREGULATIONS (accessed 3 January 2022).

McNaught, A., AbilityNet (2019). Accessibility Maturity Model. Alistair McNaught Consultancy Ltd. Available at: https://www.learningapps.co.uk/moodle/xertetoolkits/play.php?template_id=2196#page1 (accessed 4 January 2022).

Office for Students (2019). Beyond the bare minimum. Are universities and colleges doing enough for disabled students? *OfS Insight*, issue 4. Available at: https://www.officeforstudents.org.uk/media/1a263fd6-b20a-4ac7-b268-0bbaa0c153a2/beyond-the-bare-minimum-are-universities-and-colleges-doing-enough-for-disabled-students.pdf (accessed 3 January 2022).

Rhodes, G. (2020). Accessibility statements v 4. AllAble. Available at: https://www.allable.co.uk/research/accessibility-statements-v4 (accessed 3 January 2022).

University of York (2019). Creating accessible documents workshop. Available at: https://docs.google.com/presentation/d/1F0OjnstuJVU2GX-CuGA7TaM7yflw6ucUqke7k-Xp-8Q/edit#slide=id.g5900fa8483_23_13 (accessed 3 January 2022).

Worcestershire County Council (2020). SCULPT for Accessibility. Worcestershire County Council. Available at: https://www.worcestershire.gov.uk/WCCSculpt (accessed 4 January 2022).

9 Conclusion – carpe diem – seize the day!

Anna M. Kelly

Introduction

This is the final chapter. We set out to create a book that answers the 'how' question – 'How to make access and inclusion everybody's business – How to create a university for all'? This book – *Making Inclusive Higher Education a Reality: Creating a University for All* – is informed by our experience of leading the University for All initiative in University College Dublin (UCD). This case study is underpinned by theory, evidence, and practice, and is buttressed by University policy and strategy (UCD, 2021, 2020a, 2018).

Throughout the writing of this book, we have endeavoured to remain faithful to the task of answering the 'how' question. Our experience of leading the implementation of the University for All initiative has enabled us to develop the tools to translate inclusion rhetoric to reality. Hence, we offer the reader a tried, tested, and transferable model to transform higher education and create inclusive institutions, where all students feel they belong.

We would be less than candid if we did not reiterate that there is no magic answer; there is no single action that can be taken; there in no silver bullet for this complex task of institutional transformation. However, we have first-hand implementation knowledge, and confidently offer a proven set of ingredients and contextual solutions to enable the creation of a university for all.

Throughout this book, we have used language in a deliberate way. In higher education discourse there are considerable differences in naming and defining under-represented students. Terms, such as access, equality, equity, diversity, inclusion, widening participation, are often used interchangeably. Throughout this book, we use the word 'access', which we define as meaning the participation and inclusion of groups who are under-represented in higher education. While this varies from country to country, these groups typically experience low participation on the grounds of age, disability, socio-economic status, race and ethnicity, family status, gender, or sexual orientation.

We also recognise that terms such as mainstreaming may be contested and understood differently. We use this term to mean a whole-institution systemic response that weaves access and inclusion into the fabric of the organisation at every level, recognising that it is everyone's business. Hence, mainstreaming

DOI: 10.4324/9781003253631-31

extends access beyond entry, to include an inclusive learning environment, designed for all students, and including teaching and learning, student support, and the built and technology environment. We define a university for all as an institution where all students feel they belong. Timmons (Chapter 2) supports this view and argued that the Equality, Diversity & Inclusion movement needs to be "all inclusive" and suggests that "Leaders need to ensure that there are conversations held on campuses and resources allocated that serve all groups".

The UCD University for All initiative, and this book, was prompted by Kelly (2017), whose study of implementation of access policy in Ireland's seven universities identified an 'inclusion implementation gap', despite the policy imperative that explicitly promotes the integration of access and inclusion into everyday life of the university: moving it from the institution's margins (HEA, 2015). In response to this 'gap', University for All was developed as a whole-institution evidence-based and systemic response to ensure that all students feel they belong (Kelly, 2018; Kelly and Padden, 2018b). Using an institutional lens, University for All frames the creation of a culture of inclusion necessary to embed and mainstream access in higher education. Adopting a systemic approach, University for All weaves inclusion into the fabric of the institution, engages the entire university community, and addresses all aspects of campus life – teaching, learning, support, services, and the built and technology infrastructure. In short, it moves beyond 'opening the door' to higher education and, instead, promotes universally designed inclusive systems, processes and approaches.

> Every student, wherever they come from and whatever their background, will have specific needs and requirements and we need to tailor what we do, to really meet the full range of requirements students have, without labelling them in any way.
>
> Professor Mark Rogers, UCD Registrar & Deputy President, September 2020 (UCD, 2020b)

In this context, this book distils our experience of the implementation of University for All and, importantly, it also draws on the work of international authors whose contributions offer perspectives for the USA, Canada, UK, Belgium, and Morocco. In this final chapter, we have synthesised the learning, describing Key Take Aways, and offer the ingredients to enable readers to progress their inclusion journey confidently.

Lessons from the implementation frontline

The overarching message of this book is that institutional transformation, while complex, is achievable with a developed understanding of the essential ingredients and tools to enable this change. Over the course of eight chapters, this book has taken the reader through this process, offering an insight into these ingredients, the tools to drive implementation, and the rationale for their use.

Achievement of an inclusive university for all demands institutional transformation, with increasing agreement on the need to move from concept to reality. The challenges associated with this such are considerable (Chapter 2). Williams, Russell, and Tuitt, drawing on Kennedy (2020), emphasised the need to avoid the "diversity loop" and advise "HWIs [Historically White Institutions] seeking to make excellence inclusive and antiracist must commit to moving beyond superficial performative DEIJ [Diversity, Equality, Inclusion & Justice] pretences and engage in the hard work of transforming their institutions" (Chapter 2). We concur, and this transformation is indeed hard work, and because of this reality, we draw attention to the important qualities that have proved invaluable. As such, we think courage, being comfortable with levels of ambiguity, and a healthy respect for imperfection will help sustain and overcome the inevitable obstacles that will arise. Because of the enormity of this challenge, people often ask us, 'where to begin'; we strongly recommend beginning wherever the opportunity presents – change is not a linear process. Taking a lead from George Bernard Shaw, who advised that we "don't wait for the right opportunity: create it" the critical decision is to start, to seize the day – carpe diem!

The creation of a university for all requires systemic cultural change, and calls for leadership, engagement with the university community, and the student voice. The deliberate involvement of this triumvirate of actors is necessary to ensure that all voices are heard, contextual issues are considered, and ownership is fostered. In our experience, two of these actors tend to be automatically considered for leading parts. However, increasingly, the pivotal role of students is also being recognised (Brooks et al., 2015; Czerniawski and Kidd, 2011). Students are powerful catalysts for change and their role as 'ally' is integral to the implementation process (Chapters 1 & 6).

Taking inspiration from Durkheim – the French sociologist who summarised that talent is equally distributed, opportunity is not – we recognise that students' awareness of issues of social justice and equity is essential to their educational experience, which, in turn, informs their role as implementation actor. The students' lived experience is a most effective antidote to the received wisdom and the associated assumptions, and serves as a powerful persuader (CFE Research, 2020).

Understanding the challenges of implementation are helpful when approaching the creation of an inclusive university (Chapter 2). As Pressman and Wildavsky (1984) note, "People appear to think that implementation should be easy: they are therefore upset when expected events do not occur or turn out badly" (pp. xx–xxi). Higher education institutions are complex organisations, with different traditions, missions and structures, competing priorities, external pressures, and financial constraints. As a result, implementation is intricate and multi-multi-faceted. When leading such change, we think it is important to become "hopeful implementers" (Bowen, 1982) and develop a compelling range of tactics and associated strategies, such as persistence, multiple implementation ideas, and priorities to engineering a 'bandwagon effect' (Bowen, 1982, pp. 18–20).

Recognising that higher education institutions are complex entities, we propose seven critical components (Figure 9.1) to enable the move from policy statement to embedding access in practice: 1) University Leadership and Institutional Strategic Planning, 2) Governance and Structures, 3) Evidence and Data, 4) Implementation Planning and Leadership, 5) Consultation, 6) Promotions and Communications, and 7) Staff Training and Development (Chapter 2).

A tactic that has proved pivotal in accelerating the change process is the role of evidence and data. Fleming (Chapter 3) argues that "We treasure what we measure", and proposes data collection (however imperfect), the visual representation of these data, clear accessible data storytelling, together with knowing your audience, as a powerful force in altering perceptions, attitudes, and behaviours. She illustrates this through the work of John Snow, a medical doctor who sought to understand the spread of cholera, and consequently mapped the spread of this disease, tracking it to one well, leading to the eventual acceptance in the scientific community that cholera was not spread through the air but was a deadly bacterium (Johnson, 2006). Fleming argues that "The value of data in driving change is incontrovertible", a viewpoint shared with Holness, who says "Data are important, but they must be fit for purpose and produced in ways that staff can fully engage with them", noting the importance of using data to assess the impact of on students and focus on

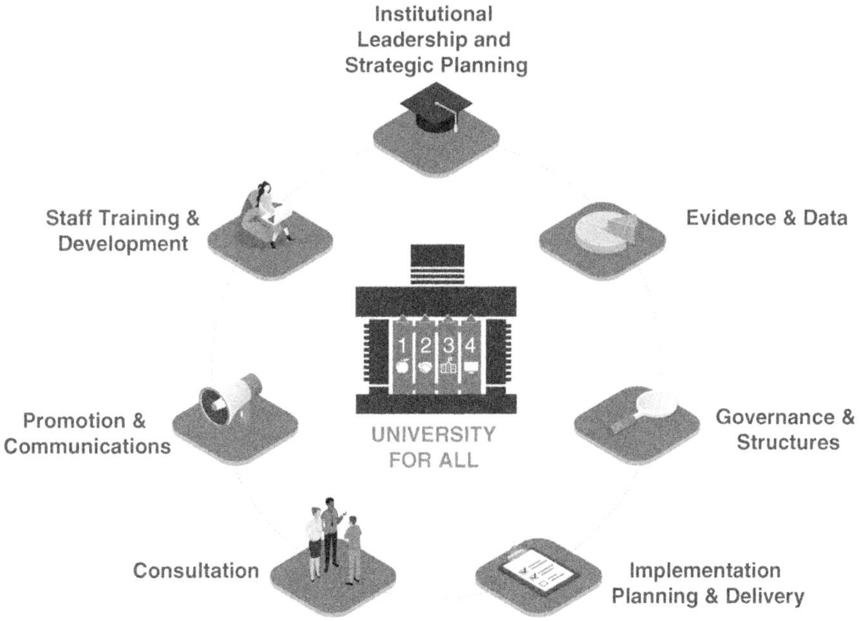

Figure 9.1 University for All Implementation Framework

how we work with students (Chapter 3). Fleming proposes a model for using data to identify and prompt action to drive change, comprising:

- Context – set the scene
- Protagonist – establish the characters
- Resolution – call for action
- Transformation – establish the solution
- Obstacle – identify the problem.

In addition to the use of data, the Toolkit for Inclusive Higher Education Institutions (Kelly and Padden, 2018a) is also a critical device to stimulate and scaffold the institutional change process. Padden (Chapter 4) discusses this self-assessment tool, designed to turn belief and vision into action. Padden observed, "If the road to hell is paved with good intentions, then higher education institutions that haven't actioned inclusion are built, brick by brick, with belief and vision that has never become reality".

This Toolkit reinforces a 'one bite at a time' approach, offering an institution-wide lens to assess inclusion progress, identify opportunities for improvement, and create bespoke action plans. The challenge of continuing to implement the change process during COVID-19 accelerated the development of a digital version, which now also includes a reporting function. The format of the Toolkit comprises four typical institutional 'pillars', as well as the foundation and scaffolding components:

- Foundations and Scaffolding: Strategic Approach and Organisation
- Pillar 1: Programme & Curriculum Design, Teaching & Learning
- Pillar 2: Student Supports & Services
- Pillar 3: Physical Campus & the Built Environment
- Pillar 4: Information Technology Systems & Infrastructure.

Characterising the Toolkit as a "living document which will evolve and adapt", designed for use by programmes, schools/departments, or professional units, Padden outlines the four key steps:

1. Seek senior leader support
2. Establish a change team
3. Conduct a University for All workshop (to discuss the relevant student data, engage the student voice, Universal Design and inclusive practice training, undertake the self-assessment exercise)
4. Develop an Action Plan.

Padden observed, "The completion of the self-assessment exercise with as many colleagues as possible is highly effective in creating awareness of inclusive practice". Concurring, Farrelly, who uses the Toolkit in the Arts & Humanities discipline, questions, "who 'does' inclusion?" – her experience suggests it often falls to early career female staff on precarious contracts. She notes that the Toolkit has "democratised inclusion work" and offers her, as Widening Participation Lead, a 'sword and shield' that ensures visibility and recognition with the academy. Also in Chapter 4, Finlay, who uses it with Social Science colleagues, reported that the Toolkit facilitates iteration and flexibility, allowing for progress and resolution of areas of tension. He also observed that participants tended to "underrate current practice", and some "participants suggested that change has to come to a considerable extent from the top, so that practice matched the university's rhetoric, and the necessary resources were provided". Flanagan (Chapter 4) uses the Toolkit within the Engineering discipline and, over a two-year period, held in-person and virtual sessions that considered Pillar 1: Programme & Curriculum Design, Teaching & Learning and Pillar 4: Information Technology Systems & Infrastructure. He observes that using the Toolkit "has impacted very positively on our inclusive practice in Engineering at UCD". He attributes this to a range of factors, including the use of specific questions, which "provoke debate and engagement among colleagues in a way that 'opening the floor' without creating context for discussion cannot efficiently do". Flanagan also draws attention to the importance of the involvement of senior leaders as critical to support, convey a sense of urgency, and maximise participation in the Toolkit workshops.

The theme of how to promote inclusion in the classroom is explored in Chapter 5. Padden advocates the adoption of Universal Design for Learning (UDL). First used with students with disabilities, it is increasingly recognised as a framework that benefits all students. She notes that "UDL is not a set of rules but rather a framework which prompts a change in thinking and practice, encouraging faculty to consider the diversity of their students before they even begin their programme". At its core, UDL concerns flexibility and choice by "providing students with multiple means of engaging with learning, accessing learning materials, and demonstrating their learning through assessment and other activities". Padden stresses the importance of UDL in effecting change in the classroom through a focus on the educator rather than perceived student 'deficits'. She also highlighted the Faculty Partner Programme, a project to accelerate the implementation of UDL by developing a Community of Practice of UDL advocates and role models across all disciplines (Chapter 5).

Aabi and Bracken offered their experience of using UDL to promote learner agency in the University of Ibn Zohr (UIZ), Morocco's largest university. They discussed the importance of learner agency in advancing inclusive practice, where, historically, practice favoured differentiating the curriculum in the absence of little research or practice in "anticipatory inclusive design". This novel case study was "championed by lecturers and learners who are keen to bring about positive change in inclusive practices" (Chapter 5), and includes UDL capacity building, learner blogs, research, and evaluation. While acknowledging the success of this initiative in developing policy and practice in UIZ, these authors cautioned against transposing UDL "directly from its initial application within schools in North America onto educational contexts that are significantly different in relation to their socio-cultural, historical and legislative pathways".

In yet another context, Yang melds two educational frameworks – Universal Design for Learning and Intercultural study – to develop a model for UDL for Culturally Inclusive Learning, which overlays the key features of each, to address: 1) engagement (why), 2) representation (how), and 3) action and expression (what) (Chapter 5). Yang observes that the world, and the higher education classroom, is increasingly globalised, and urges university educators to build an understanding of the impact of cultural dimensions on the approaches and expectations of students from cultural backgrounds different from their own. Yang notes that they must adapt their own teaching approach to ensure their teaching is culturally inclusive. This case study offers an approach to Culturally Inclusive Teaching based on UDL, an important component of which is Intercultural Development.

Fleming (Chapter 6) juxtaposes student support with the issue of the status of those who provide it. In teasing out what lies behind the term 'student support', Fleming draws on Lareau's (2011, 2003) research into parenting styles and sense of 'entitlement' among middle-class children, in contrast to those from working-class backgrounds, and concludes that "it would therefore seem reasonable to conclude that the work of those of us in Student Support is to cultivate a sense of entitlement to supports" (Chapter 6). She further develops this idea, drawing on Bourdieu's work on cultural, social, and symbolic capitol (Crossley, 2008), to make connections between the types of support offered and those preferred by students. She cites a 'capitol' analysis of the goals of 645 incoming students, carried out at the beginning of the 2019–20 academic year, which revealed that students' goals fell into the four capitol categories, which congregate in Social (291), Culture (209), Academic (138), with the goals of seven students classified as Financial. In this context, Fleming proposes that the nature, timing, sequencing, and content of student supports need careful consideration. She also questions the extent to which "supports are universally designed so that our students from the non-dominant background are not required to assimilate to succeed in education" (Chapter 6). Furthermore, she cautioned about messaging and "its potential for 'othering' and the risk of prompting students to create an alternative narrative, or what Reay and her colleagues (2009) refer to as 'reinvention'". Issues of terminology and language were also of concern, such as the commonly used concept of 'raising aspirations'; for example, Fleming favours terms such as 'raising expectations' or 'realising aspirations' as they convey a culture of inclusion and positivity. Fleming asserts that both the status of supports and those who provide them is opaque, noting that staff working in "student supports tend to be located outside the academic sphere", and that "the term 'professional' is contestable", concluding that "The location and governance of student supports therefore runs the risk of undermining or devaluing the function, efficacy, and impact of student supports and services in supporting an inclusive university" (Chapter 6). She favours adoption of the "Third Space", "to explore the emergence of broadly based, extended projects across the university, which are no longer contained within fixed boundaries, and have generated new roles and activities" (Whitchurch, 2013, 2008). In this context, Fleming calls for a move away from the debate from what was described as the "academic–administrator 'divide'" (Conway, 2012) to "reimagining of the nature of student support, and the engagement of more colleagues, both academic and professional, [that] would embed the activity and incorporate it as an integral aspect of the university mission".

Thomas, too (Chapter 6), notes, "For too long student support has been sidelined, positioned as a remedial intervention for students who are struggling and may be at risk of withdrawing, rather than a mainstream activity for all students, and to be undertaken by all staff". Thomas' research, spanning over 20 years, chronicles the evolution of supports, their delivery, as well as their role and status within the academy. At the beginning of the century, she found that "The overriding concern was to consider how student services could play a more strategic and influential role in the emerging widening participation agenda, by contributing to the retention and completion of students from 'non-traditional' student groups" (Thomas et al., 2002). A decade later, a study of the "gendered engagement with academic and pastoral support services" reported little change in the model of service delivery (Woodfield and Thomas, 2012). Thomas describes #Ibelong, developed as a model for mainstreaming student support, and involving the whole course/programme team in specific interventions: 1) Dialogue Days, 2) Team Teacher Reflection, and 3) Student Community Mentoring (Thomas, forthcoming). She highlights Dialogue Days (DD), which "bring together students, staff and student community mentors from a particular course or programme of study, and create a safe space in which to discuss diversity, belonging and success". Two types of DD are: DD1, provided to incoming students, focused on "dialogue about diversity in relation to past experiences and expectations of the forthcoming HE programme, promoting interaction between students and with staff to develop belonging and thinking about how the course can support students to be successful". The second, DD2, offered "towards the end of the academic year, reflects on the first-year experience of studying, belonging, and succeeding in HE, and empowers students to feel safe and supported in looking ahead to be successful in their second year of study, where there are increased academic demands and higher expectations of student autonomy".

Similar to Fleming's work, Thomas finds that "students benefitted by making friends, getting to know staff, gaining understanding about diversity and the importance and challenges of belonging and success; and staff developed understanding about the diversity of their students and their support needs". She also advises that accessible student supports embedded in the curriculum are needed, as is the use of a "diversity-brave" approach, enabling students to talk about difference (Chapter 6).

The learning environment was discussed by Lombard (Chapter 7), who as an Occupational Therapist is concerned with the relationship between the person, environment, and everyday performance. Lombard defines an inclusive built campus as

> one that caters to the diverse needs of the population so that as many users as possible can access, navigate and use the campus facilities without the need for specific accommodations, modifications or assistive technologies and hence can engage in all aspects of university life.
>
> (p. xxxxx)

She characterises the physical environment as part of a 'jigsaw' that must be supported by institutional policies and procedures that promote diversity and inclusion. Lombard's practice involves supporting students with disabilities, and, therefore, she is alert to the environmental impact on student "performance of and engagement in the academic, social, and personal aspects of their student role, and subsequently their level of satisfaction, enjoyment, and sense of belonging within a university" (Chapter 7). While the need for an accessible built environment has been driven by people with disabilities, it has resulted in adoption of minimum standards, rather than inclusion for all (Imrie, 2012; Ringaert, 2003; Shauyb, 2020). Pointing to the increased participation by students with disabilities in UCD (Fleming et al., 2022), Lombard reminds us that the university has "many kinds of users in a university (e.g. students, staff, visitors, research participants, service personnel)", who have diverse needs "including but not limited to users with a physical, cognitive, sensory, or mental health disability, low-income users, mature entrants, people from international backgrounds with different languages and cultures, part-time users, users who are pregnant, have a temporary illness or injury, or users of various ages and genders" (Chapter 7). Drawing on the work of Salmen (2001), Lombard advocates the adoption of universal design, which "goes beyond mere compliance" and seeks to design environments for all:

> Accessibility is a function of compliance with regulations or criteria that establish a minimum level of design necessary to accommodate people with disabilities, universal design is the art and practice of design to accommodate the widest variety and number of people throughout their lifespans
>
> (Salmen, 2011, p. 6.1)

Lombard, stressing the importance of user data to inform the campus development, cites sample responses to the physical campus and built environment survey statement in University for All Student and Staff surveys, conducted in UCD in 2020. She advises that the development of an inclusive built campus takes time; a point reinforced by Froyen (Chapter 7), who highlights real-life challenges, including the lack of a whole-institutional approach, budgetary roadblocks, and implementation obstacles. Froyen charts the evolution of Universal Design education for the built environment from policy direction (Council of Europe, 2001) to experimentation in selected universities. While embedding this work in architecture curriculums was initially slow, Froyen notes that "two decades later, a new generation seems to build on more solid social, academic, and professional foundations in a multi-disciplinary academic approach". He presents two case studies, one undertaken in UHasselt (Hasselt University, Belgium) and one describing an experimental design for "Rooms for Care & Well-being" in public spaces, noting "a diversity of trial-and-error grassroots approaches will gradually lead to a more consistent body of knowledge and experience" (Chapter 7).

Corcoran and Hamill (Chapter 7), together with Sweeney and Lowe, present such a body of knowledge in describing UCD's journey towards developing an inclusive physical campus and built environment. Sweeney and Lowe outline the approach to mainstreaming inclusion and campus accessibility. Key features include gathering data and evidence, assigning resources, fostering effective collaborative working relationships, creating awareness, developing ownership, financial commitment, incremental change, and the support of senior leaders. They present the Accessible Sensory Trail case study as an example of collaborative campus innovation. The Trail consists of several individual garden areas, where accessibility was improved, and where additional sensory planting occurred. These areas link to form a trail across campus.

Corcoran and Hamill, who work as 'campus custodians', managing the university property, discuss strategies to deal with new and legacy structures in the context of the creation of an inclusive university for all (Chapter 7). They describe the adoption of a 'new build' Universal Design (UD) process, whereby Universal Design criteria (43-point checklist), based on the University for All Toolkit (Kelly and Padden, 2018a), were developed. Now, all building designs are subject to this process, which includes accessibility workshops, a UD checklist review, and a UD feasibility report, which is augmented by on-going accessibility advice from the University accessibility consultant.

A strategy for legacy buildings is also described by Corcoran and Hamill. They have developed an Accessibility Systems Management Plan to monitor all essential building accessibility features – an approach that has served to embed inclusion in day-to-day operations. In tandem with this, they have developed a programme of 'Minor Works', which are small-scale improvements that "make impactful alterations in a legacy campus". They noted the importance of a whole-institution approach, and collaboration between the university and design teams, as central to the development of an inclusive campus.

In the penultimate chapter (Chapter 8), Elliott addresses the technological environment, highlighting the impact of digital inaccessibility on the educational experience for all students, created by inaccessible technologies, including websites, format of learning materials, and inadequate digital competence of students and faculty. He notes, however, that much that was impossible heretofore, was fast-tracked by the onset of COVID-19, which exposed educational inequalities and the 'digital divide' (AHEAD, 2020; Fitzpatrick and McStravock, 2020). Yet, students also reported an appreciation of the flexibilities that online learning offered. They reported feeling more independent as learners, and "they could fit their learning into their lives more easily" (Clarke, 2020, sec. 2). Clarke cautions against relying exclusively on tools for learning, but rather advocates adherence to pedagogical principles of design, recommending that "all online/blended or hybrid activity adheres to the principles of Universal Design" (Clarke, 2020, sec. 5). To embed Universal Design in IT systems, Elliott recommends a strategic collaborative approach, development of coherent policies, and the promotion of a partnership between students, citing the IUA EDTL, who are "engaging students as co-creators in developing digital teaching and resources" as an example of such partnership (IUA EDTL, 2021).

Recognising the need for such collaboration and partnership, O'Rourke, Teevan, and Collins, describe UCD's journey towards the development of inclusive information systems and infrastructure. Acknowledging the scale and complexity of systems that include the teaching/virtual teaching, learning, and research environment, as well as student information systems, they note, "these technologies need to be developed with the entire student body in mind" (Chapter 8). They present a case study, illustrating the implementation of Ally, a tool to assist faculty and staff in the creation of accessible content, generating alternative formats for students, providing faculty with accessibility scores on learning content, and suggesting how these can be improved. O'Rourke, Teevan, and Collins also outline measures taken to comply with the EU Directive of Website Accessibility (Government of Ireland/European Union, 2020), and where compliance is monitored by the NDA (National Disability Authority). They also describe a pilot programme using Silktide, a web-based application enabling site owners to measure and improve website performance. With over 420 websites existing under the UCD domain, O'Rourke, Teevan, and Collins stress the need for vigilance to ensure alignment with/between IT planning policy and inclusion goals.

Finally, McNaught (Chapter 8) discusses digital accessibility in the UK, which is making progress (Rhodes, 2020). McNaught observes that digital accessibility involves complex, multi-layered issues, with stakeholders at government and community levels. He advocates the promotion of good communications between all stakeholders to identify issues, barriers, and solutions. McNaught also recommends that awareness, education and training, support, and resources are needed to foster its development. He urges the creation of opportunities for sharing information on the challenges, compromises, and contradictions of the 'accessibility journey'.

The creation of such learning opportunities lies at the heart of this book: We wrote *Making Inclusive Higher Education a Reality: Creating a University*

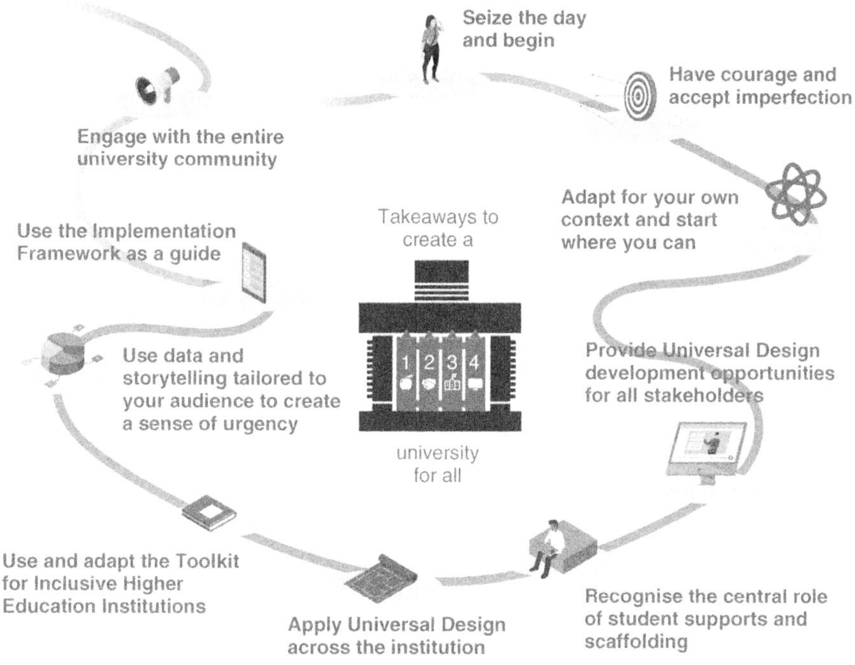

Figure 9.2 Key Take Aways for creating a University for All

for All so that higher education could benefit from our collective experience of the ebb and flow of creating an inclusive university.

To this end, we have distilled our learning into 11 lessons, which we describe as Key Take Aways (Figure 9.2): 1) Seize the day and begin; 2) Have courage and accept imperfection; 3) Adapt for your own context and start where you can; 4) Provide Universal Design development opportunities for all stakeholders; 5) Recognise the central role of student supports and scaffolding; 6) Inclusion means moving beyond compliance; 7) Apply Universal Design across the institution; 8) Use and adapt the 'Toolkit for Inclusive Higher Education Institutions' (Kelly and Padden, 2018); 9) Use data and storytelling tailored to your audience to create a sense of urgency; 10) Use the University for All Implementation Framework as a guide (Chapter 1 & 2), and 11) Engage with the entire university community.

Focal scoir – last word

Higher education institutions are increasingly reflective of society's diverse population mix, where universities and colleges are challenged to design proactively more flexibilities that meet the needs of all students and offer a learning experience that takes account of the breadth and diversity of student needs. This book, *Making Inclusive Higher Education a Reality: Creating a*

University for All, forges research and practice in the fields of Universal Design, access, inclusion, change, and institutional transformation, offering real-world insights to enable higher education to rise to this challenge.

In so doing, however, we are persuaded by the idea of evolution, not revolution. As we have said many times, higher education environments are complex entities and an evolutionary approach works best, is more sustainable, and fosters ownership and collaboration. Taking inspiration from Soren Kierkegaard, the Danish philosopher, who said, "Life can only be understood by looking backward; but it must be lived looking forward" (Bouchier-Hayes, 2005), we have looked backward. We have deepened our understanding, created new knowledge, and, now, offer it to you, the reader. We hope that it will be a force for good in the development of an inclusive future for all in higher education.

References

AHEAD (2020). *Learning from Home During COVID-19: A Survey of Irish FET and HE Students with Disabilities.* Dublin: AHEAD Educational Press.

Bouchier-Hayes, D. (2005). "Life can only be understood by looking backward; but it must be lived looking forward" — Soren Kierkegaard (1813–1855). *Irish Journal of Medical Science*, 174, 4. https://doi.org/10.1007/BF03168511

Bowen, E. (1982). The Pressman–Wildavsky Paradox: Four addenda or why models based on probability theory can predict implementation success and suggest useful tactical advice for implementers. *Journal of Public Policy*, 2, 1–21.

Brooks, R., Byford, K., and Sela, K. (2015). The changing role of Students' Unions within contemporary higher education. *Journal of Education Policy*, 30, 165–181.

CFE Research (2020). *The Role of Lived Experience in Creating Systems Change: Evaluation of Fulfilling Lives: Supporting People with Multiple Needs.* Leicester, UK: CFE Research.

Clarke, M. (2020). *Report of the Working Group on Prioritised Resourcing to Support Teaching, Learning and Assessment in the Autumn Trimester 2020/21*. Dublin: University College Dublin.

Conway, M. (2012). Using Causal Layered Analysis to explore the relationship between academics and administrators in universities. *Journal of Futures Studies*, 17(2), 37–58.

Council of Europe (2001). *Resolution Resap(2001)1 on the Introduction of the Principles of Universal Design into the Curricula of All Occupations Working on the Built Environment*. Strasbourg: CoE.

Crossley, N. (2008). Social class. In M. Grenfield (ed.), *Pierre Bourdieu: Key Concepts.*. Stocksfield, UK: Acumen.

Czerniawski, G. and Kidd, W. (eds). (2011). *The Student Voice Handbook: Bridging the Academic/Practitioner Divide.* Bingley, UK: Emerald Group Publishing.

Fitzpatrick, L. and McStravock, K. (2020). *National Reports on Students and COVID-19.* Dublin: USI.

Fleming, B., Padden, L., and Kelly, A. (2022). *Who Counts? University for All Data, Metrics and Evidence, 2021–2022*. Dublin: UCD Access & Lifelong Learning.

Government of Ireland/European Union (2020). *S.I. No. 358/2020 – European Union (Accessibility of Websites and Mobile Applications of Public Sector Bodies) Regulations 2020*.

HEA (2015). *National Plan for Equity of Access to Higher Education, 2015–2019*. Dublin: Higher Education Authority.

Imrie, R. (2012). Universalism, universal design and equitable access to the built environment. *Disability and Rehabilitation*, 34, 873–882.

IUA EDTL (2021). *Your Education, Your Voice, Your Vision – Results of the Student Campaign run by the Enhancing Digital Teaching and Learning (EDTL)*. Dublin: IUA.

Johnson, S. (2006). *The Ghost Map: The Story of London's Most Terrifying Epidemic – And How It Changed Science, Cities, and the Modern World*. New York: Riverhead Books.

Kelly, A. (2018). From the margins to mainstreaming – a universally designed and inclusive approach to access and participation in UCD. In *Ireland's Yearbook of Education. Mapping the Past. Forging the Future 2017–2018*. Dublin: Education Matters.

Kelly, A. (2017). *An Analysis of the Implementation of National Access Policy to Integrate and Mainstream Equality of Access in Irish Universities – Through the Lens of Inclusive Design (PhD)*. Dublin: University College Dublin.

Kelly, A.M. and Padden, L. (2018a). *Toolkit for Inclusive Higher Education Institutions – From Vision to Practice*. University for All Publication Series. Dublin: UCD Access & Lifelong Learning.

Kelly, A. and Padden, L. (2018b). University for All: Embedding equality of access, participation and success in higher education. In *Universal Design & Higher Education in Transformation Congress: Conference Proceedings*. Dublin: Centre for Universal Design/IOS Publications.

Kennedy, D. (2020). Moving beyond 'performative' diversity commitments. Presidio Blog. Available at: https://www.presidio.edu/blog/moving-beyond-performative-diversity-commitments/ (accessed 28 February 2022).

Lareau, A. (2011). *Unequal Childhoods: Class, Race, and Family Life*. Berkeley, CA and London: University of California Press.

Lareau, A. (2003). *Unequal Childhoods: Class, Race, and Family Life*. Berkeley, CA and London: University of California Press.

Pressman, J.L. and Wildavsky, A.B. (1984). *Implementation*. Berkeley, CA and London: University of California Press.

Reay, D., Crozier, G., and Clayton, J. (2009). 'Strangers in Paradise': Working-class students in elite universities. *Sociology*, 43, 1103–1121.

Rhodes, G. (2020). *Accessibility Statements V4* (online) Available at: https://www.allable.co.uk/research/accessibility-statements-v4 (accessed 7 February 2022).

Ringaert, L. (2003). Universal Design of the built environment to enable occupational performance. In L. Letts, P. Rigby, and D. Stewart (eds), *Using Environments to Enable Occupational Performance*. Thorofare, NJ: SLACK Incorporated, pp. 97–116.

Salmen, J.P.S. (2011). U.S. Accessibility Codes and Standards: Challenges for Universal Design. In W.F.E. Preiser and K.H. Smith (eds), *Universal Design Handbook*, 2nd edn. New York: McGraw-Hill, pp. 6. 1–6. 7.

Shauyb, T. (2020). Emergence of design standards and inclusive design. In T. Shauyb (ed.), *Inclusive University Built Environments: The Impact of Approved Document M for Architects, Designers, and Engineers*. Cham, Switzerland: Springer Nature, pp. 35–62.

Thomas, L. (forthcoming). *Dialogue Days (IO1). #Ibelong: Towards a Sense of Belonging in an Inclusive Learning Environment*. Rotterdam: Erasmus University.

Thomas, L., Quinn, J., Slack, K., and Casey, L. (2002). *Student Services: Effective Approaches to Retaining Students in Higher Education*. Stoke-on-Trent: Institute for Access Studies, Staffordshire University Press.

UCD (2018). *Equality, Diversity and Inclusion (EDI) Strategy and Action Plan 2018–2020–2025*. Dublin: University College Dublin.

UCD (2020a). *To the Rising Future, UCD Strategy 2020–2024*. Dublin: University College Dublin.

UCD (2020b). *Strategy 2020–2024 – Enabling a University for All*. Dublin: UCD Access & Lifelong Learning.

UCD (2021). *Education and Student Success Strategy*. Dublin: University College Dublin.

Whitchurch, C. (2008). Shifting identities and blurring boundaries: The emergence of third space professionals in UK higher education. *Higher Education Quarterly*, 62(4), 377–396.

Whitchurch, C. (2013). *Reconstructing Identities in Higher Education: The Rise of Third Space Professionals*. Abingdon, UK and New York: Routledge.

Woodfield, R. and Thomas, L. (2012). *Male Students: Engagement with Academic and Pastoral Support Services*. London: Equality Challenge Unit.

Appendix

OHAC

O'Herlihy Access Consultancy

Accessibility Review

Project:	()
Address:	
Review Type:	
Review Date:	
Prepared by:	

Latest revision (Rev No.X) – Date

Universal Design Considerations

The following is a list of items for consideration in order to achieve a Universal Design approach within the proposed design.

No.	*Area*	*Item*	*Within current design?*	*Design Team Comments – Feb 20*	*OHAC Comment/ Query – Date*	*Design Team Feedback*
1	External Environment	Covered walkways				
2	External Environment	Set down areas for larger vehicles				
3	External Environment	Dog spending areas				
4	External Environment	Seating/Rest points				
5	External Environment	Street Furniture/ Lighting				
6	External Environment	Surface finishes				
7	External Environment	Cycling				
8	External Environment	Shared spaces design				
9	External Environment	Accessible electric parking				
10	External Environment	Wayfinding and signage				
11	External Environment	Steps and equitable use				

No.	*Area*	*Item*	*Within current design?*	*Design Team Comments – Feb 20*	*OHAC Comment/ Query – Date*	*Design Team Feedback*
12	Entrances	Automated doors with canopies				
13	Entrances	Intercom design				
14	Waiting/reception areas throughout the building	Mixed seating to be provided throughout				
15	Waiting/reception area	Mobility scooter parking and charging				
16	Circulation	Automated doors on corridors/access strategy				
17	Circulation	Lifts larger than part M requirements				
18	Circulation	Glazing – Design – Manifestations,				
19	Circulation	Floor finishes				
20	Circulation	Stair nosings and handrails				
21	Sanitary facilities	Accessible adult changing places				
22	Sanitary facilities	Accessible changing rooms within same sex showering/changing facilities				

No.	*Area*	*Item*	*Within current design?*	*Design Team Comments – Feb 20*	*OHAC Comment/ Query – Date*	*Design Team Feedback*
23	Sanitary facilities	Mother and baby facilities				
24	Sanitary facilities	Ambulant self-contained facilities				
25	Sanitary facilities	Gender neutral facilities				
26	Other facilities	Audience and spectator facilities/Auditoriums				
27	Other facilities	Meeting rooms/ Workspaces				
28	Other facilities	Prayer facilities				
29	Other facilities	Autism friendly spaces				
30	Other facilities	Specialist room types to address accessibility – e.g. heights of workstations, demonstration rooms, etc.				
31	Other facilities	Scooter charging points				
32	Other facilities	Assistive Technology				
33	Other facilities	Café/Restaurant				
34	Signage & wayfinding	Signage and wayfinding providing a Universal Design strategy				

No.	*Area*	*Item*	*Within current design?*	*Design Team Comments – Feb 20*	*OHAC Comment/ Query – Date*	*Design Team Feedback*
35	Signage & wayfinding	Information points & kiosks				
36	Acoustics	Refer to best practice				
37	Hearing enhancements	How does the design meet good practice?				
38	Emergency egress	Safe evacuation procedure				
39	Emergency egress	Evacuation lifts				
40	Emergency egress	Visual and audible fire alarms				
41	Emergency egress	Final exit routes accessible for people with reduced mobility				
42	Emergency egress	Refuge area design				
43	Neurodiversity	Refer to best practice (finishes, lighting, operations etc.)				

Note: All standards/guidelines quoted may be subject to subsequent revisions. Where standards/guidelines are updated by amendment or revision the latest edition should be adopted.

References:

1. DEHLG (2010) Building Regulation, *2010 Technical Guidance Document M. Disability Access. Department of Environment*, Heritage and Local Government, Dublin.
2. BSI (2018), BS8300-1: Design of an accessible and inclusive built environment, Part 1: External environment – Code of practice.
3. BSI (2018), BS8300-2: Design of an accessible and inclusive built environment, Part 2: Buildings – Code of practice.
4. Inclusive Design Standards published by the London Legacy Development Corporation (LLDC) (Second edition – May 2019) – https://www.accessconsultancy.ie/Inclusive-Design-Standards-London-Legacy-Development-Corporation-May-2019

Index

Note: page numbers in italic type refer to Figures; those in bold type refer to Tables.

AbilityNet 203
academic capital 134, *135*, 212
Access and Lifelong Learning (ALL) 53
Access Leaders 7, 90, 133
access, terminology and definition 2, 206
accessibility 77, 158, 159; accessibility audits 175; accessibility maturity model for education 204; *see also* Universal Design
Accessibility Systems Management Plan 181, 215
accessible technologies 111; *see also* digital accessibility; IT (information technology) systems
actions, Toolkit for Inclusive Higher Education Institutions 75
'add-on' approach 4, 22, 23
affordability of accommodation, baseline research 8, 13
Aguirre, A.J. 29
Ahern, Aoife 94
ALL (Access and Lifelong Learning) 53
Ally software, Brightspace VLE (Virtual Learning Environment) *194*, 194–196, 216
ambiguity 26, 29
anti-Black violence, US universities' response to 4, 33–37, 208
Apple, Michael 130
Architects' Data (Bauenwurfslehre) 167
architectural design guides 167
"architecturally disabled" 165
Architecture discipline, UDL (Universal Design for Learning) 104–105
Aristotle 25
Arts and Humanities discipline, Toolkit for Inclusive Higher Education Institutions 4–5, 87–89, 210–211
Ashwin, P. 138
Asian students, attainment gap and the RAFA2 (Re-imagining Attainment for All) project 66–67, *67, 68*, 69
assessment, UDL (Universal Design for Learning) 104
assistive technology 136–137, 187; *see also* IT (information technology) systems
Association of American Universities 34
Association of Colleges, UK 203
attainment gap, RAFA2 (Re-imagining Attainment for All) project 66–67, *67, 68*, 69
audiences, for data *59*, 59–60, 62
Ayad, K. 115

Baboeram, P. 147–148
Bauenwurfslehre (Architects' Data) 167
Bendou, A. 115
Bennani, K.D. 115
BIPOC (Black, Indigenous and other peoples of colour) students, US universities 4, 33–37, 208
Black Lives Matter movement 33
Black students: anti-Black violence, US universities' response to 4, 33–37, 208; attainment gap and the RAFA2 (Re-imagining Attainment for All) project 66–67, *67, 68*, 69
Blythman, M. 29
Bologna Process, EU 23
Bourdieu, P. 5, 130–131, 132, 212
Bowen, E. 26, 29, 208

Bridger, G. 138
Brightspace VLE (Virtual Learning Environment) case study *194*, 194–196, 216
Bruner, J.S. 52
built environment 4, 5, 77–78, 155–162, *156*, **160**, *161*, 214; Estates Services case studies 162, 174–177, 178–183, 215; Universal Design Patterns case study 162, 164–172, 214–215; *see also* Toolkit for Inclusive Higher Education Institutions: Pillar 3: Physical Campus and the Built Environment
'burning platform' metaphor 4, 51, 53, 62
Butcher, J. 29

campus *see* physical campus
Campus Accessibility Officer role 175
Canada 85; EDI (equality, diversity and inclusion) policies in post-secondary education 4, 40–42
capital, Bourdieu's concept of 5, 130–131, 132, 134–135, *135*
Carson, T.L. 87–88
Centre for Creativity, UCD 182, *182*
Centre for Excellence in Universal Design (CEUD) 43, 44, 45, 175
Centre for Learning, UCD 182
Ceresnova, Z. 157
CEUD (Centre for Excellence in Universal Design) 43, 44, 45, 175
challenges, Toolkit for Inclusive Higher Education Institutions 75
champions, importance of in EDI (equality, diversity and inclusion) policies in post-secondary education, Canada 41
cholera outbreak, London, 1854 52, 209
CIT (culturally inclusive teaching) for UDL 5, 100, 118, 119–123, **120, 121**, 212; Hofstede's cultural values framework 118–119
City of Westminster College 203
Clarke, M. 188–189
class, and intergenerational patterns of social inequality 131–132, 212
Clouder, L. 111
collectivism, in cultures 119, **120**
College of Social Sciences and Law, UCD (University College Dublin) 90–91
colour-brave approach 147
communities, and EDI (equality, diversity and inclusion) policies in post-secondary education, Canada 41
Communities of Practice (CoP) *see* CoP (Communities of Practice)
commuter students 147
concerted cultivation parenting style, middle class parents 131, 132
Content Management System (Terminal 4 CMS) 197, 199
Conway. M. 140
CoP (Communities of Practice) 5, 15, 85; digital accessibility, UK 203; digital badge programme 104; Faculty Partnership Programme, UDL (Universal Design for Learning) 5, 106–107, 211
Côte d'Ivoire 111
Council of Europe, Resolution ResAP (2001) ('Tomar Resolution') 165
courage 26
COVID-19 pandemic 12, 82, 93, 102, 115, 145, 187, 210
cultural capital 130, 134, *135*, 212
culturally inclusive teaching *see* CIT (culturally inclusive teaching) for UDL
culture: definition of 118–119; *see also* CIT (culturally inclusive teaching) for UDL
curriculum design: BIPOC (Black, Indigenous and other peoples of colour) students, US universities 35, 36; decolonisation 77; UDL (Universal Design for Learning) 104, 111; *see also* Toolkit for Inclusive Higher Education Institutions: Pillar 1: Programme and Curriculum Design, Teaching and Learning
'curriculum model' 146

data, as a driver for change 4, 51–63, 73, 209–210; audiences *59*, 59–60, 62; mixed methods research 58, *58*; student engagement and retention case study 4, 65–69; student voice in 58
DDs (Dialogue Days), #Ibelong project 147–151, 213
decolonisation of the curriculum 77
DEIJ (diversity, equity, inclusion, and justice) policies, US universities 33–37, 208
Department for Education and Skills, UK 145–146

Design for All approach 24, 75, 164, 167, 170–171
Dialogue Days (DDs), #Ibelong project 147–151, 213
Diffusion of Innovation model (Rogers) 15
digital accessibility 5–6; UK digital accessibility case study 6, 188, 201–204, 216; web accessibility case study 196–199; *see also* IT (information technology) systems
Digital Accessibility Working Group, UK 202
Digital Ambassadors 7, 189
Digital Badge in Universal Design for Teaching and Learning 102–104, *103*
'digital divide' 6, 187, 216
disabilities, people with 8, 77; Morocco 110–111; online and blended learning 187, 188–189; physical campus and built environment 5, 157–158; and UDL (Universal Design for Learning) 99, 112, 113–114; and Universal Design 43, 44–46, *46*, 100
Disability Act 2005, Ireland 43, 175
disability rights movement 113–114, 157
Dis-ability Situations 164
"Disability, Work and Inclusion in Ireland" (OECD) 44
Disabled Persons Organisations (DPOs), Ireland 43
Disabled Student's Commission 202
"disproportionate burden" derogation 204
diversity *see* access
diversity-brave approach 147–148, 150–151, 213
Dolmage, J.T. 137
Donegal further Education and Training Board (ETB), Technology Enhanced Learning (TEL) Mentors 188
DPOs (Disabled Persons Organisations), Ireland 43
Dunster, Lorraine 62
Durkheim, E. 6, 208
dyslexia 158
dyspraxia 158

EAA (European Accessibility Act) 2019 44
early adopters of IT (information technology) systems 188, 195
early career academics 87–89
EASPD (European Association of Service Providers for People with Disabilities) 44
ECU 29
Edelman, Marian Wright 57
EDI (equality, diversity and inclusion) policies in post-secondary education, Canada 4, 40–42
EDTL (Enhanced Digital Teaching and Learning) Project, IUA (Irish Universities Association) 189
Education and Training Foundation, UK 203
Education for a Changing World Green Paper (Department of Education Ireland) 55
educational ecosystems model 45–46, *46*
El Jamyly, S. 112
Elhachloufi, M. 115
Embedding Student Success (National Forum) 100
Engineering discipline: Toolkit for Inclusive Higher Education Institutions 5, 93–95, 211; UDL (Universal Design for Learning) 104–105
Enhanced Digital Teaching and Learning (EDTL) Project, IUA (Irish Universities Association) 189
entitlement, middle class sense of 131, 132, 212
equality *see* access
equity *see* access
equity groups, Ireland 55, 100
EU (European Union): higher education policy and practice 23–24; Universal Design 43–44; Web Accessibility Directive 197, 216
European Accessibility Act (EAA) 2019 44
European Association of Service Providers for People with Disabilities (EASPD) 44
European Higher Education Area 24

Faculty Partnership Programme, UDL (Universal Design for Learning) 5, 106–107
Farrelly, Mary 138
FET (Further Education and Training) 101
financial capital 134, *135*, 212
Floyd, George 33, 35
Framework Law 51.17 (Kingdom of Morocco, 2019) 115
friendships, students' goals for 5, 132–133
Fund for Students with Disabilities 106

funding: BIPOC (Black, Indigenous and other peoples of colour) students, US universities 35; EDI (equality, diversity and inclusion) policies in post-secondary education, Canada 41
Further Education and Training (FET) 101
further education, UK 202, 203
Future Teacher Project 203

GDS (Government Digital Services), UK 22–203
gender, and student support services 146
Goldsmith, Selwyn 165
'good enough' data 65–66
good practice examples, Toolkit for Inclusive Higher Education Institutions 75–76
Government Digital Services (GDS), UK 22–203
Government of Flanders Equal Opportunities Team 165
Gray, S. 138

Hanesworth, P 111
Hardy, Thomas 6–7
Hasselt University, Belgium (UHasselt) 5, 167–171, *170, 171*, 215
HEA (Higher Education Authority) 1, 2, 23, 53; National Access Policy 100
Heaney, Seamus 7, 127
High Participation Systems (HPS) 127
higher education: academic roles in 138; changing patterns in 128–129; classism in 131–132; staff relationships in 140
Higher Education Authority (HEA) *see* HEA (Higher Education Authority)
Hill, M. 25, 29
Historically White institutions (HWIs), US 4, 33–37, 208
'hopeful implementers' 26, 208
hostile ignorance 131, 136
HPS (High Participation Systems) 127
Hupe, P. 25, 29
HWIs (Historically White institutions), US 4, 33–37, 208

#Ibelong project case study 5, 145–151, 213
ICD (Intercultural Development Programme), UCD Michael Smurfit Business School *121*, 121–123
Idea of a University (Newman) 21, 141
imperfection 29
implementation framework, UCD University for All 3, *3*, 24–26, **27–28**, 29, 208
Imrie, R. 157
INCLUDE (International Collaboratory for Leadership in Universally Designed Education) 110, 112, 113, 114, 115
inclusion *see* access
inclusive design 24, 74, 164
Inclusive Design Framework 24
Inclusive Practice, training for 81
Inclusive Teaching 94
individualism, in cultures 119, **120**
Individuals with Disabilities Act, US 113
inequality, intergenerational patterns of 131–132
information technology *see* IT (information technology) systems
Ingham, P. 6–7
Institute of Art, Design and Technology Dun Laoghaire 104
institutional approach to the University for All 4, 21–30, 208; inclusive post-secondary education case study 4, 40–42; physical campus and the built environment *161*, 161–162; Universal Design case study 43–46; US universities' response to anti-Black violence case study 4, 33–37, 208; *see also* Foundations and Scaffolding: Strategic Approach and Organisation; Toolkit for Inclusive Higher Education Institutions
intangibles, in institutional change 26, 29
integral design 164
intellectual disabilities, students with, EDI (equality, diversity and inclusion) policies in post-secondary education, Canada 4, 40–41
Intercultural Development Programme (ICD), UCD Michael Smurfit Business School *121*, 121–123
"International Classification of Functioning, Disability and Health" (World Health Organization) 164
International Collaboratory for Leadership in Universally Designed Education (INCLUDE) 110, 112, 113, 114, 115
'intrinsic' 4
Irish Universities Association *see* IUA (Irish Universities Association)

IT (information technology) systems 4, 5–6, 66, 78, 94, 187–188, 192–193, 215–216; Brightspace VLE (Virtual Learning Environment) case study *194*, 194–196, 216; digital accessibility case study, UK 188, 201–204, 216; implementation of accessibility tools for the Virtual Learning Environment case study *194*, 194–196, 216; online and blended learning 187, 188–190; web accessibility case study 196–199; *see also* Toolkit for Inclusive Higher Education Institutions: Pillar 4: Information Technology Systems and Infrastructure
IUA (Irish Universities Association) 188–189; EDTL (Enhanced Digital Teaching and Learning) Project 189, 216

JNU (Jawaharlal Nehru University), New Delhi 157–158
Johnson, S. 52
Jude the Obscure (Hardy) 6–7

Kelly, Anna 3, 51, 174
Kennedy, D. 208
Key Take Aways 6, 216–217, *217*
Kierkegaard, Soren 218
Knaflic, Cole Nussbaumer 52, 54
Kotter, J. 29, 51
KPIs (Key Performance Indicators), data and storytelling 53–54, 55

laptop loan schemes 14, 189
Lareau, Annette 131–132, 212
Learning and Teaching Enhancement Unit (LTEU), University of Roehampton 66
learning support services 136–137
Lisbon Declaration on Inclusive Education 2021 44
LTEU (Learning and Teaching Enhancement Unit), University of Roehampton 66

Mace, Ron 137
mainstreaming 73; terminology and definition 2, 206–207; and University for All 22, 23
Martinez, R. 29
May, H. 138
medical model of disability 157
mental health difficulties 158
meritocracy 6
middle class, intergenerational patterns of social inequality 131–132, 212
Minor Works 175, 179, 182, 215
'minority tax' 87–88
Mitra, D.L. 148
Morocco, UIZ (University of Ibn Zohr), UDL case study 5, 100–101, 110–116, *112*, 211–212
Morris, A. 88

narrative *see* storytelling, through data
National Access Policy (HEA) 100
National Centre for Universal Design, Ireland 4
National Disability Authority (NDA), Ireland 43, 44, 197, 216
National Disability Inclusion Strategy, Ireland 175
National Forum 100, 101–102, 104, 141
National Office for Equity of Access to Higher Education, Ireland 55
natural growth parenting style, working class parents 131–132
NDA (National Disability Authority), Ireland 43, 44, 197, 216
Netherlands 85
neurodiverse students 158, 176
Newman, J. 21, 141
Nurunnabi, M. 101

OBAAT ('one bite at a time') strategy 25, 210
occupational therapy 155
O'Farrell, L. 60
Office for Students, UK 202
O'Herily Access Consultancy 182
online and blended learning 187, 188–190; Brightspace VLE (Virtual Learning Environment) case study *194*, 194–196, 216; ICD (Intercultural Development Programme) 122; *see also* IT (information technology) systems
organisational culture, and UDL (Universal Design for Learning) *112*
Orr, S. 29
Owen, M. 146

Padden, L. 51, 174
parenting styles, class differences in 131–132
parking issues 12–13
PEO (Person-Environment-Occupation) Model 155–156, *156*

physical campus 4, 5, 77–78, 155–162, *156*, **160**, *161*, 214; Estates Services case studies 162, 174–177, 178–183, 215; Universal Design Patterns case study 162, 164–172, 214–215; *see also* Toolkit for Inclusive Higher Education Institutions: Pillar 3: Physical Campus and the Built Environment
'Plus-One' mindset 87, 88; and UDL 107
post-secondary education, inclusive 4, 40–42
power distance, in cultures 119, **120**
Pressman, J.L. 25, 29, 208
professional development: TTR (Team Teacher Reflection), #Ibelong project 147, 149–150, 151, 213; for UDL (Universal Design for Learning) 101–104, *103*, 111
Professional Development Framework (National Forum) 101–102
programme design *see* Toolkit for Inclusive Higher Education Institutions: Pillar 1: Programme and Curriculum Design, Teaching and Learning
Public Sector Bodies (Websites and Mobile Applications) (No. 2) Accessibility Regulations 2018 (UK) 202

Rabbitte, Anne 23
racial and ethnic groups, hostile ignorance towards 131, 136
RAFA2 (Re-imagining Attainment for All) project 66–67, *67, 68*, 69
Raheja, G. 157–158
Rainford, J. 136
Reasonable Accommodations 77, 100
Reay, D. 6, 131, 136, 212
resources: EDI (equality, diversity and inclusion) policies in post-secondary education, Canada 41, 42; Toolkit for Inclusive Higher Education Institutions 76
Rickett, B. 88
Rogers, E. 15
"Rooms for Care and Well-being" 5, 167, 169–171, *170, 171*215
Rosewell, K. 138
Rumsfeld, Donald 26
Ryttberg, M. 140

Saint-Exupéry, Antoine de 142
Salmen, J.P.S. 159
sanitary facilities *see* "Rooms for Care and Well-being"
scaffolding: storytelling through data *54*, 54–55, 57–58, *65*; student supports and services 127, 128; *see also* Foundations and Scaffolding: Strategic Approach and Organisation; Toolkit for Inclusive Higher Education Institutions
SCM (Student Community Mentoring), #Ibelong project 147, 150, 151, 213
self-assessment statements, Toolkit for Inclusive Higher Education Institutions 75, 79, 81, 90
Sensory Garden Project 176
Shaw, George Bernard 24–25, 208
Shuayb, T. 157
signage, accessible 176
Silktide 4.0 software 198–199, 216
silo approach 22
SISWeb 193
Slovak University of Technology, Bratislava 157
Snow, John 52, 209
social capital 130, 132, 134, *135*, 212
social model of disability 157, 164
Social Reproduction Theory 130–131
Social Science disciplines, Toolkit for Inclusive Higher Education Institutions 5, 90–91, 211
SOLAS, Ireland 44
solutions, Toolkit for Inclusive Higher Education Institutions 75
Staffordshire University 145–146
stakeholders: IT systems and infrastructure 6; and UDL (Universal Design for Learning) 111
storytelling, through data 4, 51, 52–54, *53*, 209–210; story scaffold *54*, 54–55, 57–58, *65*
Student Community Mentoring (SCM), #Ibelong project 147, 150, 151, 213
student engagement and retention 128; UK data case study 4, 65–69; *see also* #Ibelong project
Student Experience Map, UCD *128*, 128–129, *129*, 137, *137*
Student Goals, UCD *133*, 133–134, 141
student mentors 148, 150, 151
Student Success Strategy 141
student supports and services 5, 127–136, *128, 129, 133, 135*, 212–213; BIPOC (Black, Indigenous and other peoples of colour) students, US universities 34, 36; #Ibelong project case study 5, 145–151, 213; staff status 5, 138–141,

139, 212, 213; student engagement and retention data case study 65–69; Universal Design for 136–138, *137*; *see also* Toolkit for Inclusive Higher Education Institutions: Pillar 2: Student Supports and Services
student voice: as catalyst for change in a University for All 6–7, 208; in the data story 58, *58*; ICD (Intercultural Development Programme) 122; physical campus and built environment 157–158, 176; in the Toolkit for Inclusive Higher Education Institutions 81, 82; in the UIZ (University of Ibn Zohr), Morocco, UDL case study 113–115
Student Voice Conference, Morocco 114–115
Student Welcome event 7
success, celebration of students with intellectual disabilities, Canada 41
Suryanwanshi, S. 157–158
symbolic capital 130, 212

teaching qualifications 101; *see also* professional development
Team Teacher Reflection (TTR), #Ibelong project 147, 149–150, 151, 213
Technological University Dublin 45
Terminal 4 CMS (Content Management System) 197, 199
Third Space *139*, 139–141, 213
Thomas, L. 29, 132, 134, 137–138
Tierney Building, UCD 180, *181*
'Tomar Resolution' (Council of Europe Resolution ResAP) (2001) 165
Toolkit for Inclusive Higher Education Institutions 4–5, 6, 15, 73, *74*, 85, 210–211; Arts and Humanities discipline 4–5, 87–89, 210–211; baseline research 7–14, **9**, *9*, **10**, *10*, **11**, *11*, *12*, **13**, *13*, **14**; bottom-up planning 90–91; development of 74–75; digital interactive toolkit *83*, 83–84, *84*; Engineering discipline 5, 93–95, 211; implementation 79–82, *80*, 209, *209*; marginalised and underrepresented staff 87–89; Social Sciences and Law disciplines 5, 90–91, 211; structure of 75–78; student voice in 81, 82; target users of 79
Toolkit for Inclusive Higher Education Institutions; Foundations and Scaffolding: Strategic Approach and Organisation 4, 21–30, 76–77, 210; baseline research 8–9, **9**, *9*; inclusive post-secondary education case study 4, 40–42; Universal Design case study 43–46; US universities; response to anti-Black violence case study 4, 33–37, 208
Toolkit for Inclusive Higher Education Institutions: Pillar 1: Programme and Curriculum Design, Teaching and Learning 4, 5, 66, 77, 93–94, 99–108, 210, 211; baseline research 9–11, **10**, *10*; UDL for CIT (culturally inclusive teaching) case study 5, 100, 118–123, **120, 121**, 212; UIZ (University of Ibn Zohr), Morocco, UDL case study 5, 100–101, 110–116, *112*, 211–212
Toolkit for Inclusive Higher Education Institutions: Pillar 2: Student Supports and Services 4, 5, 66, 77, 127–142, 210, 212–213; baseline research **11**, *11*, 11–12; #Ibelong project case study 5, 145–151, 213
Toolkit for Inclusive Higher Education Institutions: Pillar 3: Physical Campus and the Built Environment 4, 5, 77–78, 155–162, 210, 214; baseline research *12*, 12–13; Estates Services case studies 162, 174–177, 178–183, 215; Universal Design Patterns case study 162, 164–172, 214–215
Toolkit for Inclusive Higher Education Institutions: Pillar 4: Information Technology Systems and Infrastructure 4, 5–6, 66, 78, 94, 187–190, 192–199, 210, 211; baseline research *13*, 13–14, **14**; implementation of accessibility tools for the Virtual Learning Environment case study *194*, 194–196; UK digital accessibility case study 188, 201–204, 216
Trow, M. 127
TTR (Team Teacher Reflection), #Ibelong project 147, 149–150, 151, 213
Tuitt, F. 29

UCD (University College Dublin), Belfield Campus *179*, 179–183, *180*, *181*, *182*
UCD (University College Dublin), Information Technology services department 187–188, 192–199; Brightspace VLE (Virtual Learning Environment) case study *194*,

194–196, 216; implementation of accessibility tools for the Virtual Learning Environment case study *194*, 194–196; online and blended learning 187, 188–190; web accessibility case study 196–199
UCD (University College Dublin), Michael Smurfit Business School, ICD (Intercultural Development Programme) *121*, 121–123
UCD (University College Dublin), University for All 7, 15–16, 73, 99, 206, 207; baseline research 7–14, **9**, *9*, **10**, *10*, **11**, *11, 12*, **13**, *13*, **14**; cynicism and scepticism around 14–15; data as a driver for change 4, 51–63, 209–210; development of model 24; Faculty Partnership Programme 5, 106–107, 211; implementation framework 3, *3*, 24–26, **27–28**, 29, 208; institutional approach 21–30; introduction and overview of 2–3, *3*, 4, 22; Key Take Aways 6, 216–217, *217*; physical campus and the built environment 5, 157, 159–161, **160**; policy context 23–24
UD Living Lab 165, *166*
UD2Care (Universal-Design-to-Care) 165
UDE (Universal Design in Education) 43
UDEP ("Universal Design Education Project") 165, *166*
UDL (Universal Design for Learning) 5, 91, 99–101, *101*, 211; baseline research 9–11, **10**, *10*; CIT (culturally inclusive teaching) case study 5, 100, 118–123, **120, 121**, 212; Faculty Partnership Programme 5, 106–107, 211; good practice case studies and disciplinary change 104–105; Ireland 4, 43, 44–45; professional development for 101–104, *103*; removal of barriers 107–108; UIZ (University of Ibn Zohr), Morocco, case study 5, 100–101, 110–116, *112*, 211–212
UHasselt (Hasselt University, Belgium) 5, 167–171, *170, 171*, 215
UIZ (University of Ibn Zohr), Morocco, UDL case study 5, 100–101, 110, 115–116, 211–212; context 110–113, *112*; student perspectives 113–115
UK: digital accessibility case study 6, 188, 201–204, 216; #Ibelong project 5, 145–151, 213; student engagement and retention data case study 4, 65–69
UNCRPD (United Nations Convention on the Rights of People with Disabilities) 43, 44, 110
Universal Design 6, 24, 43–46, 74, 77, 100; national guidelines for 175; physical campus and the built environment 5, 157, 158–161, **160**, 162, 164–172, 174, 175, 178, 182–183; for student supports and services 136–138, *137*; training for 81; Universal Design Patterns case study 162, 164–172, 214–215; *see also* UDE (Universal Design in Education); UDL (Universal Design for Learning)
"Universal Design Education Project" (UDEP) 165, *166*
Universal Design for Learning *see* UDL (Universal Design for Learning)
Universal Design in Education (UDE) 43
Universal Design of Shared Educational Campuses in Ireland 45
"Universal Design Rooms for Care & Well-being in public spaces" 169–171, *170, 171*, 215
Universal-Design-to-Care (UD2Care) 165
universities, terminology and definition 2, 207
university access services 162
University College Dublin *see* UCD (University College Dublin)
university estate services case studies 162, 174–177, 178–183, 215
University for All *see* UCD (University College Dublin), University for All
University League Tables 62
University of Alberta, On Campus programme 40
University of Botswana 188
University of Calgary, Flanagan Foundation Initiative 189
University of Connecticut Office for Diversity and Inclusion (ODI) 33
University of Ibn Zohr, Morocco *see* UIZ (University of Ibn Zohr), Morocco, UDL case study
University of Prince Edward Island 41
University of Regina 40, 41
University of Roehampton 66
University of York 203
US (United States): disability rights 113; HWIs' (Historically White institutions') response to anti-Black violence 4, 33–37, 208

Van Horn, C. 25
Van Meter, D. 25
VLEs (Virtual Learning Environments), Brightspace VLE case study *194*, 194–196, 216

WAI (Web Content Accessibility Guidelines) 197
web accessibility case study 196–199; *see also* IT (information technology) systems
Weber, Max 138, 140
Wejchert, Andrzej 180, *180*
Welcome events, UCD 132–133
What Works? student retention and success programme 147
Whitchurch, C. 138, 139
widening participation *see* access
Wildavsky, A.B. 25, 29, 208
Woodfield, R. 146
Woodrow, M. 29
Worcestershire County Council 203
working class: intergenerational patterns of social inequality 131–132, 212; student support 135–136, 212
World Health Organization 164, 171
WP (Widening Participation) data *see* data, as a driver for change

Printed in Great Britain
by Amazon

35169338R00145